CONFLICT AND DECISION-MAKING

IN SOVIET RUSSIA

A CASE STUDY OF AGRICULTURAL POLICY

1953-1963

SPONSORED BY THE

PRINCETON CENTER
OF INTERNATIONAL STUDIES

FOR A COMPLETE LIST OF THE BOOKS SPONSORED BY THE
PRINCETON CENTER OF INTERNATIONAL STUDIES
PLEASE SEE THE BACK OF THE BOOK

CONFLICT
AND DECISION-MAKING
IN SOVIET RUSSIA

A CASE STUDY
OF AGRICULTURAL POLICY

1953-1963

BY SIDNEY I. PLOSS

PRINCETON UNIVERSITY PRESS

PRINCETON, NEW JERSEY

1965

To Kaja

CONTENTS

CONFLICT AND DECISION-MAKING

IN SOVIET RUSSIA

A CASE STUDY OF AGRICULTURAL POLICY

1953-1963

". . . a political science which is faithful to its moral commitment of telling the truth about the political world cannot help telling society things it does not want to hear. This cannot be otherwise in view of the fact that one of the main purposes of society is to conceal the truth about man and society from its members. That concealment, that elaborate and subtle and purposeful misunderstanding of the nature of man and of society, is one of the cornerstones upon which all societies are founded."—Hans J. Morgenthau*

*In *Approaches to the Study of Politics*, edited by Roland Young, Evanston, Ill., 1958, p. 72.

INTRODUCTION

WESTERN INTERPRETATIONS of Soviet official conduct are often rooted in assumptions about the unique role of Communist ideology and a single will's domination of policy-making in the USSR. The ideology has been misrepresented as something homogeneous which tightly unifies the outlook of Soviet leaders, inhibits the emergence of narrow, specialized interests in their midst, and so restricts their policy choices as to make it unprofitable to study whatever conflict may exist in the one-party system. The representatives of the primacy-of-ideology school overlook the enormous diversities in the vast body of Communist theory and the many levels of understanding to which its vague operative clauses are susceptible. The regime's own ideological functionaries alert one to the danger of mistaking the form of party doctrine for its more elusive substance when they intimate that such theory is fashioned to meet the exigencies of current-day politics. Significantly, the example offered is the most illustrious work of party philosophy: "In order correctly to understand the theoretical content of V. I. Lenin's book *Materialism and Empirio-Criticism*, one must first of all know when and why, for what political, practical purpose, this book was created—that is, he must know the specific phase of CPSU history."[1] The same might readily be said of the "ideological" pronouncements of even less

---

[1] S. T. Kaltakhchyan in *XXII S"yezd KPSS i Zadachi Kafedr Obshchestvennykh Nauk. Materialy Vsesoyuznogo Soveshchaniya Zaveduyushchikh Kafedrami Obshchestvennykh Nauk Vysshikh Uchebnykh Zavedeniy. 30 yanvarya-2 fevralya 1962 goda* (22nd CPSU Congress and Tasks of Social Science Departments. Materials of the All-Union Conference of Heads of Social Science Departments of Higher Educational Institutions. January 30-February 2, 1962), Moscow, 1962, p. 432.

1

theoretically minded leaders of Soviet Communism like Joseph Stalin and Nikita S. Khrushchev.

Other students of Soviet affairs have investigated the formal structure of the ruling Communist party and on that basis made equally seductive generalizations about the dynamics of national policy-making in Soviet Russia. The foremost is that the party's senior secretary is the unchallenged leader of policy because the party Rules entrust the central administrative body of the party "to direct current work, chiefly the selection of personnel." Any party member whose career fortunes are supposedly dependent on the mercies of the senior secretary might not be expected to voice policy courses alternative to his, at least for very long. However, Secretary-General Stalin was effectively challenged on the rates of agricultural collectivization in 1929-1930 and the equally important question of party purges in 1932; as late as the February-March 1937 Central Committee session, many Committee members questioned the wisdom of Stalin's proposals to introduce extraordinary mass terror.[2] First Secretary Khrushchev, likewise denied the right to terrorize upper-level defaulters, was consistently opposed on policy matters in 1953-1957 by members of the party Presidium whose subsequent removal from the leadership

[2] Cf. Leonard Schapiro, *The Communist Party of the Soviet Union*, New York, 1960, pp. 392-393; B. N. Ponomarëv *et al.*, *Istoriya Kommunisticheskoy Partii Sovetskogo Soyuza (Izdaniye vtoroye, dopolnennoye)* (History of the Communist Party of the Soviet Union [2nd, supplemented edition]), Moscow, 1962, p. 445; *Voprosy Istorii KPSS* (Problems of CPSU History), No. 1, 1964, p. 33; and *The Crimes of the Stalin Era, Special Report to the 20th Congress of the Communist Party of the Soviet Union by Nikita S. Khrushchev, First Secretary, Communist Party of the Soviet Union. Annotated by Boris I. Nicolaevsky*, Supplement of *The New Leader*, New York, 1962, pp. S25-26.

allowed their identification.[3] Such opposition to the senior secretary is not likely to have transpired if unlimited power resided in his office. Historical precedent should caution against overinterpretation of the party Rules.

An Australian student of politics, J. D. B. Miller, has judiciously suggested that the only way to learn about the nature of the decision-making process in any country is to examine actual cases.[4] The aim of the present study is to further our understanding of contemporary Soviet politics by reconstructing from the official record disputes over agricultural policy in the post-Stalin period. Answers, however tentative, are sought to the questions: (1) Who makes important decisions? (2) What political or governmental bodies participate in one way or another in adopting the decisions? and (3) What positions and attitudes do the major personalities involved in the formulation of policy assume? Agricultural policy has been chosen as the avenue to understanding since it is a preoccupation of the leadership which impinges on the traditionally central issues of method of government and resource allocation, as well as the interrelated subject, foreign relations.

The difficulty of undertaking this kind of study is identical with the reason for the aforementioned delusive commentary about Soviet policy-making, viz., the tediousness of penetrating the elaborate smokescreen around the inner workings of Kremlin politics. For almost the

---

[3] A good introduction to this period is George D. Embree, *The Soviet Union Between the 19th and 20th Party Congresses, 1952-1956*, The Hague, 1959. The *post facto* designation of oppositionists is touched on in Roger Pethybridge, *A Key to Soviet Politics: The Crisis of the Anti-Party Group*, New York, 1962.

[4] *The Nature of Politics*, London, 1962, p. 275.

span of a generation, 1929-1958, an artificial calm normally prevailed over the surface of political life in Soviet Russia. That life remained concentrated in the Communist party's Central Committee and, for the most part after 1936, in a segment of the Committee's Politburo-Presidium. No longer was there any forthright airing of the party leaders' divergent viewpoints on the organization's strategy, tactics, and internal management. The Bolshevik version of "cabinet secrecy" was proclaimed by Stalin in 1929, on the eve of a nation-wide campaign of modernization which required popular sacrifice of even the necessities of life, iron discipline in the bureaucratic elite, and not the slightest hint of disarray in the political command structure. Stalin told the April 1929 Plenum of the CPSU(B) Central Committee and Central Control Commission: "We must take appropriate measures forbidding individual members and alternate members of the Political Bureau, when speaking publicly, to deviate in any way from the line of the Party and the decisions of the Central Committee or of its bodies. . . . We must take appropriate measures so that press organs, both Party and Soviet, newspapers as well as periodicals, should fully conform to the line of the Party and the decisions of its leading bodies."[5]

After the personal dictatorship of Stalin was created in the purges of 1937-1938 and "monolithism" fully glorified, regime propagandists ordinarily limited irregularities in the elite to the indulgence of junior-grade officials in empire-building, suppression of criticism and self-criticism, and religious observances.[6] Alternatively, party intellectuals working in the mass media were criticized

[5] J. Stalin, *Problems of Leninism*, Moscow, 1953, p. 373.
[6] See P. Pospelov, *Bol'shevik*, No. 23, 1951, pp. 10-11.

for "ideological" errors without any inkling that their real mistake was to have fostered in cryptic terms the solutions to practical problems advocated by defeated groupings in the system of closed politics.[7] The professions of total unity in the Kremlin were as obscurantist as so much other Stalinist propaganda. It is always the despot's method of rule to utilize divide-and-conquer techniques with courtiers of differing outlook, and after World War II conflicts in the Moscow hierarchy over issues of policy and power were both legion and ferocious.

After Stalin, an unwritten code of factional conduct known as "collective leadership" was put into practice. The act may be dated to the Central Committee session in July 1953 which endorsed the ruling Presidium's arrest or murder of security chief L. P. Beriya.[8] The phraseology of the abstracted decree of the session indi-

[7] See Harrison E. Salisbury, *Moscow Journal: The End of Stalin*, Chicago, 1961, pp. 308ff. While not agreeing with each of Mr. Salisbury's conclusions and interpretations, I think that he has made a far greater contribution to our knowledge about Soviet political reality than have his critics.

[8] The session's decree has remained confidential but its main points are outlined in the party *History*: "The plenum of the party Central Committee which was held in July 1953 approved the decisive actions directed towards eliminating the criminal activity of Beriya and his accomplices. The plenum adopted measures for the strengthening of party guidance over all links of the state apparatus, for ensuring effective supervision of the work of all bodies and agencies, including the organs of state security. The Central Committee took a firm course towards reestablishing and developing the standards of party life worked out by V. I. Lenin and tested by experience—foremost, the principle of collectivity. Only the collective political experience of the entire party, it says in the decision of the July plenum, the collective wisdom of the Central Committee, relying in its activity on the Marxist-Leninist theory, the initiative and activeness of the leading cadres and party masses, ensure the correctness of the leadership of party and country, the unshakable unity and solidarity of the party ranks, and successful building of communism" (Ponomarëv *et al., op. cit.*, p. 644).

5

cates that now the touchstone of individual ascendancy on policy questions was the ability of a Presidium member to secure a consensus of opinion among his dozen or so colleagues, or in the Central Committee itself with its 125-150 voting members, who in turn were subjected to varied pressures by the elite at large. Perhaps ten or fifteen thousand people articulated their demands behind the scenes in the hope of finding a measure of satisfaction.[9] In step with the new trend of wider participation, regime literature provided for inner-party diversity of opinion and, notwithstanding the party Rules' strictures against canvassing and the formation of voting blocs ("factionalism"), some kind of bloodless conflict. The existence of such references in the party press, as well as their incidence at particular times, may be taken as a reliable measure of the actual state of affairs behind the façade of "monolithic unity." Thus, in 1954, the notion of turbulence inside the party was given unaccustomed attention by one ideological functionary:

> The Communist party has never glossed over differences inside the party; it has overcome them by means of struggle. Yet Engels said that in a genuinely proletarian party contradictions cannot be glossed over but always are resolved in struggle. Only by means of struggle for the principled Marxist-Leninist line has the Communist party guarded itself and the proletariat against the pressure and influence of the bourgeoisie and its agents in the labor movement. Only as the result of irreconcilable struggle with anti-party and anti-revolutionary elements has the Communist party over-

[9] The figure is suggested in Franz Borkenau, "Zur Methode der Sowjet-Forschung," *Philosophisches Jahrbuch der Görres Gesellschaft*, 62.2, Munich, 1953, pp. 394-406.

come inner-party contradictions, attained the unity and solidarity of its ranks, and ensured victory over the enemies of the toiling masses. The overcoming of inner-party differences by means of struggle is a developmental pattern of the Communist party.[10]

Similarly, in April 1957 an expert on party organization wrote that "insofar as the party is an animate political organism, there always will be clashes of different viewpoints. 'In the party there always will be arguments and struggle,' V. I. Lenin pointed out, 'they must only be confined within party limits' (*Works*, Vol. 7, p. 416)."[11] A few weeks later, no less an authority on political infighting than Khrushchev referred to one of its aspects during an interview with Turner Catledge, managing editor of the *New York Times*, which the CPSU Central Committee daily *Pravda* ran on May 14, 1957:

> *Catledge:* I am very much interested to know how decisions are adopted by leading bodies in the Soviet Union and what procedure is followed in adopting these decisions which become the expression of the views of the collective leadership of the Soviet Union. Does the Presidium of the Central Committee of the Communist party of the Soviet Union meet regularly? How does it adopt decisions? Are minutes taken of the sittings of the Presidium? Do you have clashes of opinion at meetings of the Presidium?

> *Khrushchev:* The Presidium of the CPSU Central Committee meets regularly at least once a week. The

[10] N. I. Shatagin, *Edinstvo Partiynykh Ryadov—Glavnoye Usloviye Sily i Mogushchestva KPSS* (Unity of the Party Ranks Is the Main Condition of the Power and Might of the CPSU), Moscow, 1954 (approved for publication September 7), p. 9.

[11] G. Shitarëv, *Kommunist*, No. 5, 1957 (approved for publication April 9), p. 33.

Council of Ministers also meets at least once weekly. Plenary meetings of the CPSU Central Committee are convened at least twice a year.

More often than not, when questions are examined at meetings of the Central Committee Presidium, different points of view are expressed, as the members of the Presidium strive to examine the problem under discussion as thoroughly as possible. During the discussions, the members of the Presidium usually arrive at a unanimous point of view. If on some question unanimity cannot be reached, the problem is decided by a simple majority vote.

Of course, very heated debates sometimes arise. But that is quite natural in a democratic discussion.

These statements tending to legitimate inner-party conflict indeed reflected its existence at the apex of the dictatorship: the first was made shortly before G. M. Malenkov resigned as chairman of the USSR Council of Ministers, clearly at the insistence of victorious opponents in a running political battle, and the second and third immediately preceded the denouement of a lengthy conflict in the party Presidium over all facets of national policy.

However, while the regime's propaganda was tailored to allow for the clashes occurring within the hierarchy at the time, the substantive nature of the arguments was as usual concealed from the general public. A number of factors help to account for the secrecy. Firstly, chaos might break loose if the many disaffected elements in the population knew that the supreme bosses were quarreling over matters affecting their livelihood. Secondly, there is reason to believe that in Communist states lower-echelon bureaucrats are reluctant to implement policies which they suspect may soon be overturned by a shifting balance of forces at the center. B. Koehler, formerly a candidate member of the Politburo and secretary of the Czech C.P. Central Committee, has said as much in a reference to feuding cliques in a party's directorate: "Such groups, even if they are not large, seriously hamper the development of initiative in implementation of the political party line."[12]

Despite the usual outward placidity, fierce conflict was unremitting in the supreme councils of the party. It was waged in the manner which Valentin S. Zorin, a commentator of Radio Moscow, has averred to be typical of disputation in the U.S. Republican party: "This struggle is usually carefully veiled from the eyes of outsiders, camouflaged in every way, conducted noiselessly and secretly. And only now and then, when passions reach an especially great white-heat, do they suddenly burst forth into the open, in the form of some kind of scandal, and then, until a new explosion, become submerged and invisible to the unsophisticated eye."[13] This is a good description of the circumstances surrounding the electrifying announcements which intermittently flowed from the Kremlin about the "anti-party actions" supposedly just detected on the part of highly placed figures like Bukharin (1929), Ryutin and Slepkov (1932), Eysmont, Tolmachev, and Smirnov (1933), Beriya (1953), Malenkov, Kaganovich, and Molotov (1957), and Marshal Zhukov (1957). The losers in policy disputes of the Stalin era sometimes unobtrusively paid with their lives (Posty-

[12] *Rude Pravo* (Prague), November 23, 1961.
[13] *Monopolii i Politika SShA: Monopolii i Vnutrennyaya Politika Respublikanskoy Partii SShA v 1953-1960 gg.* (Monopolies and US Policy: Monopolies and the Internal Politics of the US Republican Party, 1953-1960), Moscow, 1960, p. 65.

shev in 1940 and Voznesenskiy in 1950), were reprimanded in secret party directives (Khrushchev in 1951), or merely dropped from the Politburo (Andreyev in 1952). After the purge of Beriya in June 1953, these unlucky individuals sometimes met with no worse a fate than demotion in rank (Malenkov in 1955), while their clients, in the revived Lenin tradition, were sent into "diplomatic exile" (Ponomarenko in 1955). Whatever the hazards involved, intensive conflict persisted in the Soviet leadership from 1929 to 1958.

The June 1957 purge in the party Presidium allegedly spelled an end to such "reprehensible" modes of leadership behavior as "intrigue, cliquishness, and factionalism."[14] This myth was debunked a few months later, when a conspiratorial decision was reached to exclude Marshal G. K. Zhukov from the Presidium and remove him from the post of defense minister while he was on tour abroad. Apprehensive officials had to be reassured that the top leadership functioned "in a spirit of harmony and solidarity."[15] But what might be called the "language of conflict" scarcely fell into disuse following Khrushchev's victory in 1957.

The "language of conflict" is compounded of several principal elements: (1) statements which tend to legitimate political argument; (2) rebukes of anonymous personalities for dissidence; (3) shadings of textual emphasis; (4) modification of standard terminology; and (5) a

---

[14] *Kommunist*, No. 10, 1957, p. 10.

[15] V. Churayev, *ibid.*, No. 17, 1957, p. 32. *Turkmenskaya Iskra* (Organ of the Communist Party of Turkmenia), January 18, 1959, reports that a provincial party conference recently heard criticism of a local party secretary who "followed the path of intrigue" and "hampered the harmonious and coordinated work of the province committee bureau."

leader's reticence about some question which his associates have commented on. As in 1954 and 1957, a leading party propagandist declared in the August 1960 issue of the party study journal; "Apparently *each and every* labor party of a great land can develop only in internal struggle, in full accord with the general trend of dialectical development. . . . There will be articulated various opinions which often diverge. And this is quite natural. 'The struggle of shadings in the party is *inevitable* and essential,' wrote V. I. Lenin."[16] In the weeks immediately prior to this statement, the most sweeping overhaul of the party command since 1957 had been executed in phases and Soviet foreign policy was drastically altered. Once more, early in 1961 the same propagandist stressed the normality of overcoming inner-party differences "by means of struggle."[17] Various shifts in party and government posts concurrently pointed to friction in the leadership. Besides, another integral component of the "language of conflict" had since appeared in communications media.

This other component is refutation of the mistaken viewpoints of unspecified "comrades," "officials," "economists," "Communists," "planners," and even "people" who may later turn out to be members of the party Presidium. The device of oblique ridicule evidently is intended to discredit and isolate the chiefs of splinter groups in the Central Committee without having the conflict brought into the streets. A few examples may be

[16] Ye. I. Bugayev, *Politicheskoye Samoobrazovaniye* (Political Self-Education), No. 9, 1960, pp. 33ff.

[17] Ye. I. Bugayev, *O Nekotorykh Zakonomernostyakh Razvitiya Marksistko-Leninskoy Partii* (On Some Developmental Patterns of a Marxist-Leninist Party), Moscow, 1961 (approved for publication January 31), p. 23.

cited. Khrushchev remarked at the 20th party Congress in 1956: "Some comrades might ask if we are right to reclaim virgin lands in drought areas."[18] The leaders of the dispersed grouping of Malenkov and Molotov were later accused of trying to prove that expenditures in assimilating virgin lands in the semi-arid zone of the country would not be recouped and that the undertaking was economically useless.[19] Also at the 20th Congress, Khrushchev criticized "some wise people" who recently had proposed to diminish the growth rates of heavy industry.[20] Other speakers employed the pejoratives "benighted economists" and "benighted Communists."[21] Later, "the pseudo-economist Malenkov" was charged with the "anti-Leninist assertion" that "the preponderant development of heavy industry is not obligatory."[22] Or again, "Some people might say," Khrushchev noted in May 1957, " 'Why reorganize [industrial and construction] management? After all, our industry is working well. What more do you want?' "[23] Khrushchev's reorganization scheme had encountered the resistance of Malenkov and Molotov.[24] The reliability of this device of oblique reference as an indicator of high-level conflict is shown by the fact that it was persistently utilized even when the exalted status of the mysterious troublemakers had become known: in 1955-1956, although Molotov publicly retracted his statement that only the foundations of so-

[18] *Pravda*, February 15, 1956.
[19] Cf. "On the Anti-Party Group of Malenkov, G. M., Kaganovich, L. M., and Molotov, V. M.," *ibid.*, July 4, 1957, and Khrushchev, *ibid.*, December 16, 1958.
[20] *Pravda*, February 15, 1956.
[21] M. A. Suslov, *ibid.*, February 17, 1956, and F. R. Kozlov, *ibid.*, February 16, 1956, respectively.
[22] L. F. Il'ichëv, *ibid.*, October 26, 1961.
[23] *Ibid.*, May 8, 1957.
[24] "On the Anti-Party Group. . . ," *ibid.*, July 4, 1957.

cialism had been built in the USSR, Khrushchev not long afterward attributed this minority view simply to "some officials."[25]

Molotov's statement may be assumed to have been the expression of a concrete debate about policy. It minimized the progress of Soviet society and implied the need for a more circumspect line of policy. Such forthright criticisms in the public papers of leaders are rarities. Their open effort to win friends and influence elite opinion usually takes the form of textual nuance and marked reticence on current issues. The prototype of such behavior is clearly revealed in the preface which Lenin wrote in April 1917 for his *Imperialism, The Higher Stage of Capitalism*. Lenin noted that, when he wrote the book in 1916, the existence of censorship had required him to insinuate (*pisat' namëkami*) the political crux of his subject matter. The censorship rules operative in the Soviet Communist party since 1929 have constrained its endlessly feuding leaders to revive this manner of political discourse.

Those in the outer circle of the elite take it for granted that without scrutiny for points of nuance and emphasis, the underlying message of most press articles cannot be comprehended. As one of them remarks: "It has become ordinary in some discussions or articles to regard writers of the older generation, and even of the middle generation, as traditionalists (and this has become virtually 'reprehensible'!), and to proclaim the young ones to be innovators. Of course, this is not said directly, but in some 'generalizing' articles *one senses that kind of 'subtext'* " (italics added).[26] The "subtext" is by no means unfathom-

[25] Cf. *Kommunist*, No. 14, 1955, pp. 127-128; and *Pravda*, February 15, 1956.
[26] L. Remmel'gas, *Literaturnaya Gazeta* (Literary Newspaper), February 26, 1963. "Subtext" is a translation of *podtekst*.

able to outsiders. There were foreign analysts like Robert C. Tucker, who at the time compared the December 21, 1954, editorials of *Pravda* and *Izvestiya* and concluded that shadings of emphasis signified a leadership dispute over resource allocation; the judgment was supported by Malenkov's resignation of the premiership a few weeks later, amidst heavy criticism of his distinctive outlook on investment priorities, and the aforementioned remark at the 22nd party Congress.

The act of manipulating the sequence of terminology in conventional formulas is a dimension of the textual shadings. Thus a book reviewer expresses concern in this regard:

> In these same economic textbooks there are various formulations of the demand of the basic economic law of socialism. In P. Nikitin's textbook the following definition is given: "The immediate goal of socialist production is a fuller satisfaction of the constantly growing needs of the entire society through uninterrupted and rapid development of socialist production on the basis of superior technology." In the textbook *Political Economy*, authored jointly, what is *essentially an entire different formulation* [italics added] is presented: "The typical traits of *the basic economic law of socialism* include uninterrupted expansion and perfection of production on the basis of superior technology with the aim of fuller satisfaction of the constantly growing needs and all-around development of all members of society."[27]

The change in terminological sequence from consumption . . . production to production . . . consumption had sharply differentiated the writers' subtexts.

[27] G. Zinchenko, *Voprosy Ekonomiki* (Problems of Economics), No. 9, 1960, p. 135.

Deleted phraseology in reprinted material may also be analyzed from the political angle. A glimpse into factional editing practices is afforded by a party historian who deals with the conduct of Kamenev, Molotov, and Stalin as editors of *Pravda* in March 1917:

> . . . even Lenin's published text was "cut" in the editorial office in order that it might conform with the opinions of Stalin and Kamenev. This is readily seen by comparison of the genuine text of one of Lenin's letters with the version printed in *Pravda*.

Lenin writes:	*In "Pravda" this passage reads:*
"The government of Octobrists and Cadets, of Guchkovs and Milyukovs, *cannot*—even if it sincerely wished (only infants can think that Guchkov and L'vov are sincere)—*cannot give the people peace, bread, or freedom*" (V. I. Lenin, *Works*, Vol. 31, p. 20).	"The government of Octobrists and Cadets, of Guchkovs and Milyukovs, *cannot*—even if it wished —give peace, bread, or freedom" (*Pravda*, March 22, 1917).

Having expunged the parenthetic phrase, the editorial office distorted the thought of Lenin's text, implying that Lenin had allowed that Guchkov and Milyukov could sincerely desire peace, bread, and freedom for the people. Thus, the editorial office of *Pravda* weakened the political sharpness of Lenin's description of the Octobrist and Cadet government. This was also true of other excisions from Lenin's article.

Lenin writes:

"Only the capitalists and their toadies, the social-patriots and social-chauvinists,—or, to speak of political names familiar in Russia, only the Guchkovs, L'vovs, Milyukovs, and Shingarevs, on the one hand, only the Gvozdevs, Potresovs, Chkhenkelis, Kerenskys, and Chkheidzes, on the other,—can deny or gloss over this fact" (V. I. Lenin, *Works*, Vol. 31, p. 13).

In "Pravda" this passage reads:

"Only the capitalists and their toadies, the social-patriots and social-chauvinists, can deny or gloss over this fact" (*Pravda*, March 21, 1917).

The editorial office deleted the entire concluding portion of the phrase wherein Lenin proceeds from general categories to specific criticism of the figures of the bourgeois government and of the Mensheviks. The editorial office of *Pravda* further "rectifies" Lenin by substituting a doubly "general" presentation of the question in place of criticism which is objective and comprehensible to the toilers.

Lenin writes:

"Otherwise the Guchkovs and Milyukovs will restore the monarchy and not deliver any of the 'freedoms'

In "Pravda" this passage reads:

"Otherwise the people will be deceived. Promises are cheap. All bourgeois intriguers in *all* bourgeois

they have promised. All bourgeois intriguers in all bourgeois revolutions have 'fed' the people promises and stupefied the workers. Our revolution is a bourgeois revolution. Therefore, the workers must support the bourgeoisie, according to the Potresovs, Gvozdevs, Chkheidzes, and Plekhanov, who spoke yesterday" (V. I. Lenin, *Works*, Vol. 31, p. 20).

revolutions have 'fed' the people promises and stupefied the workers. Our revolution is a bourgeois revolution. Therefore, the workers must support the bourgeoisie, according to the utterly worthless politicians from the camp of the Liquidators" (*Pravda*, March 22, 1917).

And here too the "rectifications" emasculated Lenin's criticism of the Guchkovs, Milyukovs, and defensive-war types like Chkheidze.[28]

The pitfall of reading the Soviet press in terms of Western values was avoided in May 1957 by Victor Zorza, who believed that the silence of a leader on a topical issue registered his disagreement with the expressed viewpoint of his colleagues. Zorza reported that the failure of certain members of the party Presidium to subscribe in public to Khrushchev's proposal to reorganize industrial and construction management denoted high-level opposition to the plan. Zorza was later proved to have been correct. It is noteworthy that as the proof was forthcoming, K. Fedin, secretary of the USSR Writers' Union, stated this particular rule of internal political communication:

Two alternatives are possible: to share the responsibility of the editorial board to which you belong, or to

[28] A. V. Snegov, *Voprosy Istorii KPSS*, No. 2, 1963, pp. 23-24.

explain in what things you differ from your colleagues and why, and thus dissociate yourself from responsibility for their actions. To do neither means to repudiate your responsibility to the reader. A third position—that of silence—can only mean an intention to say to the reader: "See, everyone is 'for,' and we are 'against.' "[29]

The rule was still in force at the time of the December 1958 CPSU Central Committee session. T. A. Yurkin, a ministerial official, or a state functionary, told how in 1954 he and other Committee members had attended expanded meetings of the party Presidium for discussion of Khrushchev's virgin soil program and witnessed the first secretary's arguments with Molotov, Malenkov, and Kaganovich. "But," Yurkin added, "Bulganin ordinarily was silent."[30] L. R. Korniyets, an agricultural procurement officer, elaborated vindictively: "When the group [of Malenkov and Molotov] opposed this most urgent and vitally important measure of the party—I have in mind assimilation of the virgin lands—Bulganin was silent, that is, acted like a double-dealer."[31]

The "language of conflict" points to the existence of debate in the leadership, helps to clarify active political issues, and suggests the positions of individual leaders. But it tells nothing about the character of the disputes and the motivations of the protagonists. Specifically, are the

[29] *Pravda*, June 16, 1957 (*Current Digest of the Soviet Press*, New York, Vol. IX, No. 24, pp. 13ff.; source cited hereafter as CDSP).
[30] *Plenum Tsentral'nogo Komiteta Kommunisticheskoy Partii Sovetskogo Soyuza, 15-19 dekabrya 1958 goda, stenograficheskiy otchët* (Plenum of the Central Committee of the Communist Party of the Soviet Union, December 15-19, 1958, Minutes), Moscow, 1958, p. 409 (source cited hereafter as *Plenum I*).
[31] *Ibid.*, p. 518.

exchanges bland or acrimonious, and do the contenders merely struggle for power or are their battles tests of antagonistic conviction? Here, valuable insights may be gleaned from party literature. A propagandist remarks that Soviet Communists "argue not about which world outlook to support—their world outlook is Marxism-Leninism—and not about whether the party's general line is correct or incorrect—its correctness is proved by life and does not evoke doubts—but about *how best to resolve problems of everyday policy and practice, which choices to make in order more successfully to resolve one or another specific task* . . ." (italics added).[32] The profession of universal belief in the ideology and acceptance of the broad course of policy cannot be taken to mean that the arguments are neither bitter nor consequential. Both parties to the Sino-Soviet dispute of 1956-1963 repeatedly affirmed their devotion to "Marxism-Leninism" and the "general line" of the Communist movement as enunciated in the documents of the 1957 and 1960 world conferences of the Communist parties. But a rancorous division persisted over tactical alternatives on which the fate of world peace might have depended. Just how high feelings run in the course of leadership disputes in Soviet Russia may be gauged from the facts that a "policy of revenge" in relations between Presidium members is entirely credible to elite audiences, and that once disputes are resolved, job reprisals and awards are usually meted out to the entourages of feuding chieftains.[33] As in any polity, questions of power and policy are intertwined. A member of the

[32] N. Lomakin, *Partiynaya Zhizn'* (*Party Life*), No. 7, 1960, p. 16.
[33] On the tradition of political patronage, or *"sheftsvo,"* see Borkenau, *op. cit.* I have since learned that it is also discussed in Franz Borkenau, "Getting at the Facts Behind the Soviet Façade," *Commentary*, Vol. 17, No. 4 (April 1954), pp. 393-400. On malice

party Presidium implausibly alleged at the 22nd Congress that the group of Malenkov and Molotov coveted only power; the revised version of his speech in the minutes of the Congress more convincingly links power and policy.[34] A logical inference is that certain key positions in the party bureaucracy are better suited than others for the mounting of policy initiatives and must be captured through struggle. In particular, the administrative board, or Secretariat, of the party Central Committee has been a focal point of contention in view of its important role with respect to staff studies.

Clearly, there would be no struggles if all leaders shared the same values. Their behavior is actually determined by all kinds of considerations. Party doctrine requires that policy be formulated in such a manner as to

---

in the Presidium, see "Saburov's Declaration at the XXI Party Congress," *Soviet Studies*, Vol. xi, pp. 220-221.

[34] Cf. O. V. Kuusinen's speech in *Pravda*, October 27, 1961, and *XXII S"yezd Kommunisticheskoy Partii Sovetskogo Soyuza, 17-31 oktyabrya 1961 goda, stenograficheskiy otchët* (22nd Congress of the Communist Party of the Soviet Union, October 17-31, 1961, Minutes), Moscow, 1962, Vol. ii, p. 390. The pertinent texts are:

Pravda, October 27, 1961

. . . from the very outset it was obvious that the main urge of this group was to remove from the Central Committee Presidium Comrade Nikita Sergeyevich Khrushchev—continuator of the cause of Lenin—and to seize all leadership in its hands.

Minutes, approved for publication December 22, 1961:

. . . in the first instance, this group sought the removal from the Central Committee Presidium of Comrade Nikita Sergeyevich Khrushchev—continuator of the cause of Lenin—and strove to seize all leadership in its hands *in order to have the opportunity to change the policy of the party, which was charted by the 20th Congress* (italics added).

promote harmony between classes and ethnic groups, ensure national security, and maximize national wealth with minimum expenditure of labor and resources.[35] But Khru-

[35] The doctrine of the "primacy of politics over economics" is officially defined as follows: "The Communist party considers that not one of its decisions on problems of economics and culture which is of nation-wide importance can be executed without the decisions having an effect on the political condition of the country, on the relations between the working class and the peasantry, on the relations between the peoples of the USSR. Therefore, the party and Soviet government in making their decisions examine problems foremost from the political standpoint, that is, take into account the relations between classes and nations. The correct political approach to any matter of state requires foremost a clear-cut answer to the question of whether or not the given measure facilitates strengthening of the Soviet state, strengthening of the working class's alliance with the peasantry, the friendship of the peoples of the USSR, and the building of communism. The political approach to the solution of the tasks of economic and cultural organization expresses the concern of the party for the political condition of the country, for facilitating to the utmost the strengthening of the Soviet state and for mobilizing the forces of the multinational Soviet people for the building of a communist society" (Bol'shaya Sovetskaya Entsiklopediya [Large Soviet Encyclopedia], Moscow, 1955, Vol. 33, p. 558).
An ideological functionary's amplification of the doctrine throws light upon some of the specific issues at stake: "Take, for example, the solution of problems like the development of industry and agriculture, the allocation of capital investments between branches of the economy and spheres of cultural life, between various regions of the country, the fixing of prices of manufactured goods and agricultural products, etc. These are not only economic but also political problems, since their solution concerns the interests of different social groups—workers and office employees, the kolkhoz peasantry, and the interests of different nations which form the Soviet Union. The party solves all these problems so that the interests of any social group are not infringed upon and the alliance of the working class and peasantry will be unswervingly strengthened and the friendship of the peoples be reinforced" (G. Glezerman, Kommunist, No. 7, 1963, p. 32). The 1961 party Program instructs that "The immutable law of economic development is to achieve in the interests of society the highest results at the lowest cost" (Pravda, November 2, 1961).

21

shchev's opponents of 1956-1957 have been plausibly accused of anti-peasant bigotry, Great Russian chauvinism, underestimation of Soviet military power, and delaying tactics.[36] Moreover, there is evidence that personalities at the policy-making level may champion the interests of one institutional agency over another and keep considerations of personal prestige foremost in their moves.[37]

[36] Cf. Khrushchev, *Pravda*, December 16, 1958, I. Vinnichenko, *Literaturnaya Gazeta*, February 20, 1962, and V. Stepanov, *Izvestiya*, February 8, 1963, all concerning the group's anti-peasant prejudice; M. O. Mnatsakanyan, *Voprosy Istorii KPSS*, No. 10, 1963, p. 6, with reference to the group's "chauvinistic position" of mistrusting indigenous personnel in the borderlands; and, on Molotov's underestimation of Communist Bloc power, N. M. Druzhinin, ed., *Sovetskaya Istoricheskaya Nauka ot XX k XXII S"yezdu KPSS: Istoriya SSSR; sbornik statey* (Soviet Historical Science from the 20th to the 22nd CPSU Congress: USSR History; A Collection of Articles), Moscow, 1962, p. 494.

[37] Some members of the Malenkov-Molotov group had wrongfully attempted to "substantiate the primacy of state agencies over party agencies" (*Kommunist*, No. 10, 1957, p. 5). While in charge of railroads, Kaganovich and Molotov had sought preferential treatment for that sector of the economy (cf. *Izvestiya*, May 8 and 10, 1962). A. I. Kosygin, a member of the party Presidium, told the 22nd CPSU Congress that "Often in the solving of economic problems the position of the members of the anti-party group was dictated not by economic or technical expediency, but by considerations of personal prestige" (*Pravda*, October 23, 1961). Khrushchev alluded to the importance of the prestige factor in a memorandum (*zapiska*) of March 31, 1961, which he submitted to the party Presidium. After urging the creation of a representative farm inspectorate and advisory board in Moscow, he remarked: "True, it might be said that such an agency is to some extent a repetition of the Council for Kolkhoz Affairs which existed a few years ago. It must be recognized that even the Council for Kolkhoz Affairs called to order certain local leaders. And it was abolished not because it failed to justify itself, but because Malenkov, who was then responsible for agriculture, did not want to have a Council for Kolkhoz Affairs which was headed by A. A. Andreyev, who incontestably knew more about kolkhoz production than he did. Precisely for that reason, Malenkov strove to abolish the Council for Kolkhoz Affairs" (N. S. Khrushchev, *Stroitel'stvo Kommunizma v SSSR i Razvitiye*

In sum, the empirical data for study and interpretation of Soviet politics are neither meager nor prohibitively incomplete. A proved reliability attaches to the jargon of Communist discourse, which a Soviet historian has rightfully deplored as "the cement-like language." If this language is carefully examined over periods of time, in conjunction with the career patterns of party leaders, issues and leadership alignments can be reasonably established. A margin of error is inevitable in this kind of analytical enterprise. But to ignore the data and appeal beyond them is to value intuition rather than induction in the attempt to comprehend Soviet behavior.

The original plan of this study called for its limitation to the events of 1958-1963, or the five years since Khrushchev and his group defeated the consortium of Malenkov and Molotov. But a perusal of background material showed a continuity of issues and decision-making roles which necessitated an introductory review of postwar arguments over Stalin's conventional agricultural policy, the despot's influential valediction on the chronic "peasant question," and relevant aspects of the leadership struggle of 1953-1958. Accordingly, Chapter I deals with the Stalin heritage of policy tradition, postwar disputes, and personal maneuvering, while the ongoing controversies are treated in Chapter II (1953-1958). Separate chapters are devoted to the events of 1958, 1959, and 1960 because Central Committee meetings were then convened annually to discuss farm problems and the transactions revolved around specific clusters of issues. The

---

Sel'skogo Khozyaystva [Building of Communism in the USSR and Development of Agriculture], Moscow, 1963, v, 349; source cited hereafter as *S.K. v SSSR i R.S.Kh.*).

managerial and investment conflicts of 1961 and 1962 seemed to require joint discussion in view of their association with the new party Program. The section devoted to "Conclusions" will present hypotheses about the broader implications for Soviet politics which issue from the record of upper-level strife over agriculture in the post-Stalin period.

The reasoning of the present study derives almost entirely from an examination of the leading national papers of Soviet Russia, as distinct from the specialized agricultural press. I have felt that the actual state of affairs in the countryside, which has underlain the policy proposals of at least some leaders, may be adequately known by studying the central press together with the production and management reports of Western experts like Naum Jasny, Arcadius Kahan, J. Miller, Alec Nove, Solomon M. Schwarz, and Lazar Volin.

A foremost debt of gratitude must be expressed to Solomon M. Schwarz and Boris Nicolaevsky, whose commentaries on Soviet agriculture, integrating as they do the inseparable problems of politics and economics, have literally inspired me. I am also most grateful to Set Mardirosian, whom I regard as the most knowledgeable American-born student of Soviet politics. Mr. Mardirosian in the course of my work has offered incisive criticisms of a substantive kind and generously made available his extensive notes of Soviet materials which bear on the subject. Valuable suggestions have also been made by James Billington and Carl Linden, to whom I am thankful.

PRINCETON, NEW JERSEY
SEPTEMBER, 1964

CHAPTER I

THE LEGACY OF STALINISM

THE ESSENTIALS of Stalin's own special theory of government banefully influenced the development of Soviet agriculture for nearly a quarter-century. "Stalinism" insisted on a scale of economic priorities geared toward comprehensive build-up of the heavy engineering and armaments industries. It deemphasized the short-term satisfaction of consumer needs and granted powers of enforcement to a highly centralized bureaucracy. In agriculture, Stalinism meant output without state inputs for the necessary amounts of machinery and chemical fertilizer.[1] It meant a subsistence reward for the work of the

[1] These figures demonstrate the low priority of agriculture in Stalin's investment program:

	Investment (in billions of 1962 rubles and in comparable prices)		
Years	In the entire economy	In agriculture (by state and kolkhozes)	In agriculture in percentage to all capital investment in the economy
1938-June 1941 ..	16.4	2.0	12.2
1946-1950	38.0	5.4	14.2
1951-1953	38.9	5.7	14.7
1953	13.9	1.9	13.7

SOURCE: V. Khlebnikov, *Voprosy Ekonomiki*, No. 7, 1962, p. 50. The state's share of the total agricultural investment is 50-60 per cent.

As a consequence of this relatively meager input, the technical equipment of agriculture in the Stalin period was far below the

greater part of the agricultural labor force, which was involuntarily enrolled in nominal cooperatives known as collective farms, or kolkhozes.[2] Stalinism also denoted

1955 level, which a Soviet commentator observed to be "inadequate." His comparative data are as follows:

	1940	1950	1955
Tractors (in 15 h.p. units)	531,000	595,000	844,000
Tractor power (in terms of millions of h.p.)	10.3	14.0	21.6
Trucks, including fuel trucks	228,000	283,000	544,000
Grain combines	181,700	211,200	388,000

SOURCE: T. Koval', *Kommunist*, No. 2, 1957, p. 52.

In practical terms, this signified basic mechanization of the sowing and harvesting of grain and certain specialized crops. Kolkhoz tasks in 1952 were mechanized as follows: sowing grain —87 per cent; combine harvesting—70 per cent; plowing fallow land—96 per cent; fall plowing—97 per cent; sowing cotton—98 per cent; and planting sugar beets—95 per cent (N. S. Khrushchev, *Pravda*, September 15, 1953 [CDSP, v, 39, p. 11]). Although grain farming reached the highest level of mechanization, labor-consuming processes like gathering straw and chaff and cleaning of grain on threshing floors had not yet been mechanized. Animal husbandry and potato and truck farming were branches in which manual labor predominated. Only on some kolkhozes had such labor-consuming processes as preparing feed and piping water been mechanized (I. Laptev, *Pravda*, September 19, 1953 [CDSP, v, 38, p. 10]). As late as 1959, six times less chemical fertilizer was available in the Ukraine and Moldavia than was used in the US (T. Koval', *Kommunist*, No. 15, 1959, p. 36).

[2] On the organization of farming, see Alexander Vucinich, *Soviet Economic Institutions: The Social Structure of Production Units*, introduction by Sergius Yakobson, Hoover Institute Series, Series E:Institutions, Stanford, 1952. The average amount of cash annually paid by a kolkhoz in 1952 was 623 (old) rubles, or about $60.00, per household (Lazar Volin, *Problems of Communism*, Vol. VIII, No. 1, 1959, p. 39. Unless noted otherwise, the January 1, 1961, exchange rate of 10 old to one new ruble will be used). Supplementary payment-in-kind was unpublicized, perhaps because in many cases it never exceeded the prewar iron ration of one or two kilograms of grain offered by 30 per cent of the kolkhozes for each "labor-day," or accounting unit of

a method of rule whereby the vast majority of agricultural technicians were employed in offices, relaying downward the centrally designated plans for kolkhozes, which listed hundreds of production goals, not differentiated according to local soil and climatic conditions.[3] Moreover, heavy agricultural equipment was isolated in state-run Machine and Tractor Stations (MTS), which independently performed basic farm operations, mainly in return for a part of the crop.[4] The ruinous effect of such practices is apparent from data which show that in the period 1928-1953, when the number of urban consumers increased by over 50 million, gross agricultural production rose only 7 per cent and the output of livestock products declined.[5]

---

personal labor (G. A. Chigrinov cites this figure from the Archive of the USSR Commissariat of Agriculture, in *Voprosy Istorii KPSS*, No. 1, 1962, p. 129). At the time, 1937, a workday averaged 1.28 "labor-days" in 430 surveyed kolkhozes; 194 annual "labor-days" per able-bodied collective farmer and 438 per household were officially reported (Naum Jasny, *The Socialized Agriculture of the USSR: Plans and Performance*, Stanford, 1949, p. 417).

[3] Khrushchev, *Pravda*, September 15, 1953.

[4] On the MTS, see Lazar Volin, *A Survey of Soviet Russian Agriculture*, Agriculture Monograph 5, U.S. Department of Agriculture, Washington, D.C., 1951, pp. 67-68; and Jasny, *op. cit.*, pp. 293-294.

[5] The following figures indicate this lag in gross agricultural production using 1928 as the base year:

	1937	1940	1950	1953
Gross Agricultural Production	96	98	106	107
inclusive of:				
tillage	117	117	124	115
livestock	73	77	87	98

SOURCE: Khlebnikov, *op.cit.*, p. 49.

I am grateful to Professor Warren W. Eason for his estimates of the urban population on January 1, 1928, and January 1, 1953, the latter inclusive of territories annexed after 1939.

In the general setting of the depressed condition of agriculture during the final years of Stalin's reign, conflicting tendencies were at work on the policy-making level. Some members of the Politburo who appreciated the critical situation in the countryside urged that the regime's traditional course be modified in the direction of increased reliance on economic levers instead of administrative orders, and relaxation of central controls over kolkhozes. This movement of new ideas was current among leaders whose daily responsibilities were in the planning sector and who must have viewed the lag of agriculture as a threat to the further progress of rapidly advancing industry (Voznesenskiy) and those who were versed in the complexities of governing an important farm region (Khrushchev). Countervailing sentiment predominated among executives whose humdrum concerns were related less to problems of economic efficiency than to maintaining strict social discipline under central authority (Malenkov and Beriya). The competitive strivings of these reformist and orthodox-minded personalities to gain the despot's favor and his own vested interest in embroiling lieutenants in unremitting conflict with one another precluded any stable accommodation of the rival influences and helped to invest general policy with an air of uncertainty. The hesitation would prevail until the Malenkov-Beriya partnership, which since 1949 had held sway on a foundation of terror, first under Stalin and then among his heirs, was broken in the early summer of 1953 and a relatively freer climate obtained in an expanded arena of hidden politics.

The Empiric Ascendance (1946-1949)

Responsibility for ensuring the recovery of agriculture

from wartime losses fell to Nikolay A. Voznesenskiy, a theoretical economist born in 1903, who in the last decade had served as chief planner in Leningrad, chairman of the USSR State Planning Commission (a Committee since 1948), deputy premier, alternate member of the Politburo, and co-chairman of the State Defense Committee in charge of military procurement. Voznesenskiy's disposition toward seeking realistic solutions to the problems of a dislocated command economy was reflected in his writings, which underscored the importance of money relations, market prices, and the calculation of profits and losses.[6] This empiric approach, which ran counter to the voluntarist mainstream of Stalinist thought, made its imprint on agricultural policy in 1947 and early 1948, when Voznesenskiy reached the height of his success with promotion to full membership in the Politburo and receipt of a Stalin Prize for his book *The War Economy of the USSR in the Period of the Patriotic War*. The remedies for production ills which Stalin then approved at the behest of his main economic advisor included greater material encouragement of work in the socialized sector, defense of the collective farmers' right to conduct private activities, wide use of consumer cooperatives as commission agents to dispose of farm surpluses in the town, and enhanced autonomy and payment for on-the-spot technicians. At the same time, definite limits to rationality were imposed by Stalin's capricious temperament. He angrily rebuffed Khrushchev's intimations that peasant tax rates were excessive and that agrotechnical practices designed to conserve chemical ferti-

[6] See P. J. D. Wiles, *The Political Economy of Communism*, Cambridge, Mass., 1962, pp. 104ff.; and G. Sorokin's article on the sixtieth birthday of Voznesenskiy in *Pravda*, December 1, 1963.

lizer were untenable. In keeping with Stalin's divisive tactics, Khrushchev was provided with an opportunity to overcome an intrigue of Malenkov's against his pragmatic viewpoint on agrotechnology and made the best of it. But more doctrinaire policies crystallized in 1948 after the death of Voznesenskiy's patron, A. A. Zhdanov.

Any lingering hope of the war years that the kolkhoz system of mixed and private subsidiary farming, with heavy emphasis on the former, would be superseded by exclusive reliance on individual initiative was dashed in September 1946 by the state decree ordering restoration to the kolkhozes of property and livestock which the peasants had unlawfully seized in the recent upheaval.[7] A Council on Kolkhoz Affairs headed by Politburo member A. A. Andreyev was established in the government on October 8, 1946, to enforce the disciplinary edict through a network of representatives in the localities functioning as central controllers, independent of local agencies.[8] But within the framework of the kolkhoz system there was considerable room for the government to maneuver between the extremes of relative tolerance and stark regimentation.

The preferability of moderation was obvious to Khrushchev, who sketched the contours of agricultural policy in the immediate postwar years in a speech delivered on January 18, 1946, at a conference in the Ukraine.[9] Khrushchev began his party political career in industry, but

[7] "Against Violations of the Kolkhoz Charter," James H. Meisel and Edward S. Kozera, eds., *Materials for the Study of the Soviet System*, 2nd revised and enlarged edn., Ann Arbor, 1953, pp. 388-394.

[8] *Ibid.*, p. 395.

[9] "More Rapidly Restore Agriculture of the Soviet Ukraine," *Partiynoye Stroitel'stvo* (Party Organization), No. 2, 1946, pp. 28-44

after appointment to leadership of the Ukraine in 1938 he evolved into a full-fledged agronomist whose lively interest in kolkhoz details attracted the notice of foreign visitors.[10] Yet on the eve of the war, Khrushchev had successfully promoted various measures which aimed at raising material inducements and personal responsibility for kolkhoz labor, recruiting more energetic and knowledgeable people into the central agricultural agencies, and granting some measure of independence to farm technicians within the limits of the central plans.[11] Khrushchev in January 1946 reaffirmed his belief that kolkhozes might be put on a sounder economic and political footing by a proper combination of personal and societal interests. He boosted anew the "link" system of organizing labor in small units, which enabled precise measurement of the costs and results of work and appropriate impact on earnings.[12] The example of 4,000 kolkhozes in the Ukraine

[10] Cf. *S.K. v SSSR i R.S.Kh.*, II, 425; John Maynard, *Russia in Flux*, New York, 1948, p. 410; and Milovan Djilas, *Conversations with Stalin*, New York, 1962, p. 122. These observations of Maynard capture one aspect of Khrushchev's style: "A good sign is that some of the Communists are beginning to study the details of agriculture, and learning to talk to farmers in farmers' language. Here is a scrap from a long speech by Khrushchev, Secretary of the Central Committee of the Party in the Ukraine, with the *voces populi* interjected: 'You must have your coarse-wool sheep as well as your fine. A jacket from a coarse-wool Rumanian sheep is good for fifteen years' wear. (Applause.) I can't imagine what life in the village would be like without a sheepskin jacket. (Laughter.) . . . You must do better with your buckwheat. Trofim Denisovich Lysenko (a famous popularizer of new farming methods) says, grow millet instead. Millet? But what about your bowl of porridge? (Laughter.) And don't you want buckwheat for the sake of your bees? No honey this morning! What? (More laughter.)'"

[11] The proposals and decrees of 1939-1940 are reviewed by Chigrinov in *Voprosy Istorii KPSS*, No. 1, 1962, pp. 137-139. A. I. Mikoyan is named as a supporter of the changes.

[12] The importance of the "link" for tending labor-intensive

which regularized incentives by offering supplementary payments, another of Khrushchev's prewar innovations,[13] was likewise held up for emulation. Khrushchev drew on one of Stalin's conciliatory pronouncements of the mid-1930's to emphasize the admissibility of a private plot for each kolkhoz household.

The moderate spirit of Khrushchev's speech was reasserted in the report of Andreyev to the February 1947 CPSU(B) Central Committee Plenum, which raised Voznesenskiy to full membership in the Politburo.[14] Andreyev insisted that each kolkhoz household dispose of its own cow for private use. He disclosed that a memorandum (*zapiska*) on grain farming had been submitted to the government by P. I. Doronin, who became party first secretary of Kursk Region, Khrushchev's birthplace in the Ukraine, shortly after Khrushchev took charge of the territory in 1938 and who served with Andreyev and Khrushchev on the board of the council on Kolkhoz Affairs. Andreyev only remarked that the proposals from Kursk concerned pay for work in kolkhozes. But articles which Doronin later wrote for the organizational magazine of central party headquarters[15] leave no doubt

---

crops like sugar beets and tobacco, but its unsuitability in grain farming, was pointed out in a law adopted after Khrushchev's arrival in the Ukraine, viz., the decree of the USSR Council of People's Commissars and CPSU(B) Central Committee of December 31, 1940, "On Supplementary Payment of Collective Farmers for Raising Yields of Agricultural Crops and Productivity of Livestock in the Ukrainian SSR," in *Istoriya Kolkhoznogo Prava* (History of Kolkhoz Law), Moscow, 1958, ii, pp. 165-175.

[13] *Ibid.*

[14] Accounts of the Plenum are in *Pravda*, February 28, 1947, and March 7, 1947.

[15] "Examine Deeply the Economy of Kolkhozes," *Partiynaya Zhizn'*, No. 17, 1947, pp. 6-15; and "Questions of Organizing Labor in Kolkhozes," *ibid.*, No. 1, 1948, pp. 20-24.

that he was pressing for adoption of the small-scale work unit in grain farming, too. Doronin's memorandum may therefore be regarded as the origin of the April 19, 1948, decree of the USSR Council of People's Commissars which authorized the incentive-directed "link" in grain farming.[16] Still another concession to peasant self-interest which resulted from the plenum was broader allowance for consumer cooperatives to act as commission agents in disposing of kolkhoz surpluses in urban markets. The cooperative shops paid higher than official state purchase prices for foodstuffs bought under decentralized procurement and offered urban consumers a state-controlled alternative to the free, kolkhoz market in supplementing their purchases.[17] In the early part of 1947, 19,000 commission shops opened in cities and worker villages, and meat sales by urban cooperatives ranged from one-fifth to one-quarter of the total of such sales.[18]

Stalin came forward at the 1947 Plenum with one of his rare overt interventions of the day. Andreyev revealed that during the session Stalin recommended that agriculture experts not actually working in farms and MTS but in administrative posts remote from the barnyards should receive a quarter less pay than those in operational jobs. This would have logically complemented a recent directive prohibiting anyone from rescinding or altering agrotechnical measures formulated by kolkhozes, together with agronomists, without the knowledge of the special-

[16] "On Measures for Improving Organization, Raising Productivity, and Regularizing Wages in Kolkhozes," *Istoriya Kolkhoznogo Prava*, II, pp. 309-317.

[17] See John T. Whitman, "The Kolkhoz Market," *Soviet Studies*, Vol. VII, pp. 384-398, which notes that in 1948 turnover on the kolkhoz market amounted to about 15 per cent of total retail trade.

[18] B. Braginskiy, *Partiynaya Zhizn'*, No. 13, 1947, p. 53.

ists involved or permission of the district representatives of the Ministry of Agriculture.[19] But Stalin was not prepared to heed local technicians after the Ukrainian granary had undergone its worst drought since the famine of 1921. The dictator had already rebuked his overlord in the Ukraine for advocating appeasement in internal affairs. After Khrushchev made an inspection tour of the hinterland at the close of the war, he reported to Stalin that a village cousin had complained about the high tax on private apple orchards. According to Khrushchev, Stalin "replied that I was a *narodnik*, [peasant socialist] that mine was the *narodnik* approach, and that I had lost the proletarian class instinct."[20] Now Stalin doubted Khrushchev's competence to function as the master agronomist of his domain.

The argument over agrotechnical policy which was touched off at the 1947 Plenum had serious implications not only for grain production, vitally important as that was, but also for investment policy and personal relationships in the ruling group. It furthermore disclosed the intimate association of the notables of politics and science in Soviet Russia.[21] The dispute raised the question of the appropriateness of the grassland crop rotation system, a method of farming to compensate for the scarcities of chemical fertilizer and machinery and to maintain soil fertility and structure, combat wind erosion, and provide an economical source of feed for livestock. (The system calls for successive periods of sown grass and cultivated

[19] State Plan for Development of Agriculture in 1946, *Pravda,* March 9, 1946.
[20] *Kommunist,* No. 12, 1957, pp. 12-13.
[21] The particulars of this argument are in *S.K. v SSSR i R.S. Kh.,* I, 137-139, II, 107, and VI, 57-58 and 177-180.

crops, with a minimum of two or three consecutive years of perennial grasses and clover to be included in crop rotations averaging from 7 to 9 years in length.) Khrushchev had told Stalin even before the war that conditions in the Ukraine were not suitable for the cultivation of spring wheat, which was planted in conjunction with the grassland system. The cultivation of winter wheat was deemed more feasible in the southern environment, but at the 1947 Plenum the Siberian agronomist Mal'tsev recited figures attesting to the high yield of spring wheat in the eastern areas. When Politburo members adjourned to a nearby room during an intermission, Stalin, disheartened by the recent poor harvest in the Ukraine, turned on Khrushchev for objecting to the extensive planting of spring wheat in his region. Stalin ordered that the decree of the Plenum record a serious lag in spring wheat production in the Ukraine, and this was done. The impersonal phraseology of the critical notation was ignored in domestic political quarters and the mere act of criticism was taken to represent Stalin's displeasure with Khrushchev and his Ukrainian subjects in general. As Khrushchev recalls the incident: " . . . the Plenum condemned the Ukrainian leaders for failure to appreciate spring wheat. True, my name was not mentioned. But all who knew even the slightest about the crux of the matter understood that it was directed against me personally. Then I said to Stalin that the Krasnodar and Rostov leaders should also be condemned since they do the same as we. But Stalin rejected my proposal. As you can see, he wanted to strike only at the Ukraine."

The differences over agrotechnology probably were a contributing factor to the removal of Khrushchev from the party first secretaryship of the Ukraine in March

1947. He retained the territorial premiership alone and was subordinated to Kaganovich, new party chief, and his deputy N. S. Patolichev, whose career fortunes indicate a connection with Malenkov. Under Kaganovich, Stalin's *diktat* in behalf of spring wheat was implemented and agricultural productivity put in jeopardy. Khrushchev requested of Stalin during a personal audience that he countermand his order for the large-scale planting of spring wheat. Stalin was reluctant to accede to the plea but finally asked that the central planners take proper action. This may have been mere duplicity, for when Khrushchev proceeded to organize a relevant discussion with kolkhoz chairmen and agronomists who backed a return to winter wheat, Stalin's dauphin arranged a press attack on Khrushchev's preference. Malenkov and A. I. Kozlov, chief of the CPSU(B) Central Committee's Agricultural Section, instructed the soil biologist Academician T. D. Lysenko to write an article degrading winter wheat and promoting the spring variety. The lesson which Khrushchev later drew from this incident was that it "demonstrates how some leaders use authoritative people for their selfish ends."

The primacy of political over technological considerations was also demonstrated in the handling of Khrushchev's proposal for land irrigation in the Ukraine. After the great drought of 1946, Khrushchev ordered that plans be drafted for the watering of lands in the southern Ukraine. The plans called for the building of a reservoir and hydropower station at Kakhovka and the irrigation of 600,000 hectares (one hectare equals 2.471 acres) by regulating the flow of the Dnieper River. The Ukrainian Politburo approved of the scheme and lodged a request with Stalin, who in turn transmitted it to Vice-Premiers

Malenkov and Beriya. Yet during the war period Beriya had vied with Khrushchev for the favor of Stalin.[22] At a session of the USSR Council of Ministers, Malenkov announced that Stalin had entrusted him with declaring that the Ukrainian plan had to be rejected because of the large capital outlays which it entailed. However, in less than a year's time, a decision was adopted to build the South Ukrainian Canal, which required several times the amount of investment needed to implement the Ukrainian plan and was ill-considered from a technical standpoint. This decision has been ascribed to the initiative of Stalin, but in quotation marks, suggesting that Malenkov and Beriya were partly responsible for it. Moreover, after the fall of Beriya, in 1954, work was halted on the South Ukrainian Canal and measures were taken to build at rapid tempo the Kakhovka power station.[23]

The thought of Malenkov's accumulating excessive power may have caused concern in Stalin's immediate circle.[24] Khrushchev managed to regain the party first

[22] According to A. N. Saburov, a partisan commander in the Ukraine during World War II: "It is quite essential to show the negative role of Beriya during the Patriotic War. Beriya had to supply the partisan units and underground organizations with communications equipment. As a careerist and political adventurer, Beriya tried to compete with the party Central Committee, showing that he supposedly did more than the Central Committee of the C.P.(B) of the Ukraine. As a result of such hostile activity on the part of Beriya, many partisan units of the Ukraine, including the units of A. F. Fedorov and S. A. Kovpak, were deprived of communications equipment at the beginning of the war" (*Voprosy Istorii KPSS Perioda Velikoy Otechestvennoy Voyny* [Problems of CPSU History of the Period of the Great Patriotic War], Kiev, 1961, p. 300).

[23] The Kakhovka affair is related by Ye. Alekseyevskiy in *Kommunist Ukrainy* (Communist of the Ukraine), No. 12, 1963, pp. 9-10.

[24] See George Paloczi-Horvath, *Khrushchev: The Road to*

secretaryship of the Ukraine in December 1947, albeit compelled to relinquish his government post. He warned Stalin of the prospect of grain difficulties in the Ukraine if spring wheat plantings continued there and succeeded in making his point. But Stalin, whose personal prestige was involved, refused to overturn the pertinent verdict of 1947 by means of an order of the Central Committee Politburo or Secretariat. He chose instead the "roundabout way" (*okol'nym putëm*) of arranging a regional conference of scientists and farm practitioners at which adherents of the grassland system would have to concede defeat. At the conference, which was held in Kiev sometime in 1949 and attended by about 500 agricultural officials, the scientists who upheld the grassland system were overwhelmed in "hot battles" that Khrushchev diplomatically audited from behind the scenes.

The conclusion which had to be drawn from the outcome of the Ukrainian wheat issue was that no real alternative existed to a policy of substantial investment in agriculture. But in the summer of 1948 Stalin's gaze was fixed on the external problems of quarantining his satellite empire in East Europe against the virus of independence spreading from Yugoslavia, and of dislodging the Western powers from their Berlin salient within the empire. Concurrently, on August 31, 1948, Zhdanov, the benefactor of Voznesenskiy and Stalin's deputy in the Central Committee Secretariat, died suddenly. Stalin might have been expected to have named as his new aide a figure who was not merely reputed to be "hard" and "dogmatic," as had been true of Zhdanov, but could be relied upon to ferret out of the bureaucracy men eager to tackle

Power, London, 1960, pp. 116-117. This book is the best political biography of Khrushchev which is available to date.

the acute domestic needs of the hour. That repressive function was allotted to Malenkov, who for the first time in several years was listed as a member of the Secretariat on July 20, 1948. Malenkov's identification with the "conservative" viewpoint in the recent skirmish over the grassland method provides reason to believe that he was instrumental in launching at the end of 1948 the series of long-term investment projects which were predicated on the illusion that the short-term situation in agriculture was not critical. These enterprises, which came to be known in time as "The Great Stalin Projects for Remaking Nature," were inaugurated on October 24, 1948, when the press carried the decree of the USSR Council of Ministers and CPSU(B) Central Committee "On the Planting of Protective Forest Belts, the Introduction of a System of Crop Rotation with Grasses, and the Construction of Ponds and Reservoirs, with a view to securing high and stable crop yields in the steppe and mixed forest-and-steppe districts of the European part of the USSR."[25] The results of the afforestation plan to combat drought would not be known until the trees had grown sufficiently to start fulfilling their task, which might take ten or fifteen years; the climate of part of the territory scheduled for tree planting was so dry that failure was likely despite the greatest care; and kolkhozes were saddled with an enormous financial burden, since they had to pay for seedlings and the use of machinery supplied by the state and repay an undisclosed amount of state credits.[26]

The phase of relative liberality now drew to a close. Its characteristic feature was the adoption of a series of

[25] Meisel and Kozera, *op. cit.*, pp. 468-469.
[26] Naum Jasny, *Soviet Studies*, Vol. III, p. 154.

measures to reward diligent work in both the private and socialized sectors. The policies of one-cow-per-household, commercial trade, and the small work unit in grain farming were all directed toward that end. The leaders most closely associated with these incentive policies were Khrushchev and Voznesenskiy. There is no direct evidence of conflict on the need to generate productivity, but there is word that Khrushchev incurred the hostility of Malenkov and Beriya when he made various technological proposals, one of which required the immediate outlay of large sums of state funds. This hostility may be ascribed at least partly to motives of personal rivalry. However, in only a few months' time the incentive policies would be entirely scrapped and Voznesenskiy along with many of his supporters purged, while Malenkov and Beriya functioned as Stalin's chief lieutenants in Moscow. This confluence of events provides the first indication of leadership differences not merely on personal grounds, but also on policy conceptions. On the one side, there existed a desire to raise productivity by materially stimulating individual initiative; on the other, a belief in the efficacy of collectivist exhortation. Stalin's prejudice for the latter alternative was notorious, but in 1947-1948 he heeded the advice of colleagues attuned to the realities of national life. The timing of his change of mind concerning incentives—early in 1949—suggests that external and military concerns then intruded brashly into the policy kitchens.

THE DOCTRINAIRE RESURGENCE AND ITS OPPOSITION (1949-1953)

On March 5, 1949, Voznesenskiy was summarily dismissed from the government cabinet pursuant to a directive of Stalin.[27] Six weeks later the administrative will-fulness in economic management which was so alien to the young planner's style of work was tacitly condoned in official relations with the peasantry. The party and government decree outlining a Three-Year Plan of Animal Husbandry which was published in *Izvestiya* on April 19, 1949, obliged local authorities to secure "in the shortest possible time" a clear-cut predominance of collectivized animal holdings.[28] This summons led to the decimation of collective farmers' herds and in 1952 the number of large horned cattle in the country diminished by 2,200,000 animals and cow herds by 550,000 animals, evidently because the peasants put their own food needs ahead of those of communally owned livestock, for which the state procurement prices were nominal.[29] Moreover, the April 1949 decree required a sizable expansion of the sown area of perennial and annual grasses on kolkhozes.[30] This forcing of grassland crop rotation is attributable to a massive diversion of resources to the armaments industries in response to Stalin's perception of a military threat on the Western borders of his empire. A striking decline of the growth rate of the light and food indus-

[27] The last days of Voznesenskiy are reviewed by his alter ego V. V. Kolotov in *Literaturnaya Gazeta* (Literary Newspaper), November 30, 1963.

[28] The decree is condensed in Meisel and Kozera, *op. cit.*, pp. 438-443.

[29] Cf. Jasny, *Soviet Studies*, Vol. III, p. 154; and *Pravda*, September 13, 1953 (CDSP, v, 37, pp. 3ff.). In 1950, the state procurement price for a kilogram of kolkhoz beef was 33 kopecks, or less than 2 per cent of the retail sales price (*Kommunist*, No. 9, 1962, p. 44).

[30] The sown area of perennial grasses on kolkhozes was to increase to not less than 5,800,000 hectares in 1949, to not less than 8 million hectares in 1950, and to 11 million hectares in 1951; annual grasses on kolkhozes were to reach a minimum of 3,200,000 hectares in 1949, 3,500,000 in 1950, and 4 million in 1951.

tries in 1949 points to remilitarization of the economy at that time.[31]

A further radicalization of agricultural policy occurred in August 1949, when urban food sales by cooperatives were discontinued and commercial trade outlets restored to the Ministry of Trade, which was forbidden to pay kolkhozes higher than state purchase prices for their above-quota products.[32] The unity of organization and policy normally discernible in Communist behavior was total as a result of the success achieved by Malenkov and Beriya in conducting their anti-reformist intrigues. A purge of moderates on the editorial staff of the Central Committee's theoretical and political magazine was formalized by the decree which the Politburo or Secretariat issued in the Committee's name on July 13, 1949, "On the Journal *Bol'shevik*." This document remained confidential until quoted in full by Secretary Mikhail A. Suslov in a *Pravda* article of December 24, 1952, which reopened the casebook on the former chief editor of *Bol'shevik*.[33] The decree alleged that the leaders of *Bol'shevik* had resorted to editorial chicanery in order to preach the gospel

[31] The production of "Group A" (weaponry and capital goods like steel, pig iron, coal, oil, electricity, and cement) rose 22 per cent in 1947, 29 per cent in 1948, and 25 per cent in 1949; the output of "Group B" (light and food industries) increased by 21 per cent in both 1947 and 1948, and in 1949 slumped to 8 per cent (*Narodnoye Khozyaystvo SSSR v 1958 Godu* [USSR National Economy in 1958], Moscow, 1959, p. 139).

[32] Whitman, *op.cit.* Since the commercial trade system went into effect, the prices in kolkhoz marketplaces had fallen by an average of 29 per cent. The suspension of commercial trade activity probably resulted from Stalin's refusal to compensate the peasant for what he could obtain by tightened procurement policies rather than from control of the kolkhoz market.

[33] "Concerning the Articles by P. Fedoseyev in *Izvestiya*, December 12 and 21" (by M. Suslov, *Pravda*, December 24, p. 2; reprinted in *Izvestiya*, December 25, p. 2), CDSP, IV, 50, pp. 14-15.

of reformism. Their "inadmissible work methods" were explained as follows: "New text is inserted into articles reaching the magazine without the knowledge of the authors of these articles, the new text being such as to alter radically the content of these articles." Substantively, the editors had mistakenly praised Voznesenskiy's *War Economy of the USSR*—that is, lionized the intellectual apostle of reformism. Under the prodding of Suslov, the expelled Fedoseyev indeed confessed that as chief editor of *Bol'-shevik* he had abetted "eclectic" ideas about political economy. Among the lesser dignitaries released from the staff of the journal was F. Koshelev, whose contributions on agricultural policy followed the lines advocated by Khrushchev in the early postwar period.[34] The principal beneficiary of the realignment in *Bol'shevik* was S. M. Abalin, who was to hold the chief editorship until the eclipse of Malenkov after the death of Stalin.[35]

The doctrinaire inquisition swept far beyond the limits of the propagandist community. Voznesenskiy and thousands of his supporters at various levels of the bureaucracy were remorselessly persecuted. Beriya endeavored to convict Voznesenskiy on a writ alleging the loss of classified documents in the State Planning Committee, a crime punishable by confinement in a reformatory labor camp for a term of up to ten years. Voznesenskiy and several of his associates were secretly tried in a military court, but the charges against the main defendant were suddenly dropped for some obscure reason. Late in the autumn of

[34] See in particular "On Overcoming the Antithesis Between Town and Country in the USSR," *Bol'shevik*, No. 22, 1948, pp. 43-62.

[35] Abalin was removed as chief editor of *Kommunist* (the renamed *Bol'shevik*) sometime between October 17 and November 10, 1955.

1949, Voznesenskiy was rearrested in connection with an anti-Stalin plot "uncovered" by Beriya and Malenkov in the Leningrad power structure.[36] Voznesenskiy was again tried secretly and executed in 1950, when capital punishment, abolished in 1947, was officially restored for "traitors, spies, and those seeking to undermine the state." The surface manifestation of these events was the publication in *Bol'shevik* of articles which indirectly asserted that military requirements took precedence over civilian needs and warned that advocacy of economic decentralization might prove lethal.[37]

The triumph of Malenkov and Beriya loomed so large that the despot must have pondered the thought of his own vincibility. Khrushchev the empiricist was recalled to Moscow in December 1949, at the zenith of the doctrinaire upsurge. He was to share membership in the Central Committee Secretariat with Malenkov and his orthodox confederates Suslov and Ponomarenko, and to be appointed head of the territorial party organization. Stalin's assumption that Malenkov and Khrushchev, each of whom bore a grudge against the other, would consume a

[36] Cf. Khrushchev's speech in *Pravda*, August 28, 1957, and the editorial note appended to the article commemorating the sixtieth birthday of Voznesenskiy in *Pravda*, December 1, 1963, which disclose Malenkov's role in "the Leningrad Affair."

[37] "The foreign policy of any state is a continuation of its internal policy and is determined by the nature of the state. As a continuation of internal policy, foreign policy in a number of instances assumes dominant importance. 'In conditions of world war ["Cold War"?—S.P.],' Comrade Stalin points out, 'foreign policy is the basis of any sort of policy, the center of all state life' (*Works*, III, 85)." (S. Zhudin, *Bol'shevik*, No. 20, 1949, p. 36.) The Right Oppositionists of the late 1920's, who backed the policy of concessions to private interest represented by Lenin's "New Economic Policy" and were executed or driven to suicide in the late 1930's, were alluded to by M. Leonov in *ibid.*, No. 21, 1949, p. 32.

good share of their energies in internecine feuds and thereby ensure the safety of the throne, was confirmed by the record of conflict over agriculture in the next three years. Stalin watched the contention of the men of rival outlook, nodded in different directions almost simultaneously, but throughout clung to his belief that the country had to be made ready to face a new military challenge. Ultimately, dissatisfaction with austere material and oppressive spiritual conditions grew so intense among people in all walks of life that Stalin in desperation chose to stake his personal fortunes on a new campaign to extirpate the partisans of internal relaxation.

The rational technique of guaranteeing more exact payment of labor in grain farming through the use of small-scale work units was denounced in an unsigned article which appeared in *Pravda* on February 19, 1950.[38] The article alleged that "links" obstructed the use of complex machinery and split the kolkhozes into small production cells, dispersing their resources. While this article for all intents and purposes revoked the April 19, 1948, decree traceable to Khrushchev and his collaborator Doronin, Andreyev in particular was blamed for inspiring the "links" in grain cultivation by public statements made as early as 1939 and as late as the end of 1949. A squirming confession of guilt was wrung out of Andreyev six days later and run in *Pravda* on February 28, 1950.[39] On the one hand, he pleaded that "I have never intended that the brigades should be replaced by links, but the inaccurate formulations of my statements in regard to the relation-

[38] "Against Distortions in Kolkhoz Labor Organization," translated in CDSP, ii, 10, p. 12; *Soviet Studies*, Vol. ii, pp. 72-79; and Meisel and Kozera, *op. cit.*, pp. 568-571.

[39] Translated in *Soviet Studies*, Vol. ii, pp. 79-80; and Meisel and Kozera, *op. cit.*, p. 571.

ship of the link to the brigade led to interpretations of this kind." On the other, Andreyev agreed with *Pravda's* criticism "both of the distortions committed by the Kursk Regional [party] Committee, and of my own wrong viewpoint. . . . " Doronin recanted in *Pravda* of March 2, 1950, averring that the "link" in grain farming was an "anti-mechanizational" hindrance. Three weeks later, on March 22, 1950, *Pravda* reported that a plenary session of the Kursk Regional Party Committee had reproached its bureau and itself for the formation of "links" in grain farming. The real target of these unsigned attacks on kolkhoz labor incentives was Khrushchev. He stayed true to the principles of rewarding peasants for work in the communal sector and political cronies for their personal loyalty (Doronin was named party boss of Smolensk Region in 1954, replacing the Malenkov protégé, B. F. Nikolayev). But by early 1950 Khrushchev was too strong for his opponents in the hierarchy to risk a frontal assault on his position.

Khrushchev, to be sure, was powerful enough to make a live political issue of a grandiose scheme to modernize tens of thousands of the country's backward villages in the immediate future. In speeches made on March 16, 1950, to the Moscow Regional Soviet and on March 31, 1950, to a conference of leading farm personnel—both of which were summarized in *Pravda* on April 25, 1950[40]—he tabled proposals to consolidate the many medium and small-sized kolkhozes into large-scale units and provide them with elementary urban amenities like electric lighting and plumbing. Khrushchev insisted that larger farms would be better able to utilize machinery, scientific data,

---

[40] Meisel and Kozera, *op. cit.*, pp. 572-574.

and fertilizer than the dwarf kolkhozes. He adduced data to show that cash income from each hectare of plowland and investment funds were much greater on the larger collectives. The solution to low productivity lay in enlarging the kolkhozes and building well-arranged villages with good living and recreational conditions. The kolkhozes, he held, were also entitled to build their own subsidiary enterprises for the manufacture of brick and tile, which they ordinarily bought from state agencies at high cost. Khrushchev envisioned model plans for administrative, public, and recreation buildings, as well as homes for collective farmers, and argumentatively stated that "this question is ripe." Ts. Stepanyan, an ideological functionary who was to incur the wrath of doctrinaire inquisitors in the final months of Stalin's rule, shortly lent his voice to Khrushchev's cause:

The cultural and living conditions of the toilers of agriculture are changing basically. The kolkhoz village is gradually overtaking the town. In accordance with the tasks of building communism and the achievements of the agricultural and building sciences, not only isolated villages but the villages of entire districts are in a planned manner turning into "kolkhoz towns." In the course of improving the cultural and living standards of the kolkhoz village there are emerging agro-cities, which allow for the intelligent and productive use of the achievements of science and technology in the organization of labor and improvement of the cultural and living standards of the population. An example is the Cherkassy District of Kiev Region, Ukrainian SSR. Instead of the 30 villages in this district there will be 12 agro-cities. On the seventieth birthday of Comrade J. V. Stalin [December 21, 1949] the world's first agro-city was founded.[41]

The policy of kolkhoz amalgamations was approved by Stalin and legalized in decrees of July 9 and 17, 1950, by the USSR Council of Ministers.[42] The number of kolkhozes was officially claimed to have diminished in 1950 from 252,000 to 123,000.[43] But the verbal drive for rural reconstruction was overshadowed by a series of government decrees authorizing more of the costly and long-term reclamation projects.[44] Notwithstanding a government and party decree noting certain errors of V. R. Vil'yams, main scientific advocate of the grassland system, and Lysenko's reversal on winter wheat in *Pravda* in July 1950, the Ukraine was designated the primary region among those compelled eventually to increase over tenfold the area under grasses.[45] L. G. Mel'nikov, Khrushchev's successor as party leader in the Ukraine, nonetheless maintained in *Pravda* of December 14, 1950, that a program of rural reconstruction was of "great importance at the present time," and called for the development of kolkhoz building facilities. The underlying purpose of the kolkhoz mergers—to effectuate the pooling of scarce capital resources in the farms—was commended a few weeks later by virtue of a decree promoting the creation

[41] *Bol'shevik*, No. 8, 1950, pp. 11ff.

[42] *Direktivy KPSS i Sovetskogo Pravitel'stva po Khozyaystvennym Voprosam* (Directives of the CPSU and Soviet Government on Economic Problems), Moscow, 1958, pp. 521-534.

[43] Volin, *op. cit.*, p. 52.

[44] These edicts of August-December 1950 are in Meisel and Kozera, *op. cit.*, pp. 469-477.

[45] The decree concerning Vil'yams is noted by Khrushchev in *Pravda*, March 6, 1962; and the grass plan for the Ukraine in *USSR Information Bulletin* of November 3, 1950, pp. 673-674, cited in Meisel and Kozera, *op. cit.*, p. 469.

of interkolkhoz electric power systems.[46] Khrushchev himself championed the village improvement program in speeches of January 1951 which were abridged in *Pravda* on March 4, 1951.[47]

Stalin decisively intervened in the matter of rural reconstruction on March 5, 1951. At his behest, the editors of *Pravda* informed readers that, through an oversight in the printing office, word had been omitted that Khrushchev's article of the previous day was offered only for purposes of discussion and did not express a consensus of official opinion.[48] Malenkov and Beriya evidently had presented Stalin with defamatory estimates of Khrushchev's project. Regional leaders whose career patterns make them identifiable as dependents of Beriya condoned local press attacks on either hasty amalgamations or the remodeling of kolkhoz villages.[49] Malenkov ordered the drafting of a confidential letter of the Central Committee, addressed to local party cadres, which assailed Khru-

---

[46] "Regulation on Procedure for Constructing and Operating Inter-kolkhoz Power Stations and Power Nets," USSR Council of Ministers' decree of February 3, 1951, in *Direktivy KPSS. . .*, pp. 557-569.

[47] Meisel and Kozera, *op. cit.*, pp. 574-577. In this article Khrushchev recommended that personal allotments in the new communities be limited to smaller dimensions, but added that these would still be large enough for a dwelling, an orchard of 15-20 trees, and a small kitchen garden for growing vegetables. In addition, the remaining part of the area of personal allotments stipulated by the Kolkhoz Model Statute would be removed beyond the limits of the settlement, in an area immediately adjacent to it. Khrushchev elaborated that this would not run counter to the farmers' interests but facilitate planning of the settlement and greatly reduce the manpower and monetary expenditure on the project.

[48] The editorial note is in Meisel and Kozera, *op. cit.*, p. 577; and Stalin's role is disclosed by L. F. Il'ichëv in *Pravda*, October 26, 1961.

[49] See the regional press citations of March 21, 1951, and May 26, 1951, in Schapiro, *op. cit.*, p. 516.

shchev's *Pravda* article of March 4, 1951, as "anti-Marxist," "harmful," and "erroneous."[50] Khrushchev was forced to retract his views at a conference of the Moscow Regional Party Committee held on the eve of the 19th party Congress.[51] At the Congress, Malenkov in his capacity of keynote speaker rebuked "some of our leading workers" (Khrushchev), who proposed the building of kolkhoz towns and had "forgotten the principal production tasks facing the collective farms and have put to the forefront their derivatives, narrow utilitarian tasks, problems of amenities in the collective farms."[52] Malenkov also claimed that building materials produced in kolkhoz subsidiary enterprises were more expensive than those turned out by state industry and urban cooperatives, and he advised that the peasants' efforts be directed entirely to the completion of agricultural tasks.

The fiasco over rural modernization humiliated Khrushchev, but could not serve to overthrow him. The ebullient leader's continued usefullness to Stalin as a counterweight to Malenkov and Beriya was demonstrated by the career fortunes of one of his liegemen from the Ukraine, A. A. Yepishev. Yepishev was named deputy chief of the Ministry of State Security at some time in 1951—perhaps after the agro-cities incident—and func-

[50] P. A. Satyukov, *Pravda*, October 27, 1961. Satyukov added that Molotov as well as Malenkov was responsible for the letter and that D. T. Shepilov enthusiastically participated. The July 1949 decree on *Bol'shevik* noted that Shepilov as chief of Agitprop had proved incapable of correct supervision of the magazine, advising that Voznesenskiy's book be used as a political training text. Shepilov was to ally himself with Khrushchev in the struggles of the early post-Stalin years and then reenter the camp of Malenkov.

[51] *Moskovskaya Pravda* (Moscow *Pravda*), September 28, 1952.

[52] *Pravda*, October 6, 1952, translated in Meisel and Kozera, *op. cit.*, p. xxxvi.

tioned as an observer of the clients of Beriya and Malenkov who ran the organization. Yepishev kept his portfolio until 1953, when Beriya assumed operational
control of the security service and routed him back to
the Ukraine.[53] Nor did Khrushchev cease to promote criticism of complacency and authoritarian centralism in agriculture. His spokesman among the literati was Valentin
Ovechkin, who just after the war was on the editorial
staff of the party daily in the Ukraine[54] and knowledgeably forecast changes in agricultural policy after the
death of Stalin.

Ovechkin in *Literaturnaya Gazeta* of July 24, 1952, rebuked authors who pretended to see an absence of disparities in the countryside and simply shunted basic problems to the background. He followed up with a sketch
called "District Routine" which appeared in the September 1952 issue of the literary monthly *Novyy Mir*.[55]
The hero of the story, a district party committee's second secretary, clashes with the senior secretary over the
latter's bullying of kolkhoz personnel. The Stalin-Khru-
shchev difference concerning tax rates on peasants' apple
orchards is fictionalized when the imperious official con-
trasts his healthy "proletarian way" with the junior's
"peasant fairness." The hero also dispenses Khrushchev's
distinctive remedies for managerial ills in agriculture. He
demands that operational decision-making be pushed
downward through regional party staffs, granting more
authority to district leaders so that local weather peculi-

[53] On the record of Yepishev, see S. Bialer, *Sotsialisticheskiy
Vestnik* (Socialist Courier), New York, No. 3/4 (775-776), 1963,
pp. 55-56.
[54] See *Pravda Vostoka* (Organ of the Communist Party of Uzbekistan), September 22, 1964.
[55] A partial translation is in "Document—A Contrast in Types
of Party Leadership," *Soviet Studies*, Vol. IV, pp. 447-468.

arities can be taken into account. He urges reduction of the number of bureaucratic offices and underlines the importance of sound chairmen in helping to solve the problems of economically weak farms. Moreover, the hero disagrees with a new trend of installing as farm chairmen specialists with diplomas instead of meritorious rank-and-filers. Khrushchev would later remark: "It sometimes happens that although a man has not had a specialized education, he has worked many years in agriculture and become so intimately involved in it, come to love it so, that he is not inferior to a good agronomist in the level of his knowledge."[56] The tyrannical secretary in Ovechkin's story was just as closely associable with Stalin in a review that Marietta Shaginyan wrote for *Izvestiya* of October 26, 1952. He was described as learning about the affairs of the district from figures and written reports, was disinterested in the views of the people, and "He bites their heads off for no reason at all, does not notice or praise anything good, makes things difficult instead of helping." How similar to Khrushchev's latter-day indictment of pernicious traits in the character of Stalin! One can only wonder if the despot in his last months was providing Khrushchev with a sufficient length of rope for his self-extinction.

Unlike the sober and conciliatory writings of Khrushchev's agent Ovechkin, most pronouncements bearing on agriculture were colored by fantasy and intimidation. This could not have been otherwise in conditions of spiraling military expenditures.[57] Stalin himself tried to dampen

[56] *Pravda*, March 28, 1962 (CDSP, xiv, 14, pp. 8ff.).
[57] The percentage of total state investment officially admitted to be absorbed in armaments production was 18.5 in 1950, 21.3 in 1951, and 23.8 in 1952. Western analysts estimated that from 52 to 77 per cent of the Soviet Union's "gross investment" was more

reformist enthusiasm in the months from February to September 1952 by signing, if not personally composing, rejoinders to criticisms of his harsh economic policies which were voiced at or shortly after the discussion of a draft textbook on political economy held in November 1951 under the surveillance of Malenkov. The notes were published on the eve of the 19th party Congress as J. V. Stalin's *Economic Problems of Socialism in the USSR*.[58] Abalin appropriately trumpeted the release of this compendium of orthodox dogmas, with shrill calls for "political vigilance" against "bourgeois ideology" which had enticed "certain elements in the party" and produced a new bunch of "opportunists, traitors, skeptics, and capitulators."[59] By doctrinal fiat, Stalin made permanent the priority status of heavy engineering over that of the light and food industries and expressed his will to tighten central control of the peasantry. In the course of his monologue, Stalin revealed that one of his critics outside the Kremlin had appealed to the Politburo at large to start creating badly needed material incentives for the citizenry.

The statistician Yaroshenko affirmed at a plenary ses-

---

or less related to armaments production (Meisel and Kozera, *op. cit.*, p. 519, n. 3).

[58] *Bol'shevik*, No. 18, 1952, pp. 1-50. The chapters are entitled "To Participants of the Economics Discussion. Remarks on Economic Problems, connected with the November 1951 Discussion," February 1, 1952; "Reply to Comrade Notkin, Aleksandr Il'ich," April 21, 1952; "On the Errors of Comrade Yaroshenko, L. D.," May 22, 1952; and "Reply to Comrades Sanina, A. V., and Venzher, V. G.," September 28, 1952. A rumor current in Moscow at the time ascribed the authorship of *Economic Problems* to D. I. Chesnokov, one of Stalin's favorite propagandists.

[59] Cf. the editorial article, "All-Conquering Weapon of Ideas of the Party of Lenin-Stalin," *Bol'shevik*, No. 17, 1952, pp. 8-15; and S. Abalin, "On the Communist Party Rules," *ibid.*, pp. 38-49.

sion of the economics conference in November 1951 and in a letter of March 20, 1952, sent to members of the Politburo, that Marx's theory of the normalcy of preferential development of heavy industry was applicable only to capitalist economies and was inappropriate under socialism. Yaroshenko added that to think differently would be "dogmatic." Stalin's scholastic riposte was that Lenin in a critique of a work by Bukharin had stated that Marx's formula had to be observed under socialism and its higher phase of communism. That Yaroshenko was articulating the sentiment of many experts is clear from the report of P. F. Yudin at a meeting of the USSR Academy of Sciences held on January 31, 1953. Yudin was one of Stalin's most trusted ideologues who graduated from the Institute of Red Professors in 1931, and instructed there in philosophy and party history from 1932 to 1938, when it was a hotbed of Stalinist machinations.[60] At the 19th party Congress, Yudin was awarded membership in the party Central Committee and appointed to the commission assigned to revise the 1919 party Program in conformity with the basic theses of *Economic Problems*. He told academicians at the end of January 1953:

If, for example, Yaroshenko was an exception, a solitary case, mentally deranged, it would hardly be worthwhile to pay attention to him. But Yaroshenko in one way or another has more fully and in a concentrated manner expressed harmful views which to a certain extent are current among some scientific workers. Yaroshenkoism, therefore, is not fortuitous but an ideological menace which has to be confronted and pitilessly exposed. This must be kept in mind. Among our scien-

[60] See *Kommunist*, No. 4, 1962, p. 77.

tific workers are people who, if not blood brothers, are at least ideological cousins of Yaroshenko. The danger of Yaroshenkoism is that these views are residues of Trotskyite-Bukharinist-Bogdanovist views, thoroughly hostile to our party and incompatible with Marxism-Leninism.[61]

Perhaps for his brash tactic of petitioning members of the leadership other than Stalin, as much as for his heretical viewpoint on investments, Yaroshenko was arrested.[62]

Still another wave of the groundswell of opinion in behalf of improving living standards was the proposal of the economists Sanina and Venzher to allow the kolkhozes to purchase heavy farm machinery and channel the state's savings into the consumer goods industries. A recommendation to merge the equipment of MTS and kolkhozes in conjunction with Khrushchev's plan for the amalgamation of small kolkhozes had been made two years earlier in the Ukraine.[63] Stalin argued, firstly, that the kolkhozes could not sustain the fiscal losses of any massive renewal of farm equipment (implying that farm incomes would remain low). Secondly, kolkhozes ought not become the owners of basic tools, as this would confer upon them a privilege reserved for state enterprises. Thirdly, the switch would result in a flurry of buying and selling, which was incompatible with the doctrinal goal of a moneyless economy. A post-Stalin commentary holds that at heart the autocrat dreaded the thought of ma-

---

[61] *Ibid.*, No. 3, 1953, pp. 58-59.

[62] See *XXII S"yezd i Zadachi Kafedr Obshchestvennykh Nauk*, p. 487.

[63] See Yudin's criticism of A. Pal'tsev's brochure *Roads of Transition from Socialism to Communism* (in Russian), Kiev, 1950, in *Kommunist*, No. 3, 1953, p. 59.

chinery-armed kolkhozes defying the state. The commentator is Ivan Vinnichenko, an itinerant journalist proud of his close ties with Ukrainian leaders and an advocate of measures that occasionally became policy under the sponsorship of Khrushchev. He writes: "You may recall the basic objection to the MTS reorganization. It was that after the sale of machinery to the kolkhozes the state would be deprived of the chief economic lever in guidance of the kolkhoz system. No one quoted Stalin to this effect, but . . . This indeed was one of his basic dogmas! He simply did not trust the kolkhoz peasantry and, therefore, feared to release it from his grip, tried to subordinate kolkhozes to centralized administrative rule, both economically and organizationally" (ellipses in text).[64] Stalin rounded out *Economic Problems* with a plan to decrease the peasantry's cash earnings through the gradual elimination of kolkhoz marketplaces and the direct exchange of manufactured goods *(produkto-obmen)* instead of the free sale of villagers' privately raised commodities.

Malenkov next told the 19th party Congress that agriculture was on the upgrade. "The grain problem," he declared, "formerly considered the most acute problem, has thus been solved successfully, solved once and for all." In reality, matters stood quite differently. The quantity and grade of bread for popular consumption were grossly deficient and the shortage of animal feed was acute. State grain procurements in 1952 totaled 2,118,000 poods (one pood equals 36 pounds), or 107 million poods less than in 1940, when there was a bread shortage in Mos-

[64] *Literaturnaya Gazeta,* February 20, 1962.

cow owing to underproduction.[65] Letters examined in party headquarters after the 19th Congress inquired why bread was sold with admixtures if the grain problem was solved. Stalin called the party Presidium into session and threateningly accused numerous leaders of engaging in all but sabotage.[66] The heir-apparent Malenkov now fell under a cloud of suspicion; Stalin's henchman Chesnokov was named co-editor of *Kommunist* to counterbalance the Malenkovite Abalin.[67] Beriya too was harassed after *Pravda* on January 13, 1953, announced that "some of our soviet agencies and leaders" had been remiss in apprehending "a terrorist group of physicians" in the Kremlin dispensary. Meanwhile, the pitiless squeezing of the countryside went on. New measures were introduced in early 1953 to increase the taxation of household plots in kolkhozes.[68] Stalin in February 1953 rejected a proposal of Khrushchev and Mikoyan to create farm incentives by raising the state procurement prices for livestock products.[69] As the interrelated crisis in the elite and in the nation ripened, on March 5, 1953, Soviet media reported that Stalin was dead.

In perspective, the conflicts over agriculture in 1949-

[65] On procurement, see *S.K. v SSSR i R.S.Kh.*, I, 86.

[66] Khrushchev, *Plenum Tsentral'nogo Komiteta Kommunisticheskoy Partii Sovetskogo Soyuza, 5-9 marta 1962 goda, stenograficheskiy otchët* (Plenum of the Central Committee of the Communist Party of the Soviet Union, March 5-9, 1962, Minutes), Moscow, 1962, p. 18 (source cited hereafter as *Plenum IV*).

[67] The unprecedented appointment was made between November 1 and 25, 1952. Chesnokov lost the post by April 16, 1953, when Malenkov and Beriya were ascendant.

[68] A. Nove, *Soviet Studies*, Vol. v, p. 164.

[69] *The Crimes of the Stalin Era*, p. S 58, where Khrushchev refers to the proposal as "our project"; and *Pravda*, March 7, 1964 (CDSP, xvi, 10, p. 3), where Khrushchev tells of a special price commission composed of Mikoyan, N. G. Ignatov, himself, and "others."

1953, like their forerunners, turned on the issue of the relative importance of production and consumption as this affected the citizenry at large. One section of the leadership remained committed to Stalin's traditional belief in the desirability of a hortatory approach to stimulate the agricultural work force, while another espoused concessions to its material self-interest. That Malenkov and Khrushchev still adhered to the opposing positions, respectively, offers additional reason to view the power struggles as battles of divergent outlook as well as personal advantage. At the same time, adversaries in the production-consumption dispute were wedded to rival theories about the style of government. Those of the austerity school obscured the parlous condition of agriculture and were resigned to the managerial devices of authoritarian centralism. In contrast, the conciliatory group strove to reveal the actual state of affairs in the countryside and promote a measure of local spontaneity. Differing appraisals of civic loyalty, with all that implied for the use of police powers, were inherent in such circumstances. It could also be seen from Khrushchev's persistent agitation in behalf of rural modernization even after the outbreak of the Korean War that the forces of internal accommodation were not distracted from their goals by the real or imaginary threat of war. The priority item on their timetable was that of domestic reconstruction. On a broader plane, the events of the period suggest that if Stalin's "governing formula" did rest on "a moving equilibrium of alternating phases of repression and relaxation,"[70] the competition between his rival lieutenants may be regarded as one of the important determinants of the shifting balance.

[70] Merle Fainsod, *How Russia Is Ruled*, Cambridge, Mass., 1953, p. 500.

CHAPTER II

ALLEVIATING
THE GRAIN CRISIS
(1953-1958)

VARYING PERCEPTIONS of the scope of the agrarian crisis engendered by Stalin's inflexible domestic and foreign policies, along with considerations of personal prestige, determined the nature of relevant proposals advanced in the Kremlin following the death of the autocrat. The duumvirate of Premier Malenkov and First Deputy Premier Beriya, and then Malenkov alone, consistently obscured the vast dimensions of the crisis, repeating the premier's boast to the 19th party Congress that the chronic insufficiency of grain was only a memory. Malenkov, under compulsion to compete with his rival Khrushchev for influence in elite circles once Beriya was eliminated in June 1953, hastily improvised an economic platform which should have appealed to the urban upper classes. They stood to gain from an accelerated output of high-priced consumer durables and the removal of bread grains from government stocks, and from meat and dairy purchases effectuated abroad. The stabilization of defense expenditures and slight reduction of inputs in heavy engineering which Malenkov promoted to meet his consumer goods targets were grossly inadequate for commencing the very expensive and time-consuming process of developing an up-to-date chemical fertilizer industry, without which his propaganda in behalf of increased crop yields was so much empty talk. The modest rise of farm and peasant income which Malenkov encouraged offered hope of supplying towns with more potatoes and vegetables, but not with better grades of bread and flour or nearly enough meat. Administratively, the rule of Malenkov augured for the kolkhozes a highly centralized pattern of control which in the direly neglected field of rural electrification surpassed even the Stalinist variety. On the whole, Malenkov's claim that the fulfillment of his platform would result in an abundance of foodstuffs for the population at large within two or three years' time was bereft of meaning insofar as the quality of the basic diet of the ordinary citizen was concerned.

The alternative set forth by Khrushchev was an emergency program of sowing to wheat large massifs of virgin and fallow soil in the semi-arid and underpopulated zone of the country. This program was intended to relieve the acute shortage of higher-grade bread and flour in the cities and increase the feed supply for livestock on the farms, all in the immediate future and at relatively low cost. Of course, the program's basic assumption of a grain problem tended to discredit Malenkov on grounds of complacency. In stages, and over the opposition of Malenkov and his governmental deputies, Presidium members Molotov and Kaganovich, Khrushchev's short-term plan attracted a majority in the ruling party Presidium. The plan evidently was adopted as economically sensible in view of the critical situation in agriculture, the narrow margin of unearmarked resources owing to the weight of the military budget, and the foreign trade commitments of the state.

At the same time, Khrushchev persisted in his attempts to liberate technical expertise in the countryside from the restraints of authoritarian centralism. These strivings were resisted within the leadership prior to the enforced retirement of Malenkov from the premiership in 1955, and, thereafter, foremost by Molotov and Kaganovich. Their drastic remedy for agricultural ills was to transform the relatively more loosely run kolkhozes into state farms which were tantamount to ministerial estates. Khrushchev as party first secretary also generated tension within his own power base by insisting that the members of the party's professional staff operate as a technically functional unit rather than follow the rule of the late Stalin period and merely disseminate abstract doctrine. Throughout, rival leaders solicited backing for their distinctive views in the faction-torn communities of propagandists and applied scientists.

Khrushchev now emerged as the foremost initiator of policy, but events in the early summer of 1957 indicated that he would have to rule through the party Central Committee and not above it, as was true of Stalin after 1936. The agronomist leader knew well the climatic and other limitations of his virgin soil program and verbally moved toward a shift of considerably more resources from heavy engineering to the industries servicing agriculture. Thereby he unwittingly offered to adversaries in the Presidium a trenchant debating point which helped to rally them into a bloc that momentarily dominated the normally supreme organ of authority. Khrushchev retained executive power through transfer of the dispute to the wider forum of the Central Committee, but at the cost of jettisoning his new agropolitical objective. The first secretary defensively allied himself with heavy engineering partisans who were less suspicious of his character traits than those of opposition leaders like Malenkov and Molotov, who had been instrumental in devising rather than implementing Stalin's blood purges of the elite. The oligarchic arrangements which Khrushchev and his group improvised in June 1957 in order to rescue themselves from personal disaster and the prolongation of coalition government were at once a mark of factional ingenuity and the origin of considerable vacillation in policy over the long run.

HESITATION (MARCH-JULY 1953)

The tenor of regime propaganda on agricultural themes shortly after the death of Stalin lends credence to Khrushchev's assertion that Malenkov and Beriya then wielded sufficient power to have been able jointly to realign the leadership in conformity with their wishes.[1] The exploitative approach which gained increasing prominence after Malenkov and Beriya succeeded in their cabal against the Voznesenskiyites was initially manifest in an article passed by the doctrinaire team of Abalin-Chesnokov a few days after the announcement of Stalin's death.[2] According to the article, kolkhozes were not entitled to own heavy equipment, engage in subsidiary industrial activities, or undertake internal remodeling projects. Theirs was a strictly productive function justified in terms of an urban supremacist theory that "As we advance to communism, the leading role of the town in relation to the village will increase." Stalin and Malenkov were rendered homage in this article, which reaffirmed all of the oppressive dogmas of full-blown Stalinism less "products-exchange." This curious omission suggested an incipient

[1] See Giuseppe Boffa, *Inside the Khrushchev Era*, New York, 1959, p. 27.

[2] A. Kuropatkin, "On Eliminating the Contrast Between Town and Country in the USSR and Ways to Overcome the Essential Difference Between Them," *Kommunist*, No. 4 (March 9), 1953, pp. 53-67.

cleavage in the Malenkov-Beriya alliance. That Beriya for
tactical reasons may have been seeking to ingratiate himself in reformist quarters is distinctly possible in view of
the fortunes of one G. P. Kosyachenko during and after
the period of the security chief's race for ascendancy in
the "collective leadership." Kosyachenko was named
head of the State Planning Committee on March 6, 1953,
although he was a non-member of the party Central
Committee who only a month earlier had confessed to
participation in the Voznesenskiy heresy. The appointment was made to the disadvantage of M. Z. Saburov,
who had assumed command of the Planning Committee
upon the removal of Voznesenskiy and suddenly returned to the post on June 29, 1953, or a few days after
the purge of Beriya, which broadened Malenkov's freedom of action.[3]

Whatever the opportunistic qualms of Beriya, his fel-
low-duumvir remained a staunch devotee of convention-
alism. Malenkov's predominance in the government newspaper and his good connections in scientific institutes,
which were demonstrated in the Ukrainian wheat controversy of 1947-1948, found expression in the basic output of *Izvestiya* and the monthly journal of the Academy
of Sciences' Economics Institute, *Problems of Economics.*
These publications usually extolled grassland crop rotation and shelter-belts, averred that the grain problem was
solved once and for all, and gave no encouragement to
farms that looked forward to possessing their own brick-
yards.[4] The neo-Stalinist complexion of *Problems of Eco-*

[3] On Kosyachenko and the Beriya purge, see Embree, *op. cit.,*
pp. 32, 57, and 108, n. 1.
[4] Cf. P. Logacheva, *Izvestiya,* March 18, 1953 (CDSP, v, 11, p.
22); A. Krayeva, *Voprosy Ekonomiki,* No. 5 (May 12), 1953, p.
52; and S. Tsegoyev, *ibid.,* No. 6 (May 28), 1953, p. 34. Professor

nomics was especially notable in its issue approved for printing on April 10, 1953. This reported on a meeting of the Economics and Law Division of the Academy's Economics Institute which was held on January 7-10, 1953, and devoted to Stalin's *Economic Problems*.[5] The Institute director, K. V. Ostrovityanov, drew on Suslov's aforementioned article in *Pravda* to malign the Voznesenskyites. A. M. Rumyantsev, another rapporteur, labeled as a "bourgeois degenerate" the consumer-goods partisan Yaroshenko. A paper on the future of kolkhozes was read by Ye. S. Karnaukhova, an economist, but the editors of *Problems of Economics* never did fulfill their promise to present it in a future issue. Karnaukhova must have been espousing the merits of a universal system of state rationing, since her brochure of the same period on socio-economic prospects depicted "products-exchange" as a phenomenon which was "becoming the chief means, the decisive link of improving production relations in the countryside, and that means in all society as well."[6]

The banner of anti-Stalinism first rose in the Central Committee daily *Pravda*, whose chief editor Shepilov had previously oscillated between the empiricist and doctri-

---

N. Avdonin of Lysenko's All-Union Academy of Agricultural Science demanded speedier introduction of the grassland system in *Pravda*, March 27, 1953 (CDSP, v, 13, pp. 22-23). Khrushchev in a speech of April 8, 1957, criticized Avdonin for favoring injunction over persuasion (*S.K. v SSSR i R.S.Kh.*, II, 409).

[5] *Voprosy Ekonomiki*, No. 4, 1953, pp. 78-95.

[6] *On Eliminating the Essential Difference Between Town and Country* (in Russian), State Publishers of Political Literature, Moscow, 1953, as quoted by A. Vishnyakov, spokesman of a leadership grouping opposed to "forced social change," in *Kommunist*, No. 10, 1953, p. 34. The author of the brochure evidently had in mind the so-called *otovarivaniye*, an arrangement whereby the state obtained certain specialized crops at low prices and in return delivered consumer goods to the farms, also at low prices.

naire groupings in party headquarters. Shepilov's most recent attachment to Khrushchev was to become amply clear just after the fall of Beriya and in the dispute over virgin lands at the close of 1953 and early in 1954. Now, in the spring of 1953, he displayed his loyalty to Khrushchev by running materials which tended to undermine the reputations of his neo-Stalinist adversaries. A *Pravda* article of May 14, 1953, which dealt with party political training overlooked Stalin's final treatise on national goals. A fortnight later, a district party secretary advised in *Pravda* that kolkhoz chairmen consult the rank and file before making any decisions. This had long been a cause of Khrushchev and his spokesman Ovechkin, and they would take it up again in the months ahead.[7] *Pravda* on May 29 supported the downtrodden principle of material incentive by rebuking "certain propagandists" who advocated "products-exchange" as a substitute for buying and selling.[8] Work on the extremely costly and long-range "Great Stalin Projects for Remaking Nature" had been canceled immediately after Stalin's death, but not until June 10, 1953, did *Pravda* stress the need to concentrate investment "in the central thickly populated areas of the country where capital investment can provide the most economic results *in the shortest time*" (italics added). This amounted to criticism of Beriya and Malenkov, who in major addresses in 1951 and 1952 had lauded Stalin's wasteful ventures in the hinterlands.[9]

[7] Cf. the review of "Peasant Professor," a play by Ovechkin and Genady Fish, which appeared in the November 1953 issue of *Novyy Mir*, in *Soviet Studies*, Vol. VI, pp. 77-91; and Khrushchev in *Kommunist*, No. 2, 1954, pp. 57ff.

[8] The agitation for "products-exchange" was later said to be most vehement in the oral pronouncements of "some comrades" (I. Vyaz'min, *Voprosy Ekonomiki*, No. 4, 1954, p. 27).

[9] See *Pravda*, November 7, 1951, and October 6, 1952.

Khrushchev then entered into a series of tactical alliances to weaken Malenkov and remove Beriya. He first joined with Beriya to strike down his successor in the Ukraine and co-champion of rural modernization, Mel'nikov, who had since backed Malenkov. Among other things, Mel'nikov was accused of faulty direction of regional agriculture.[10] Khrushchev would attack Mel'nikov for vocal opposition to the widespread planting of corn for silage in the Ukraine during 1950-1953 at a party meeting held in Kiev shortly after Malenkov lost his premiership.[11] Also, Mel'nikov's replacement as party leader of the Ukraine was A. I. Kirichenko, who rose to nation-wide prominence after Khrushchev defeated his major rivals for power in 1957. The subsequent fall of Beriya at the hands of Malenkov and Khrushchev sometime around June 25, 1953 provided the Khrushchev group with an opportunity to point up the immediacy of the food problem. Shepilov's *Pravda* on July 10, 1953, included in its indictment of Beriya a charge that he had "done everything to obstruct the solution of very important and urgent agricultural questions." Ovechkin rushed in to prescribe the remedies of wage incentives, on-the-spot guidance, and lectures devoid of abstraction but rich in practical content.[12] With Khrushchev's group clamoring for change in the villages, Malenkov as the most influential oligarch of the day had to take some kind of action.

The Time Factor
(August 1953-February 1955)

The opening speech on agricultural affairs at the delayed meeting of the USSR Supreme Soviet held in August

[10] *Pravda Ukrainy*, June 13, 1953.
[11] Speech of February 18, 1955, in *S.K. v SSSR i R.S.Kh.* ii, 13.
[12] *Pravda*, July 20 and 23, 1953.

1953, in order to give formal ratification to the annual state budget, was delivered by A. I. Kozlov.[13] Kozlov, who had done the bidding of Malenkov as chief of the Central Committee's Agricultural Section and later helped to draft Stalin's confiscatory Three-Year Plan of Animal Husbandry,[14] was named USSR Minister of Agriculture and Procurements on March 15, 1953. At the budgetary session he rightfully identified low yields as the gravest production failing, but in listing major crops he varnished the deplorable state of grain output by ranking potatoes, vegetables, flax, and oil-bearing cultures ahead of wheat in order of importance. Kozlov also endorsed anew the traditional livestock feed of succulent grasses. This was a fitting prelude to Malenkov's reassurance to the session that "Our country is fully supplied with grain."[15] True, Malenkov called for a more rapid increase in grain production to satisfy the population's need for bread, speedier development of animal husbandry, and supply of grain to districts which concentrated on technical crops. But he withheld ominous data and his specific policy proposals aimed at rectifying a "grave lag" in the production of potatoes and vegetables. Various tax and procurement adjustments which would increase the incomes of farms and peasants by more than 1.3 billion rubles in 1953 and more than 2 billion over a full year were designed chiefly to pull up the backward potato and vegetable sectors. The procurement prices for grain were not raised, although they were almost as abysmally depressed as those for kolkhoz beef.[16] The planned in-

[13] *Izvestiya*, August 8, 1953 (CDSP, v, 34, p. 15).
[14] *S.K. v SSSR i R.S.Kh.*, II, 113.
[15] *Pravda*, August 9, 1953 (CDSP, v, 30, pp. 3ff.).
[16] In 1953 the state paid kolkhozes the same price—about 90 kopecks—for a quintal of grain surrendered in compulsory delivery and for one acquired by purchase (which ordinarily brought a

creases in consumer goods production which internal trade minister and Presidium member Mikoyan later outlined revealed no serious intention to offset the farmers' greater purchasing power with a proper assortment of industrial goods.[17] The more rapid growth of the light and food industries in 1953 and 1954 was to redound to the advantage of the more affluent sections of the urban population. It would be achieved through slowing down expansion of the defense industries, shifting a number of machine-building plants to the production of consumer goods, tapping state reserves, and importing meat and dairy products.[18]

Considering the weak technical base of agriculture, the increment of state and kolkhoz investment in that branch from 1.9 billion rubles, or 13.7 per cent of all investments in the economy, in 1953, to 2.8 billion, or 17 per cent of the total, in 1954,[19] was hardly apt to facilitate Malenkov's professed task of securing in the next two or three years an "abundance" of foodstuffs for the public, if this bounty was thought of in terms of a sounder diet. Malenkov, however, apparently conceived of an adequate diet for the common man along the primitive lines which Khrushchev scorned in a speech of July 11, 1954: "If we only call for a struggle for communism and people live in dugouts and eat black bread with kvass [A drink made from rye bread and malt—S.P.], and we fail to improve people's lives, then some people may reflect, 'Perhaps this

higher price); the cost of producing a quintal of grain in the better-managed state farms was about four rubles (M. Terent'yev, *Voprosy Ekonomiki*, No. 9, 1963, p. 5).

[17] See the charts in Embree, *op. cit.*, pp. 87-88.

[18] Cf. *Voprosy Ekonomiki*, No. 9, 1953, pp. 10ff.; R. W. Davies, "Reports and Commentaries—The Investment-Consumption Controversy: Practical Aspects," *Soviet Studies*, Vol. vii, pp. 59-74; and *S.K. v SSSR i R.S.Kh.*, i, 342-343.

[19] Khlebnikov, *Voprosy Ekonomiki*, No. 7, 1962, p. 50.

indeed is communism—kvass with bread.' (*Stir in the hall.*)"[20]

The managerial aspect of the premier's speech of August 8, 1953, was blatantly etatist. The interkolkhoz power systems authorized in 1951 were in effect repudiated, as preference was given to the connection of MTS and farm power grids with the state outlets. This scheme, which is reminiscent of Vinnichenko's complaint that Stalin "tried to subordinate kolkhozes to centralized administrative rule, both economically and organizationally," was soon upheld by one of the foremost theorists of the reactionary wing in the party leadership. I. D. Laptev, who eventually would be exposed for his unsuccessful factional activities, in February 1954 placed articles in two periodicals which berated one S. P. Matskevich for having argued in 1952 that local electrical resources were more desirable than large-scale, state facilities.[21]

It can be seen that Laptev in actuality was attacking Khrushchev. The issue of rural electrification was somehow raised by Professor John Bernal in an interview with Khrushchev on September 25, 1954. Bernal observed that the agricultural exhibition in Moscow was displaying models of small electric-power stations and, after conjecturing that large-scale stations were more economical, inquired why this was so. Khrushchev agreed that the power derived from the smaller stations was much more expensive and explained that industry consumed almost all the output of the larger stations, thus making it incumbent on farms to build their own stations, whose output was still less costly than that of simple motors.[22] This dis-

[20] *S.K. v SSSR i R.S.Kh.*, I, 357.

[21] *Voprosy Ekonomiki*, No. 2, 1954, p. 13; and *Sotsialisticheskoye Sel'skoye Khozyaystvo* (Socialist Agriculture), No. 2, 1954, pp. 31ff.

[22] *S.K. v SSSR i R.S.Kh.*, I, 363-364.

pute over optimum limits of rural autonomy raged within a framework of acceptance of the kolkhoz system by the participants. But the outcome was nonetheless consequential for the work and leisure situation of large numbers of village inhabitants.

Almost as soon as Malenkov responded to Khrushchev's challenge to come up with a farm program, his cautious outlook on production and management was subjected to questioning. A Central Committee plenary session on agriculture was called for September 3, 1953, at the request of Khrushchev.[23] The senior party secretary read the keynote report,[24] whose political importance was its scrupulously detailed cataloguing of agricultural failings, which differentiated it from all of the regime's post-Stalin critiques and facilitated the evolution of an intra-elite consensus in behalf of tackling basic problems. Khrushchev from the outset scaled down Malenkov's heady estimate that "Our country is fully supplied with grain." He declared that "We are *in general* satisfying the country's need for grain crops, in the sense that our country is *essentially* supplied with bread . . ." (italics added). Several farm areas other than the traditional wheat producers were mentioned as having extensive possibilities for growing this badly needed crop. They were the central Black Earth provinces, the Volga region, forest steppes of the Ukraine,[25] and a number of the non-Black Earth belt areas. Western Siberia and Kazakhstan were not cited in the report, although in the distress period of 1928-1932

[23] V. Polyakov, *Kommunist*, No. 16, 1962, p. 55; and *Pravda*, November 11, 1962.

[24] "On Measures for Further Development of USSR Agriculture," *S.K. v SSSR i R.S.Kh.*, I, 7-84; and *Pravda*, September 15, 1953 (CDSP, v, 39, pp. 11ff.).

[25] Mentioned in the version of Khrushchev's report in *Pravda*, September 15, 1953, but not in *S.K. v SSSR i R.S.Kh.*, I, 43.

new lands in those more arid regions had been put under the plow on a large scale.[26] Khrushchev was well aware of this, since he met privately with officials from the northern provinces of Kazakhstan during the September 1953 Central Committee session and discussed with them the possibilities of assimilating virgin lands and creating large state farms in the steppes of that region.[27] The findings of these consultations were embodied in the Plenum's decree, which called for the production of an unspecified amount of hard wheat in Kazakhstan and Western Siberia, as well as in the regions enumerated in Khrushchev's report.[28] This modification of Khrushchev's remarks on the opening day of the plenary session foreshadowed the main thrust of his impending attack on the agro-political front.

The technical inclination and work style of the agricultural bureaucracy headed by Malenkov's dependent, A. I. Kozlov, were particular objects of Khrushchev's criticism. He advised against indiscriminate application of the grassland system and urged that vigorous steps be taken to expand the area sown to corn for silage, harking back to practice in the Ukraine during his term as viceroy. Khrushchev excoriated the Ministry of Agriculture for its inflated staffs, bureaucratic duplication and idleness, red tape in settling pressing problems, ignorance of the true state of local affairs, and stereotyped technical counseling. He proposed that the ministry drastically curtail its supervisory activity and focus on planning for the various branches of farming, material and technical supplies

[26] See Frank A. Durgin, Jr., "The Virgin Lands Programme, 1954-1960," *Soviet Studies*, Vol. XIII, pp. 255-280.

[27] A. S. Shevchenko, Khrushchev's personal secretary and an agronomist, tells of this meeting at party headquarters in *Pravda*, November 17, 1960.

[28] *Pravda*, September 13, 1953.

and financing, organizing farm procurements, selecting, placing, and training personnel, and dealing with problems of propaganda and application of advanced experience and scientific achievements. Khrushchev predicted atrophy of the ministry's local arms: "As the organizing role of MTS in collective farming is increased, the present need for district agricultural and procurement agencies obviously will decrease. It is sufficient to include several workers for planning and reporting in the district executive committee setup, but use must be made of the basic cadres of specialists in MTS and collective and state farms." The plenary session's decree agreed that "the established practice of placing the leadership of MTS and kolkhozes in the hands of agricultural agencies no longer conforms to the growing demands and changes which have occurred in agriculture." Shortly afterward, the government cabinet ordered dissolution of the district agricultural administrations and the transfer of their various technical services to MTS.[29]

Khrushchev lacked faith in the ability of ministerially trained agronomists to discard standard teachings and embrace his innovating methods. The local party officials were to assume *de facto* charge of farming and introduce those methods. Yet before the September 1953 Plenum, numerous booklets on the new agronomy were compiled at party headquarters and transmitted to the secretaries of district party committees.[30] At the session, Khrushchev denounced party officials who restricted themselves to ideological babble and left daily management of the economy to state administrators. This emergent concept of the technically functional party was utterly un-Stalinist.

[29] Z. S. Belyayeva, *Sovetskoye Gosudarstvo i Pravo* (Soviet State and Law), No. 7, 1955, pp. 12-13; and Ye. V. Shorina, *ibid.*, No. 8, 1955, p. 18.
[30] *S.K. v SSSR i R.S.Kh.*, I, 129.

A sharp delineation of party-state functions was enforced in the final years of Stalin's reign with order-giving authority put squarely in the laps of the state bureaucrats and exhortation defined as the role of party operatives. Indeed, Stalin's relevant admonitions to the February-March 1937 CPSU(B) Central Committee Plenum were cited by the author of a post-Stalin article which warned party functionaries against direct management of kolkhozes.[31] The changeover upon Khrushchev's assumption of leadership of the party Secretariat in March 1953 was resented within that body's administrative staff and on the intermediate level. A territorial party leader whom Khrushchev interrogated about the cabbage crop replied: "I am not a collective farmer but the secretary of a party regional committee."[32] Now the secretaries of district party committees and their deputies would have to spend all of their working hours in MTS so as to provide "concrete guidance" of kolkhozes. The organizational leeway of the secretaries was extended through abolition of the post of centrally designated MTS deputy directors for political affairs. To be sure, the bureau of the district party committee, "headed by the first secretary," was enjoined to do nothing less than "manage the entire economic and cultural life of the district" (Khrushchev). The editors of a party newspaper and chiefs of agitprop and science-culture sections in all party offices were similarly directed to campaign for advanced farming techniques.[33]

Important as Khrushchev's report and appointment as Central Committee *first* secretary turned out to be, this by no means established him as the dictator of agrarian

[31] See V. Suslov, *Kommunist*, No. 5, 1953, pp. 56-57.

[32] *S.K. v SSSR i R.S.Kh.*, II, 126.

[33] Cf. *Pravda*, December 4, 1953 (CDSP, V, 49, pp. 22-23); and *Izvestiya*, February 2, 1954 (CDSP, VI, 1, pp. 3-5).

policy. The decree of the September Plenum did not approve of his efficiency recommendations to draft 50,000 urban personnel as farm chairmen and subordinate MTS chief engineers to regional agricultural administrations instead of to MTS directors. Khrushchev did not prevail in the urban draft until after Malenkov was stripped of his premiership and even then the quota, which put a drain on state funds, was reduced to 30,000 personnel.[34] Moreover, the plenary decree stated that the Ministry of Agriculture, in addition to the tasks which Khrushchev outlined for it, should supervise fulfillment of the state plan for farming and observance of the Kolkhoz Statutes and assume leadership of MTS. Quite appropriately, Malenkov shifted A. I. Kozlov to leadership of the USSR Ministry of State Farms and restored to the top of the USSR Ministry of Agriculture and Procurements I. A. Benediktov, who had directed the forerunner of that agency at the close of the Stalin era.[35] Meanwhile, technological conservatism remained predominant in the state bureaucracy's scientific adjunct. *Problems of Economics* neglected the merits of silage corn and announced that the state planners were looking forward to a big rise in grass fodder over the next two years.[36] Academician Lysenko's method of planting alfalfa in conjunction with the grassland system was approbated in another article, which was to be adversely criticized once the political winds shifted more in Khrushchev's favor.[37]

[34] *Pravda*, April 15, 1955. On the payment of recruits, see *S.K. v SSSR i R.S.Kh.*, II, 51, 90, and 287.

[35] *Pravda*, September 15 and 16, 1953.

[36] A. Shcherbakov, *Voprosy Ekonomiki*, No. 10 (October 15), 1953, pp. 33ff.

[37] Cf. I. Kantyshev, *ibid.*, No. 12 (December 11), 1953, pp. 51ff.; and *ibid.*, No. 8 (July 31), 1954, p. 5.

In conformity with a general rule of Soviet politics, the factional controversy over agricultural policy heightened as economic difficulties promised to become more acute as the result of a poor grain crop stemming from unfavorable weather conditions in many regions. The per capita harvest of grain products in 1953 was 435 kilograms, or 106 less than in 1913; marketed grain produce stood at 35,800,000 tons, or 2.5 million tons less than in 1940.[38] The reaction of Malenkov was furtively to decimate the state grain reserves and pretend outwardly that the food situation was normal. "The grain problem," according to *Izvestiya* of November 12, 1953, "has been solved in the USSR. . . . " Khrushchev, on the other hand, restlessly maneuvered to win supporters prior to elaborating on his plan for emergency measures to relieve the grain squeeze. A. I. Kozlov's hold on the administrative reins of the farm system was weakened by the creation of a separate USSR Ministry of Agricultural Procurement, formed on the basis of organizations and enterprises under Kozlov's jurisdiction, and the appointment of L. R. Korniyets as USSR Minister of Procurement.[39] Korniyets worked with Khrushchev in the Ukraine and was a backer of the virgin lands program whose opinion on the question would be recorded in the party leader's relevant memorandum to the Presidium.

The most significant of a number of shifts of party personnel was the removal of V. M. Andrianov from the first secretaryship of the Leningrad Regional Committee

[38] *Kommunist Estonii* (Communist of Estonia), No. 10, 1963; and *KPSS—Spravochnik* (CPSU—Handbook), Moscow, 1963, p. 281.
[39] The decrees of November 21 and 25, 1953, are in *Vedomosti Verkhovnogo Soveta* (Gazette of the USSR Supreme Soviet), December 1, 1953, p. 1 (CDSP, v, 44, p. 9).

and his replacement by Frol R. Kozlov, in the presence of Khrushchev.[40] While Andrianov's career pointed to an association with Malenkov, Kozlov's was no less sinister. He rose in the local hierarchy following the purge which Beriya and Malenkov inspired in 1949 and was selected to perform the odious task of whipping up anti-reformist hysteria at the time of the "Doctors' Plot."[41] The train of subsequent events indicates that the Khrushchev-Kozlov relationship was an instable alliance of politicians with entirely different orientations. Khrushchev's was agricultural and decentralist, and that of the metallurgical engineer Kozlov was heavy engineering and authoritarian centralist. But at the time the interests of both roughly coincided. The tendency of Malenkov's economic policy posed a threat to the routine workings of the machine-building industry in Leningrad; Khrushchev's virgin soil plan would improve the provisioning of the northern city with foodstuffs and not really affect the region's comparatively unimportant farm economy by syphoning off West Russia's agricultural machinery for use in Kazakhstan and Siberia. These practical considerations evidently helped to seal the accord which Khrushchev and Kozlov reached at the end of 1953.

The overt expression of Khrushchev's canvassing was turgidly doctrinal but nonetheless injurious to the position of Malenkov. The premier's notoriously misleading statement about the grain problem was in keeping with Stalin's euphoric dogma of *beskonfliktnost'*, or lack of discordance between "productive relations" and the "na-

[40] *Pravda* and *Izvestiya*, November 29, 1953 (CDSP, v, 48, p. 23).

[41] See F. Kozlov, "Political Vigilance Is the Duty of the Party Member," *Kommunist*, No. 1, 1953, pp. 46-58.

ture of productive forces" under socialism. To subvert that dogma in the context of the current factional struggle was to follow the example of Khrushchev at the September 1953 Central Committee Plenum and alert the bureaucratic stratum to malfunction of the economy. The task of doing just that was assigned to Ts. Stepanyan, the ideological functionary who had argued for Khrushchev's village improvement plan in 1950 and was hazed during the reactionary press campaign of early 1953. Stepanyan in the columns of Shepilov's organ[42] tangled with "some propagandists" who "claim that complete conformity excludes contradictions and that, if contradictions arise, then complete conformity between productive forces and productive relations disappears." This view was groundless, since it regarded economic discordance as the matter of a fleeting moment instead of "a constant and inherent source of all development." Stepanyan pointed to the imbalance of industry and agriculture and insinuated that no serious upturn of consumer goods production could be attained so long as the raw materials base in the countryside was underdeveloped: "Marxism-Leninism teaches that not a single social-economic phenomenon leaves the arena of history until it has exhausted its possibilities and, conversely, *not a single economic innovation can be made until the objective conditions for it have matured.* Consistent observance of this materialist principle is the sharpest antidote for all kinds of harebrained theories, for adventurism in politics. It is impossible to hasten something for which the historical conditions have not yet matured" (italics added). When Stepanyan noted that heavy industry was the "bedrock" of the economy, it could be inferred that his patron in

[42] *Pravda*, December 7, 1953 (CDSP, v, 50, pp. 3-4).

the leadership was thinking largely of the technical outfitting of agriculture. Khrushchev indeed remarked in a
speech made about six weeks later: " . . . there will be
no communism without an abundance of products. It will
not be communism if our country has as much metal and
cement as you like but meat and grain are in short
supply."[43]

The organizational and ideological preparations completed, Khrushchev tested broader reaction to his new
lands plan. N. I. Belyayev, secretary of the Altai Territory Party Committee and a personal friend of Khrushchev (see Chapter IV), declared in *Pravda* on December
11, 1953, that several million hectares of little-productive
ranges and pastures in Siberia might be planted to wheat
without large expenditure of capital and with only a minimum of agrotechnical measures. The reservation of
"some comrades" that feed output would decline was un-
founded, Belyayev stated, since there would also be an
increased sowing of fast-growing annual grasses and silage corn. The USSR Ministry of State Farms in particular held aloof from the timely question of expanding
sown areas.[44] Malenkov's press still kept its glance on the
old farming areas and retorted to the silage-corn advocates that lupine crops were the only ones capable of as-
suring large harvests of green feed in the non-Black Earth
belt.[45]

Neo-Stalinist science and bureaucracy were then mar-
shaled to counteract the allurement of Khrushchev's virgin soil program. The USSR Academy of Sciences and

[43] *S.K. v SSSR i R.S.Kh.*, I, 144.
[44] "Utilize Vast Unused Altai Lands for Wheat," CDSP, v,
50, pp. 37-38.
[45] A. Kovtun, *Izvestiya*, December 20, 1953 (CDSP, v, 51, p. 25).

Ministry of Agriculture held a conference on kolkhoz management on December 23-28, 1953.[46] Pertinent commentaries were offered by Laptev, now designated as an associate of Lysenko's All-Union Lenin Academy of Agricultural Sciences,[47] and Professor V. S. Dmitriyev, a disciple of Lysenko who was affiliated with the Economics Institute. Laptev prefaced his remarks with a malicious aside about the onetime erroneous formation of grain "links" in Khrushchev's home region. He insisted upon the study of unutilized land in the east and referred to "the indisputable advantage of intensive agriculture in comparison to the extensive type." Laptev said in amplification that any new lands undertaking ought to be sharply limited: "This does not mean that it is not necessary to use natural resources. It is to say that the main line of development of socialist agriculture is its intensification." Dmitriyev, whose paper dealt entirely with assimilating new lands, implicitly disputed Belyayev's contention that the process was simple and economical. Special techniques were required to obtain production rises at minimal cost. One such technique which *Izvestiya* advertised on February 7, 1954, was to plow and harrow virgin lands but leave them uncropped for a year or more and then sow them to perennial grasses as well as grain.[48] Lysenko in *Izvestiya* of February 20, 1954, warned of sharp fluctuations in the crop yields from virgin lands and outlined a complex system of plowing which relied upon perennial herbaceous vegetation.[49] This agronomical

[46] Reported in *Voprosy Ekonomiki*, No. 2, 1954, pp. 109-117.
[47] *Ibid.*, No. 2, 1954, pp. 7ff.
[48] CDSP, VI, 6, pp. 28-29.
[49] CDSP, VI, 8, pp. 20 and 27. Sometime in January 1954 the Lenin All-Union Academy of Agricultural Sciences arranged a conference of scientists and practitioners on the agrotechnology

hocus-pocus was clearly intended to frustrate Khrushchev's political ambitions. The first secretary would soon act to ruin Dmitriyev's professional career and topple Lysenko from his scientific throne.

Meanwhile, the press war reached its climax. Shepilov utilized the lead-article space of *Pravda* to manipulate elite opinion in behalf of the objectives of the Khrushchev group. The *Pravda* leader of January 7, 1954, implored that tracts of virgin soil in Kazakhstan, the Volga region, the Urals, and Siberia be turned over to grain crops, especially wheat.[50] Not until January 22, 1954, did Khrushchev submit his relevant proposals to the party Presidium. (An afterthought of the outsider might well concern the futility of reading merely *Pravda* lead articles in order to estimate the correlation of political forces in Moscow.) The title of Khrushchev's memorandum of January 22, 1954, was a stark affront to Malenkov: "Ways of Solving the Grain Problem."[51] Malenkov was likewise disparaged at the very outset of the document: "A further study of the condition of agriculture and grain procurements shows that the solution of the grain problem which we have announced does not entirely correspond to the actual state of affairs in the country with respect to assurance with grain." Khrushchev presented data on state grain procurements of 1,850,000,000 poods as against supply outlays of 1,926,000,000, and termed "impermissible" the extraction of 160,000,000 poods from governmental stocks. This indignation would figure prominently in the oratory of Malenkov's successor when he took over the premiership about a year later.

---

of cultivating spring wheat in virgin and fallow lands of the east (L. N. Ul'yanov, *Voprosy Istorii KPSS. Sbornik Statey* (Problems of CPSU History. Anthology), Moscow, 1959, p. 211.

[50] CDSP, vi, 1, pp. 19-20.

[51] *S.K. v SSSR i R.S.Kh.*, i, 85-100.

Having painted a black picture of the grain economy, Khrushchev advised that in the next two years grain planting be expanded by 13 million hectares in the Volga region, Urals, Siberia, and Kazkhstan. He forecast that with a minimal yield of 10-11 quintals per hectare, grain production would rise by 800-900 million poods, including 500-600 million poods of marketable grain. This in effect would increase the state's grain procurements and purchases over one-third as compared with 1953. The capital inputs for the project would amount to approximately 550-600 million rubles, chiefly for construction purposes, and be recouped in one year's time. The basic quantities of machinery were to be requisitioned from the old farm areas and thus the resources allocated to agriculture under the 1954 economic plan would be essentially sufficient. Manpower to the extent of 70,000 persons was to be supplied through the compulsory draft of certain specialists and the voluntary enlistment of youth.

The memorandum foreshadowed Khrushchev's public criticism a month later of the agricultural and scientific bureaucracies for having allowed perennial grasses to edge out more nutritive grain crops in the formation of silage. His mention of the Ukrainian wheat dispute of 1947-1948 was a sign that in Khrushchev's mind his defeat at the hands of Malenkov, A. I. Kozlov, and Lysenko still rankled. The memorandum also suggested revision of the predatory table of kolkhoz payments for MTS work, which stifled work incentive and compelled many peasants to seek out employment in industry. Appended to the memorandum were a draft decree, "On Increasing Grain Production in 1954-1955 Through Assimilating Idle and Virgin Lands," a report of the USSR Planning Committee and the USSR Ministries of Agriculture, State Farms, and Procurement, a note of Academician Lysenko,

81

"On Grain Crop Yields in Idle and Virgin Lands," and newspaper articles on the relevant experience of farms. The joint ministerial report and Lysenko's contribution may have been addressed only to the technical feasibility of land expansion in the areas under consideration and have taken a generally neutral position.

A precarious balance of forces took shape in the leadership once Khrushchev submitted his proposal. Of the nine men who held membership in the party Presidium at the time, four were later identified as dissentients, viz., Molotov, Malenkov, Kaganovich, and Bulganin. The resistance of Molotov was bitterest. For three years he obstinately kept silent about virgin lands in policy speeches which touched on agriculture.[52] Molotov alone was singled out for opposition to the new lands program in the decree of the June 1957 Central Committee Plenum; the others were named at the Committee session in December 1958. Malenkov, perhaps, was not originally accused of fighting Khrushchev on the issue because of the uneven performances in Kazakhstan prior to the record harvest of 1958. That he did contest Khrushchev at this stage of the argument is certain from the stalling tactics of Lysenko which were given notoriety in *Izvestiya* as late as February 20, 1954. The aforementioned convocation of agumented meetings of the party Presidium to discuss the question is further suggestive of the bigness of the roadblocks that Khrushchev encountered, which it would have required several of his associates to throw across his path.

Of the five remaining members of the Presidium, three—K. Ye. Voroshilov (chairman of the Presidium of

[52] Cf. *Pravda*, March 12, 1954, February 20, 1956, and January 19, 1957.

the USSR Supreme Soviet), M. G. Pervukhin (USSR Minister of Electric Power Plants and Electrical Industry), and Saburov—have all been censured for adhering to the Malenkov-Molotov group in June 1957. But none has thus far been accused of challenging Khrushchev on new lands. Yet, in speeches made in March 1954 on occasion of the elections to the USSR Supreme Soviet, Voroshilov and Pervukhin joined Molotov and Bulganin in forgetting about the new lands decision, which all other Presidium members at least took into account.[53] The obstructionism which developed in Saburov's planning apparatus has been attributed to the incitement of Kaganovich.[54] Khrushchev's success in establishing rapport with certain members of Malenkov's government cabinet was also evident in the verbal behavior of Mikoyan. He spoke warmly of "sharply increasing the sowing of grains, *mainly via cultivation of virgin and waste lands* but also via increased yields, with a view particularly to supplying animal husbandry with grain fodders" (italics added). Conflicting emphasis indictive of misgivings appeared in the analogous speech of Secretary Suslov: "*The main task is to obtain higher yields of grain.* We have colossal potentialities. At the same time the party also considers cultivation of grain crops on virgin and idle lands in Kazakhstan, the Urals, Siberia, and the Volga region to be an important factor in increasing grain production" (italics added). This demonstrated that Suslov's right to

[53] The speeches are in *Pravda*, March 7-13, 1954.

[54] Anonymous experts in the State Planning Committee "declared that there was no money or materials for exploitation of the virgin lands, and opposed the allocation of funds for tractors, housing, metal, and wire. The suppliers objected categorically: they said that there will be no resources. Kaganovich headed this matter" (Yurkin, *Plenum I*, p. 408).

an independent viewpoint as a member of the Central Committee took precedence over any commitment to his nominal superior in the Committee's administrative arm.

Khrushchev overwhelmed the many opponents of his virgin soil program in the party Presidium by expanding the arena of conflict. As the champion of an innovating course in agricultural policy, he would repeatedly fall back on this stratagem when confronted with strong opposition in the smaller decision-making body. Khrushchev's essentially inferior status in the Presidium was evident in the weeks immediately following the adoption of his new lands program, when rivals curbed the impact of his speeches and denied him a free hand in running the new granary in Kazakhstan. Three of Khrushchev's addresses to conferences of agricultural workers were suppressed.[55] The ban occurred under an informal ruling that public statements by members of the party Presidium and Central Committee Secretariat be submitted to the governing junta for preliminary censorship.[56] Malenkov and Molotov apparently objected in part to the outspoken, impetuous, and pragmatic nature of the speeches. Grain procurement in the Russian Federation was cited at 416,000,000 poods below the 1940 figure. The storming of new lands, he said, could not wait until basic necessi-

[55] The speeches were delivered in Moscow on January 28, February 5 and 15, 1954, and are in *S.K. v SSSR i R.S.Kh.*, I, 101-219.

[56] After the death of Stalin, "A strict procedure was established in the CPSU Central Committee whereby not one important measure and not one speech (with publication in the press) of a member of the Presidium or of a secretary of the CPSU Central Committee is undertaken without preliminary group discussion" (M. L. Karelina, D. I. Nadtocheyev, and I. G. Ryabtsev, eds., *Lektsii po Istorii KPSS* [*prochitany aspirantam Akademii Obshchestvennykh Nauk pri TsK KPSS v 1961/62 g. vypusk pervyy*] [Lectures on CPSU History (read to candidates of the Academy of Social Sciences attached to the CPSU Central Committee in 1961-1962), part one], Moscow, 1963, p. 349).

ties were installed for the settlers, since that might take up to three years and the public now required more nourishing and appetizing foods. Khrushchev rhetorically asked his listeners: "And what is that very same communist society without sausage?" Approving laughter rang out as utopia was brought down to earth, and he continued in the same vein: "Really, comrades, in the communist society you will not tell people to go and eat a potato without butter. The communist society presupposes the creation of such conditions for our nation whereby people will be assured according to their need. Surely, the man who lives in the communist society will not ask for turnips in the grocery shop, but will demand better foodstuffs. But better foodstuffs cannot be created without an abundance of grain."

Khrushchev proceeded to propose that the function of detailed planning of various crops be transferred from the capital to the localities. "It may be said," he added on February 15, 1954, "that this, really, is a disruption of state planning, an underestimation of socialist methods of running the economy." Indeed, Malenkov was of that opinion and so long as he remained head of the government the planning reform was stymied. The underlying reason for the divergence over the change was the existence of different estimates of civil loyalty. According to Khrushchev: "When the Central Committee proposed to introduce a new kind of planning in agriculture, conservative people opposed this measure. They tried to frighten the Central Committee, saying that if we no longer planned the sowing of crops from the center, the collective farmers would stop sowing wheat and we would lose our supply of grain."[57]

[57] From speeches to the artistic intelligentsia, May-July 1957, in *S.K. v SSSR i R.S.Kh.*, II, 463-464.

Still another reason for the colleagues of Khrushchev to have suppressed his speeches of that day was to maintain his public image as a narrow-minded rustic who lacked Malenkov's supposed adroitness in the conduct of foreign relations. Actually, Khrushchev's immersion in agricultural affairs made him no less interested in diminution of external tension than was his foremost antagonist. He flexibly differentiated between realistic and warlike statesmen in the West, and from ulterior motives claimed that the former were especially impressed by rising living standards in Russia. At the same time, Khrushchev recognized the need to maintain an adequate defense posture in an uncertain world atmosphere. The worker and farm technician and, most important politically, the industrialist and general could all find something attractive in this oratorical amalgam.

The lever regulating key appointments in the agricultural sphere was still beyond control of the first secretary. Kazakhstan party leaders Shayakhmetov and Afonov had earlier failed to support proposals for an increase in planted acreage, and only on direct order from party headquarters did preparations begin to assimilate new lands in the region. Both were summoned to Moscow after the major decision was reached and asked to present their views on its implementation. They advised slow rates of land expansion and called for investments which were deemed excessive. The top leaders agreed that a purge was in order. P. K. Ponomarenko was named first secretary of the party in Kazakhstan and L. I. Brezhnev the second secretary.[58] Ponomarenko's rise and fall in the bureaucracy paralleled Malenkov's, while Brezhnev's ca-

[58] Cf. *Pravda*, February 12 and 22, 1954 (CDSP, vi, 6, pp. 23-24, and vi, 8, p. 22); and *S.K. v SSSR i R.S.Kh.*, i, 275-276.

reer fortunes and, especially, verbal behavior stamp him as a close follower of Khrushchev. That a dependent of Malenkov should have received preferential treatment in the circumstances indicated the negotiation of important bureaucratic appointments in the party Presidium rather than their imposition on order of the first secretary.

The February 23-March 2, 1954, Central Committee session on virgin lands provided Khrushchev with a forum for factional self-aggrandizement and the denigration of adversaries. His keynote report[59] restated the principal arguments in behalf of the new program and bristled with jibes at the lieutenants of Malenkov. Yet in his unpublished speech of February 5, 1954, Khrushchev had mocked V. S. Dmitriyev for his grassland proclivities. Now he broadcast that Dmitriyev, who formerly headed the Agricultural Planning Administration in the State Planning Committee, and S. T. Demidov, vice-chairman of the Committee, were zealous grasslanders who "persecuted people who raised their voices against improper planning and who suggested that the structure of sown areas be changed." Benediktov was an agronomist, an effective executive, and a man of principle, but he tolerated mistakes in the cropping pattern. "Bureaucracy," Khrushchev said regretfully, "evidently sucked him in." A. I. Kozlov, according to the first secretary, was even more to blame and had no excuses to offer in view of his lengthy ties with administrative and scientific agencies concerned with agriculture.

Vilification did not stop there, as Khushchev disclosed that after Dmitriyev was released from planning work, "he attempted to receive the learned degree of

[59] *Pravda* and *Izvestiya*, March 21, 1954 (CDSP, v, 12, pp. 3ff.); and *S.K. v SSSR i R.S.Kh.*, i, 227-286.

Doctor of Biological Sciences under the patronage of Academician T. D. Lysenko. Working in the Economics Institute, this parody of a scholar poses as a hero, instructs everyone how to manage agriculture, delivers lectures at the university, and, in a word, 'enriches' science. We were still discussing the question of developing virgin and idle lands when Comrade Dmitriyev had already hastened to deliver public lectures on this question. It is obvious that our science will not benefit from such 'learned' men." The double standard which Khrushchev applied to the conduct of Dmitriyev and his own henchman Shepilov in connection with the new lands decision is remarkable and raises doubt about the validity of the opinion that Khrushchev has dispassionately promoted policy debate within the upper stratum of Soviet society. Moreover, Dmitriyev shortly was deprived of the academic degree of Doctor of Biology, voted him on February 20, 1954, after several sharp interventions by his academic advisor, Lysenko.[60]

This feuding in the party elite soon had effects on the milieu of biological science. A *Kommunist* editorial which raked over the coals of the Dmitriyev incident demanded a general scholarly discussion of Lysenko's views on species formation.[61] *Pravda* a few months later carried an article which recalled that for a number of years the T. D. Lysenko All-Union Selection and Genetics Institute inflicted "tremendous" harm to the national economy by recommending a cutback of winter wheat sowings in the

[60] See "Letter to the Editor: Concerning a Faulty Dissertation (By Doctor of Biology S. Stankof, Professor at the M. V. Lomonosov State University in Moscow)," *Pravda*, March 26, 1954 (CDSP, vi, 12, p. 13).
[61] See "Science and Life," *Kommunist*, No. 5, 1954, pp. 3-13 (CDSP, i, 14, pp. 3-7).

Ukraine, Kuban, and other southern areas.[62] However, Lysenko in April 1954 lectured on spring wheat plantings in party headquarters to representatives assigned to new state grain farms in the virgin lands.[63] His indispensability as an expert on spring wheat is doubtful. More likely, Lysenko still drew some benefit from the patronage of someone like Malenkov. This hypothesis is further supported by the curious timing of the release of the documents of the February-March 1954 Plenum as well as their substantive content. Khrushchev's report of February 23 was not publicized until March 21. The decree of the session, adopted on March 2, was published in *Pravda* and *Izvestiya* on March 6. It furthermore reasserted the position of Malenkov that increase of yields "has been and remains the chief means of increasing grain production."[64] Not until March 28, 1954, did the split leadership release a completed version of the draft decree on new lands which Khrushchev had submitted over two months before.[65] This foot-dragging had been characteristic of Malenkov ever since the low procurement figures of 1953 were available to insiders.

The machinations of Shepilov and Ovechkin enabled Khrushchev to keep in the foreground personal ideas which might have been blurred if the spotlight of publicity had been turned on other, group decisions. Ovech-

[62] Academician N. Tsitsin, "Against Stereotyed Application of the Grass-Field System of Agriculture," *Pravda*, August 21, 1954 (CDSP, vi, 34, pp. 15-31).

[63] *Pravda* and *Izvestiya*, April 15, 1954 (CDSP, vi, 14, p. 7).

[64] The decree is in CDSP, vi, 9, pp. 3-6, 20, and vi, 10, pp. 16-20, 35.

[65] "In the USSR Council of Ministers and Party Central Committee: On Increasing Grain Production in 1954-1955 Through Development of Virgin and Idle Lands," *Pravda* and *Izvestiya*, March 28, 1954 (CDSP, vi, 13, pp. 11-14).

kin's agricultural sketches in *Pravda* of February 28 and March 1, 1954, decried highly centralized administration and so were the first to convey to the elite the reformist modifications which Khrushchev urged in his unpublished speech of February 15 and his Plenum report of February 23—unpublished until March 21—and that were formally approved in the decree of the plenary session, which appeared on March 6. Without explicitly mentioning Ovechkin, the *Pravda* editorial of March 3, 1954, approved his message. Other pleas for independence of lower-echelon technicians in agriculture were made in *Pravda* on April 17, 1954, and in the remarks of Khrushchev at the USSR Supreme Soviet meeting a few days later.[66] *Pravda* was now so accurate a register of Khrushchev's sentiment that his qualms about F. R. Kozlov became obvious once the paper's correspondent reported on a plenary session of the Leningrad Regional Party Committee: "It should be noted that neither the report of Comrade Kozlov nor the speeches by Comrade Vorobyev, chairman of the province executive committee, and Comrade Korytkov, head of the province agricultural administration, contained proper self-criticism or comprehensive analysis of mistakes and shortcomings in the work of province organizations in carrying out the resolutions of the party Central Committee September and February-March plenary sessions."[67]

The strain within Khrushchev's alliance with Kozlov is traceable partly to his rising interest in diverting resources from heavy engineering to agricultural machine-

[66] Cf. K. Ivanov, "Leninist Principles of Work of State Apparatus," CDSP, vi, 16, pp. 23-24; and *Pravda*, April 27, 1954 (CDSP, vi, 22, pp. 5-9).

[67] *Pravda*, April 23, 1954 (CDSP, vi, 16, p. 23).

building. He complained of a shortage of tractors and other agricultural equipment in Kazakhstan in a memorandum submitted to the party Presidium on June 5, 1954, after an inspection tour of the region. This shortage was bound to become more acute if the Presidium acted favorably on the draft decree which Khrushchev simultaneously distributed, calling for the assimilation of an additional 13-15 million hectares of new lands in Kazakhstan and Siberia during the next two years.[68] It is noteworthy that the new goal of 28-30 million hectares was the same amount of land that was to have been reclaimed only after many years and at large cost under the "Great Stalin Plan for Remaking Nature." The link-up of heavy industry and agriculture was explicit in the article of one A. Bechin in the issue of *Problems of Economics* signed for printing on June 22, 1954. Bechin addressed himself to the question of economic proportions, which was of "great theoretical and practical importance." He stressed the need for a higher rate of growth of heavy industry and, like Shepilov and then Khrushchev on the eve of Malenkov's demise, opposed "certain of our economists" who advocated equal rates of development of heavy and light industry. Specifically, Bechin noted the machinery requirements of agriculture and disputed the finding of "bourgeois scholars" that the volume of farm production increased at a slower rate than its costs.[69]

The opposition closed ranks and Khrushchev had to

[68] "Some Remarks About the Trip to Kazakhstan," *S.K. v SSSR i R.S.Kh.*, I, 296-305.

[69] *Voprosy Ekonomiki*, No. 7, 1954, pp. 3-16. Cf. Shepilov's article in *Pravda*, January 24, 1955, denouncing "pseudo-theoreticians" of the light industry school; and Khrushchev's repetition in *Pravda*, February 3, 1955 (CDSP, VI, 52, pp. 4-6, and VII, 6, pp. 3ff.).

play a relatively minor role at the Central Committee Plenum on agriculture held on June 23-26, 1954. Ministers of agriculture, state farms, and procurement reported on the current situation.[70] Khrushchev made a personal speech on the first day of the session but it was not published.[71] He had opted again to circumvent the Presidium and appeal to the more representative body for support of his proposal to bring 13-15 million hectares more of unused, unplowed land into the agricultural cycle. Khrushchev castigated those who took a wait-and-see attitude and failed to appreciate that "We must win time." If the main stake in grain production was put on the central areas, at least a decade would be needed to supply them with enough chemical fertilizer and at a cost of tens of billions of rubles to build the fertilizer plants. The grain of Kazakhstan and Siberia, on the other hand, was cheaper than that secured from any other region than the Kuban. Minister Benediktov was criticized in Khrushchev's speech for tolerating the waste of valuable seed in plantings of the wrong type of wheat in Siberia. Once more, Khrushchev advised that the local technicians be permitted to decide such questions. Ovechkin dutifully followed suit in *Pravda* on August 27 and 30 and September 1, 1954, with an installment of "District Routine" which favored the reduction of centralized administration. By November 1954 the concern for agricultural detail in the USSR State Planning Committee, but not the Ministry of Agriculture, had decreased.[72]

The decree of the June 1954 Plenum disregarded the

[70] *Pravda* and *Izvestiya*, June 27, 1954 (CDSP, vi, 26, p. 4).
[71] The speech is in *S.K. v SSSR i R.S.Kh.*, i, 306-336.
[72] See J. M., "The Agricultural Planning Order," *Soviet Studies*, Vol. vii, pp. 93-102.

figure of 13-15 million hectares in instructing the USSR Ministries of Agriculture and State Farms, the RSFSR government, and the government and party Central Committee in Kazakhstan to investigate the lands of northern Kazakhstan and Siberia, the Volga, and other areas, and by October 15, 1954, to submit proposals to the USSR government for the expansion of cultivated acreage, chiefly by organizing new state farms and improving the use of land in existing farms. This was a reversal for Khrushchev, as was the anonymity-cloaked decision to make serious economic concessions to grain farmers.[73] Khrushchev's recourse was to sustain his agitation in the provinces and by innuendo disparage Malenkov for his conceited approach to agriculture and resort to food purchases overseas. The Presidium suppressed these rumblings.[74] Nonetheless, proselytes were flocking to the movement of clandestine politics which stood for better living standards and increased autonomy at the bottom of the social scale.

Meanwhile, an increasing number of industrialists had become alienated by the premier's economic viewpoint, especially his intention to retool machine-building plants for the manufacture of consumer durables intended for urban civil servants and worker aristocrats. This helps to account for the notable shift in the configuration of political forces to the detriment of Malenkov early in August of 1954. The October 15 deadline for an experts' report on new lands potential was scrapped and a decision adopted on August 13 to raise the original target of 13

[73] The concessions are described in J. M., "Recent Agricultural Orders," *Soviet Studies*, Vol. VI, pp. 170-172.
[74] See Khrushchev's Novosibirsk speech of July 11, 1954, first published in *S.K. v SSSR i R.S.Kh.*, I, 337-358.

million hectares to 28-30 million by the end of 1956, 15 million of which were to be put under crop in the spring of 1955. The decision was ascribed to the party Central Committee and Council of Ministers—not in reverse order, as had hitherto been the case under the preeminence of Malenkov.[75] That the defection of a sizable portion of the economic bureaucracy enabled Khrushchev to turn the tables may be ascertained from the essay of one I. Vekua in the issue of *Problems of Economics* that was sent to the press on August 28, 1954, and attacked for "coarse theoretical and political errors" when Malenkov slipped a few months later.[76] Very much like Khrushchev at the June session of the Central Committee, Vekua held that time was of the essence in solving economic problems. But unlike the party leader, he had in mind the Malenkovian goal of a sharp rise of luxury goods in the next two or three years. Machine-building plants, he said, had to be converted more widely in order to reach the goal. It did not pay to emulate the Trotskyites, who had proposed "superrates" of industrialization which would have been fatal (had not the Stalinists later proclaimed them as their own). However, "certain business executives" approached economic tasks in a manner which was "narrowly departmentalist." Unity of the political and economic leadership, intoned Vekua, was essential. That no such unity existed would be apparent from the promotions which industrial ministers soon received for having switched their loyalties from Malenkov to Khrushchev and his new partner, the industrial-military administrator Bulganin.[77]

[75] *Pravda*, August 17, 1954.
[76] Cf. *Voprosy Ekonomiki*, No. 9, 1954, pp. 3-18; and *ibid.*, No. 1, 1955, p. 18.
[77] A good biographical sketch of Bulganin is in Boris Meissner,

In all, three conflicting outlooks on industrial prospects fragmented the leadership. Malenkov, for the sake of attaining immediate prosperity in the urban upper class, was ready to impinge on the interests of those whose status depended on the maintenance of first-rate industrial machine-building and armaments works.[78] An opposing group of extremists, headed by Bulganin, unreservedly took up the cause of heavy engineering. Khrushchev's deep commitment to the new lands project and hatred of Malenkov impelled him to unite with the Bulganin group. The economic viewpoint of Khrushchev was anything but the neo-Stalinist kind which certain foreign observers thought it to be. So much is clear from a number of the controversial actions of Khrushchev at the time. On November 20, 1954, he delivered a speech in Tashkent which came to light only in the 1960's.[79] Like other pronouncements of his which were then quashed in the party Presidium, this one too emphasized the importance of heavy industry.[80] But in a section dealing with peasant income, Khrushchev countenanced the balancing of supply and demand of consumer goods and thereby revised the austerity teaching of

---

Sowjetrussland zwischen Revolution und Restauration, Cologne, 1956, pp. 117-128.

[78] Official data report that the military's share of gross investment declined from 23.8 per cent in 1952 and 20.9 per cent in 1953 to 18.3 per cent in 1954 (462 million rubles less than in the previous year); see the 1958-1961 editions of *Narodnoye Khozyaystvo SSSR* and *Economic Survey of Europe in 1954* (Geneva), as cited in Embree, *op. cit.*, p. 126.

[79] *S.K. v SSSR i R.S.Kh.*, I, 367-396.

[80] Cf. his interview of September 25, 1954, with Professor Bernal, which *Pravda* ran on December 24, 1954; and speech of December 7, 1954, to the builders' conference, carried in *Pravda* on December 27, 1954 (CDSP, VI, 51, pp. 7-8, and VI, 52, pp. 7-14, 33).

Stalin that the demand for such commodities always exceeds their availability.[81] The generally acknowledged "liberalizer" Mikoyan was to foster this anti-Stalin concept in 1956 at the 20th party Congress.[82] Similarly at variance with Stalinist behavior were the remedial proposals which Khrushchev submitted to the party Presidium after he questioned citizens and learned of food difficulties in Eastern Siberia during a tour of the area.[83] Khrushchev's wooing of the military now took the form of a recommendation that special state farms be created in the Far Eastern provinces and subordinated to the quartermaster of the local garrison, so that the garrison could be fully supplied with necessary products.

The misleading feature of the Soviet political scene in late 1954 and early 1955 was the coinciding emergence of Khrushchev and the Stalin symbol. On December 21, 1954, the seventy-fifth anniversary of Stalin's birth, for example, the Soviet military organ in East Germany displayed a faked photograph showing Khrushchev and Bulganin with Stalin, Zhdanov, and Voroshilov. Malenkov had been cropped out of the original, which had not depicted Khrushchev and Bulganin.[84] This may be interpreted as an effort by the military establishment to demonstrate support of the new merger in the party Presidium and represent it in terms of a historical continuity of leadership. The compulsion to legitimate Khrushchev's newly won preeminence may also explain why after the decline of Malenkov in 1955 he was raised in one serial

[81] See J. Stalin, *Sochineniya* (Works), Moscow, 1949, XII, 322.
[82] *Pravda*, February 18, 1956.
[83] See "The Riches of the Far East Are Innumerable—From a Note to the CPSU Central Committee Concerning a Trip to the Far East and Sakhalin," November 29, 1954, *S.K. v SSSR i R.S.Kh.*, I, 397-409.
[84] The *Tägliche Rundschau* incident is described in Meissner, *op. cit.*, p. 114.

publication from a "comrade-in-arms" of Stalin to "one of the closest comrades-in-arms."[85] Most important was the textual content of the press materials which superficially related to the departed autocrat. The *Pravda* article of December 21, 1954, which contrasted with the same day's handouts in *Izvestiya* by emphasizing heavy, rather than light, industry, twice invoked the authority of Lenin to argue that heavy industry was the key to agricultural development.

Khrushchev hammered away at the same point in his report on livestock breeding to the Central Committee Plenum of January 25-31, 1955.[86] This was Khrushchev's moment of vindication, insofar as the new lands program had resulted in a 6 per cent increase of grain production over the 1949-1953 average in spite of drought conditions and poor harvest in the Volga basin and Ukraine.[87] The elite was told that the primary task was to force heavy industry "because only on its basis can there be an upturn of the entire economy of the country, including the light, food, and other branches of industry, and our agriculture." Khrushchev too quoted Lenin to the effect that "the solitary material foundation of socialism can be large-scale machine industry capable of reorganizing agriculture as well." In demanding an eventual doubling of the grain harvest to 10 billion poods (two-fifths of which was needed for animal feed), Khrushchev advocated foremost an increased production of agricultural machinery through existing facilities and new plant construction. The report also took into account the burden which the arms race imposed on heavy industry. The

[85] See the citations in Myron Rush, *The Rise of Khrushchev*, Washington, D.C., 1958, p. 8.

[86] *Pravda* and *Izvestiya*, February 3, 1955 (CDSP, vii, 6, pp. 3ff.); and *S.K. v SSSR i R.S.Kh.*, i, 421-492.

[87] Durgin, *Soviet Studies*, Vol. xiii, pp. 255ff.

conservation of funds for heavy industry moved Khrushchev to reject the probably lower-echelon proposal that the state allot credits to finance kolkhoz operations. But he slighted the Malenkovites by encouraging the formation of interkolkhoz building associations. The report also affirmed that hereafter controversies over agrotechnical intricacies had to be regarded as political struggles. B. G. Gafurov, the party secretary of Tadzhikistan, tried to prove that it was possible to narrow the rows in sowing cotton. But U. Yusupov, former premier of Uzbekistan, took a skeptical view. According to Khrushchev, "This, comrades, was not just an argument between Ivan Ivanovich and Ivan Nikiforovich. It was a dispute on a question of principle, on which, I should say, the further development of cotton-growing depends." The personal quirk of an individual leader had given a new dimension to the multi-sided world of Soviet politics.

The report of Khrushchev was published on the opening day of the annual budgetary session of the USSR Supreme Soviet. This event and the fiscal arithmetic outlined to the session heralded the downfall of the Malenkov government. The planned state investment in light industry was to drop by 23 per cent (from 1.4 billion rubles in 1954 to 1.2 in 1955). A 27 per cent rise of expenditures of heavy industry was contemplated (from 8 billion rubles in 1954 to 10 billion in 1955). Defense spending would rise by at least 12 per cent (10 billion rubles in 1954 and 11 billion in 1955). True, state inputs in agriculture, forestry, and agricultural procurement diminished 12 per cent (6.2 to 5.5 billion rubles).[88] But agricultural machine-building experienced a lift in 1955-1956.

[88] A. G. Zverev, *Pravda*, February 4, 1955 (CDSP, VII, 4, pp. 7ff.).

The state in 1954 provided agriculture with 137,000 tractors (in terms of 15-h.p. units) and 37,000 grain combines, with 115,000 of the tractors and 18,000 of the combines sent to the new lands; in 1955-1956, 404,000 tractors (in 15-h.p. units) and 83,000 grain combines were manufactured.[89]

The "policy of revenge" was pursued assiduously. Just as Khrushchev had to humble himself before the Moscow Regional Party Conference in 1952, recanting his discredited agro-city plan, so Malenkov, Khrushchev's tormentor of that hour, in his resignation of the premiership, read by an intermediary,[90] had to confess to bungling the supervision of agricultural agencies during the Stalin era. He was also made to hail the Central Committee as the initiator of the post-Stalin reforms of agricultural taxation. The jealousy of the Khrushchev group over the fact that Malenkov had outrun them in August 1953 after they proposed fiscal changes in Ovechkin's *Pravda* articles would likewise make itself felt following the 1957 dismissal of Malenkov from the party Presidium.[91] As early as 1955, however, Malenkov declared that only the fulfillment of the new program for a rapid up-

[89] *Pravda* and *Izvestiya*, January 25, 1955 (CDSP, vii, 2, pp. 9ff.); and Khrushchev, *Pravda*, February 15, 1956 (CDSP, viii, 5, pp. 3ff.).

[90] A translation of Malenkov's letter is in *Soviet Studies*, Vol. vii, pp. 92-93.

[91] USSR Minister of Agriculture Matskevich wrote in *Pravda* of July 12, 1957, that "Malenkov, for purposes of self-aggrandizement and in order to acquire popularity cheaply, tried to take personal credit for Party Central Committee measures reducing the agricultural tax and raising procurement and purchase prices for farm products, as well as other measures for bringing about a sharp advance in agriculture and for raising the material well-being of the collective farm peasantry and all Soviet people" (CDSP, ix, 28, pp. 23-24).

swing of agriculture would ensure a genuine rise in the production of all requisite consumer goods—thus implying that his own venture was misguided. The new premier Bulganin voiced the dissatisfaction of industrialists and generals over Malenkov's cutting into state stocks: "It would be an inexcusable mistake to slacken our attention to this very important matter or to yield to the temptation to solve particular current tasks from state reserves. An extremely important task for us is to increase state reserves of raw and other materials, fuel, and industrial and food goods."[92]

Factional gains and losses were reflected in the composition of the new government. Mikoyan, Pervukhin, and Saburov were awarded the title of first deputy premier, which weakened the executive influence of the most quarrelsome reactionaries in the inner cabinet of the state machinery, Molotov and Kaganovich. Deputy premierships were conferred on figures active in the spheres of defense, construction, and agriculture, the latter two going to men who are identifiable as clients of Khrushchev.[93] After Marshal Zhukov assumed Bulganin's post of defense minister, ten generals were elevated to the rank of marshal.[94] Conversely, one of Khrushchev's old antagonists in the agricultural bureaucracy, A. I. Kozlov, was dis-

[92] *Izvestiya*, February 10, 1955. See also *S.K. v SSSR i R.S.Kh.*, II, 64.
[93] *Pravda*, March 1, 1955. V. A. Kucherenko, new chairman of the State Committee on Construction, directed building and industrial trusts in the Ukraine, 1939-1950. P. P. Lobanov in 1953-1955 headed the RSFSR Ministry of Argriculture, which was created with the backing of Khrushchev at the September 1953 Central Committee Plenum. In 1956 he would replace Lysenko as President of the Lenin All-Union Academy of Agricultural Sciences.
[94] *Pravda*, March 11, 1955.

missed from the Ministry of State Farms[95] and reduced to the menial status of director of the Chistovskiy state farm in North Kazakhstan, where he floundered until Khrushchev's star dipped in 1960. Benediktov, the Minister of Agriculture, whose record was no less tainted with authoritarian centralism, managed to find a new *shef* and take over the state farms portfolio in Moscow, which he held for a little more than two years.[96] No agreement presumably could be reached on the appointment of a new minister of agriculture. Matskevich, first deputy minister since 1953 and a former associate of Khrushchev in the Ukraine, assumed the post only in October 1955.[97] Malenkov's retention of a seat in the party Presidium, Benediktov's continued activity at the center, and the vacancy of the top position in the Agricultural Ministry were symptoms of the ongoing fight in the Kremlin.

KHRUSHCHEV'S "RIGHT OPPORTUNISM" (MARCH 1955-JUNE 1957)

The sources of tension in the leadership during the third phase of the post-Stalin struggle over power and policy included the efforts of Khrushchev to establish more sensible forms of managing collectivized agriculture and to capitalize on successes in the production of grain and silage corn by effectuating a technological revolution in livestock breeding. Khrushchev's encouragement of the long-abused cooperative element in kolkhoz organization, his readiness to experiment with the functioning of MTS, which for a quarter-century had performed the role of

[95] *Ibid.,* March 3, 1955.
[96] *Ibid.* Benediktov's subsequent appointment as RSFSR Minister of Agriculture was reported in *Sovetskaya Rossiya,* June 8, 1957.
[97] *Ibid.,* October 19, 1955.

politico-economic gendarme of the countryside, and his challenge to the growth rate of the capital goods industries for the sake of more agricultural machine-building made him vulnerable to the charge of heading a new "Right deviation" in the CPSU. That accusation was indeed leveled against the first secretary in the crisis of authority which dawned in June 1957. The prosecuting faction scarcely lacked an alternative choice of action, which was the authoritarian centralist policy of farming through the massive conversion of kolkhozes into state farms, with MTS providing leverage, and the maximum development of the producer goods industries. The division of opinion on agrarian policy along "Right" and "Left" lines conformed to the pattern of the 1920's, had its immediate origins in the alignments discernible at the close of the Stalin era, and shaped the nature of agricultural politics in the forthcoming regency of Khrushchev.

The year-old standoff on the mechanics of agricultural planning was ended on March 9, 1955, when a decree of sufficient importance to merit the imprimatur of party and government allowed kolkhoz and MTS technicians to determine the specifics of cultivation and livestock breeding on the basis of central and republic-level plans which set forth only the volume of procurements.[98] The change in part enabled Khrushchev to bypass ministerial obstruction of his silage corn program.[99] The ministerial bureaucracy remained a focal point of Khrushchev's wrath in 1955-1957. He pledged to trim the swollen procurement staff of many of its 900,000 workers,[100] and in

[98] *Pravda* and *Izvestiya*, March 11, 1955 (CDSP, vii, 7, pp. 16-17).
[99] See *Pravda*, April 4, 1955; and the report that corn plantings rose from 4.3 million hectares in 1954 to 17.9 million hectares in 1955, in *Voprosy Ekonomiki*, No. 2, 1956, p. 80.
[100] *S.K. v SSSR i R.S.Kh.*, ii, 36.

1956 the USSR Ministry of Procurements was decentralized into a Union-republic type of body concerned mainly with the collection and storage of bread grains and the operation of flour mills. Khrushchev conceived of the Ministries of Agriculture and State Farms largely in terms of scientific research foundations and popularizers of advanced techniques.[101] But the remerger of the Ministry of State Farms with the Ministry of Agriculture, evidently to pare the topheavy staffs, with Matskevich in charge, was the limit of bureaucratic innovation.[102]

The opposite side of the same coin was Khrushchev's promotion of local initiatives such as interkolkhoz construction societies and village-remodeling work.[103] He reacted sympathetically to local appeals in behalf of a nation-wide congress of collective farmers to update the Kolkhoz Statutes and in the spring of 1957 foresaw the opening of the assembly at the end of that year or early in 1958.[104] The right for farm boards to undertake partial modifications of the standard rules and the regularization of payments through monthly advances and bonuses were

[101] In the Central Committee report which he read to the 20th party Congress, in *Pravda*, February 15, 1956 (CDSP, VIII, 5, pp. 3ff.); and *S.K. v SSSR i R.S.Kh.*, II, 210.

[102] *Pravda*, May 31, 1957 (CDSP, IX, 22, p. 27).

[103] *S.K. v SSSR i R.S.Kh.*, II, 158 (talk given on October 31, 1955, in his home village, not reported in *Pravda* until January 11, 1956); 207-209 (February 14, 1956); 377 (March 30, 1957); and 460 (May 22, 1957). *Pravda* on October 3, 1957, reported the existence of 450 interkolkhoz construction organizations and enterprises for the production of local building materials. Nearly 7,000 kolkhozes were shareholders in the organizations (CDSP, IX, 40, p. 26).

[104] *S.K. v SSSR i R.S.Kh.*, II, 23 (March 18, 1955) and 397 (April 8, 1957). The anticipated date is in the version of Khrushchev's Gorky speech of April 8, 1957, in *Pravda*, April 10, 1957 (CDSP, IX, 15, pp. 25-27).

decreed in March 1956, after Doronin voiced the line of the Khrushchev group.[105] A dissenting opinion on the feasibility of upgrading the importance of cash in kolkhoz accounting was then expressed by one M. Osad'ko, who with notable consistency would later contest the propriety of selling MTS equipment to kolkhozes.[106] Notwithstanding his liberalizing tendencies at this juncture, Khrushchev, out of prejudice and perhaps political calculation, shied away from the introduction of some measure of agricultural decollectivization. He told a conference on meat production held at party headquarters on May 17, 1956:

> I wish to express my opinion on the question of individual deliveries of meat and milk, which was spoken about here by the secretary of the Central Committee of the Communist party of Byelorussia, Comrade Mazurov. I must say directly that if we put chief reliance on the individual deliverer, it will indicate our weakness. If this "theory" is supported, it will be turned against the kolkhozes, against the kolkhoz system.
>
> We must now take a line so that in time we may stop receiving meat and milk from the individual deliverers and reckon entirely on the kolkhozes and sovkhozes. That will be a correct solution of the problem, a confirmation of both the theory and practice of the indis-

[105] Cf. Doronin's article in *Kommunist*, No. 3 (February), 1956, pp. 59-74; and the party and government decree in *Pravda*, March 10, 1956 (CDSP, VIII, 10, pp. 3ff.).

[106] Osad'ko's view that the cash indices should not be used to measure labor expenditure and production costs in kolkhozes is in *The Labor Day and Its Payment* (in Russian), State Publishing House for Agricultural Literature, Moscow, 1956, cited by D. Chersheyev in *Voprosy Istorii KPSS. Sbornik Statey*, p. 127.

putable advantages of our large socialist farms over the individual type. One cannot all the time force the collective farmers to develop their individual farmsteads, all the time demand that they deliver products to the state. It is necessary foremost and chiefly to develop the communal economy.[107]

Khrushchev was not originally prepared to support a Ukrainian suggestion reminiscent of Pal'tsev's in 1950 that kolkhoz chairmen also serve as MTS directors.[108] He soon favored testing the practice of reducing production costs by withdrawing the state allotments to MTS and instituting a self-sustaining arrangement.[109] By mid-1956, however, the party leader had gravitated to the Pal'tsev position, asking that MTS tractor brigades be brought closer to kolkhoz needs in the interest of a more rational use of equipment.[110] Trial runs at consolidating the tractor brigades with kolkhoz field units when the stations serviced from one to three large farms were held in 1956, and Khrushchev endorsed their results in March 1957 at a discussion on a Kuban farm.[111] A few days later he recommended the lowering of MTS production costs through a system of payments based on performance criteria.[112]

[107] *S.K. v SSSR i R.S.Kh.*, II, 226. On March 12, 1957, Khrushchev ascribed to "jackals of imperialism" the idea that "collectivized agriculture supposedly will not create conditions for the development of agricultural production, and especially livestock breeding" (*ibid.*, II, 338).

[108] See his February 18, 1955, speech to the Central Committee, C.P. Ukraine, in *ibid.*, II, 6.

[109] Speech of November 14, 1955, to Union-republic ministers of agriculture and members of the collegium of the USSR Ministry of Agriculture, *ibid.*, II, 163-164.

[110] *Pravda*, July 21, 1956 (CDSP, VIII, 30, pp. 19-20); and *S.K. v SSSR i R.S.Kh.*, II, 239-240.

[111] *Pravda*, March 11, 1957.

[112] *Ibid.*, March 14, 1957.

The tide of agrarian revisionism was now rising so high that the Sanina-Venzher heresy was tactfully propagandized and even put into practice. The agronomist V. Pal'man in an article furnished for typesetting on February 18, 1957, and approved for printing on March 23, 1957, implicitly favored the transfer, if not sale, of MTS tractors to kolkhozes.[113] In May 1957, a kolkhoz in Krasnodar Territory received from an MTS all equipment under terms of sale.[114] Also, on May 29, 1957, a German-language transmission of Radio Moscow reported the vertical integration of managerial functions, with one man acting as MTS director and kolkhoz chairman, which implied the transfer of equipment.

The neo-Stalinist wing of the party anathematized these innovations both overtly and in all-important secret conclaves. As early as 1954, Laptev had caught the "distortion" which one N. Smolin perpetrated in *Problems of Economics*, No. 1, 1953, when he advised the merger of kolkhoz field brigades and MTS tractor brigades.[115] A writer for the party's central study journal in March 1957 could not accept the proposal that MTS equipment be sold to kolkhozes, which was made at a recent conference of kolkhoz and MTS officials and scientific workers held under the auspices of the USSR Ministry of Agriculture and Lenin All-Union Academy of Agricultural Sciences.[116] Behind these orthodox ideological functionaries stood members of the party Presidium. Matskevich recalls that "when the question actually arose of preparing

[113] "The Two Masters," *Nash Sovremennik* (Our Contemporary), No. 2, 1957, pp. 171-202.

[114] I. Yegorov, *Literaturnaya Gazeta*, February 27, 1958.

[115] *Voprosy Ekonomiki*, No. 2, 1954, p. 12.

[116] S. Kolesnev, *Politicheskoye Samoobrazovaniye* (Political Self-Education), No. 3, 1957.

materials for the MTS reorganization, Molotov and Kaganovich literally tried to terrorize the apparatus of the Ministry of Agriculture in order to obtain, or more precisely to concoct, any sort of materials which would discredit this measure. And Shepilov and his helpers, like Academician Laptev, tried 'theoretically' to justify the 'erroneousness' of the formulated proposals."[117] A broader disclosure was made about the anti-Khrushchev group which is perfectly credible in view of the fact that the transformation of collective into state farms began in earnest in 1954-1955:

> Particularly harmful were the opinion and attitude of the splinter-factional anti-party group of Malenkov, Kaganovich, Molotov, Bulganin, and Shepilov toward collective-cooperative property. Where did their considerations end? Kolkhoz property was not regarded by them as being of full value and was therefore viewed as antagonistically opposed to national property. In connection with this they made a proposal for ever-greater reduction of the basis of the kolkhozes by a strengthening of the concentration of productive means in MTS. In addition the demand was made that in the mutual economic relations between kolkhozes and the state the scope of commercial ties be reduced and the transition to products-exchange be forced. From these considerations the conclusion was drawn concerning the necessity of transforming kolkhozes into sovkhozes.[118]

[117] *Plenum I*, p. 422. Shepilov defected from the Khrushchev group and rejoined Malenkov and Molotov, his patrons of 1951, in the final stages of the 1956-1957 conflict.
[118] Col. Sokolov, Radio Volga, March 22, 1959, *Ost Information*, March 24, 1959, Bundepresseamt, Bonn, Germany. The late Her-

The arguments over managerial forms and wage incentives were paralleled by others which concerned the allocation of state resources. The heavy-industry alliance directed against Malenkov in 1953-1954 broke up within weeks of his downfall. Academician Ostrovityanov, who deserted the Malenkov camp in 1954 and was to serve Khrushchev faithfully in the MTS controversy of 1958, revealed the fissure in *Pravda* of March 27, 1955. His article underscored the difficulties of agriculture and indirectly criticized top leaders ("economists") who were so enamored of capital goods as to be neglectful of the technical requirements of the countryside.[119] A follow-up article in Bulganin's *Izvestiya* paid relatively minor attention to agriculture and denounced as "enemies of the people" the "Right opportunists" who had pleaded for the slowing-down of industrial growth rates.[120] The proper share of investments due industry and agriculture was also treated divergently in *Kommunist*.[121] Quite significantly, Khrushchev now represented the metallurgist F. R. Kozlov as someone completely ignorant of agriculture.[122] The partisans of heavy engineering nonetheless

bert Ritvo kindly sent this item to me. On the start of farm conversions outside the "new lands" area, see Yu. V. Arutyunyan, *V Soyuze Edinom—Molot i Serp* (Hammer and Sickle in a Unified Alliance), Moscow, 1963, p. 26.

[119] "Against Vulgarized Interpretation of the Basic Economic Law of Socialism," CDSP, vii, 9, pp. 20ff.

[120] D. Kondrashev, "Heavy Industry—Basis of the USSR's Might," *Izvestiya*, March 29, 1955 (CDSP, vii, 9, pp. 23-24).

[121] N. Kolesov spoke of "the leading role of industry in relation to agriculture, the city in relation to the village, the working class in relation to all the toilers" (No. 10, 1955, p. 32). D. Nadtocheyev replied that "industry and agriculture comprise a single entity of the national economy" and that this demanded "the harmonious combination and development of all branches of the national economy and, foremost, socialist industry and agriculture" (No. 13, 1955, p. 19).

[122] *Pravda* on April 13, 1955, reported on Khrushchev's speech at

exerted sufficient influence to bring down total inputs in agriculture from 20.5 per cent of all capital investment in the economy in 1955 and 18.5 per cent in 1956 to 17.6 per cent in 1957.[123]

The record grain harvest of 1956 provided Khrushchev with a springboard to a far more expensive agropolitical goal than the assimilation of virgin lands. "The most rapid solution of the livestock problem" was called for in his speech of March 12, 1957, at a farm conference in Rostov.[124] A target date of 1961 was fixed for the specific mission of overtaking the current level of US per capita production of meat and milk when Khrushchev spoke in Leningrad on May 22, 1957.[125] The ensuing uproar in the party Presidium was anticipated, since "whenever the discussion concerned the production of meat and milk, Malenkov and Molotov and other members of the anti-

---

the zonal farm conference in Leningrad: "Comrade Khrushchev sharply criticized shortcomings in the management of agriculture in Leningrad Province. Comrade Kozlov, secretary of the Party province committee, and Comrade Vorobyov, chairman of the province executive committee, on the eve of the conference had proposed that the Seltso State Farm be visited, since they had considered it an example for others. In actual fact it turned out that the farm was being managed irrationally. The case of the Seltso State Farm, said Comrade Khrushchev, is shameful, and shows how superficially local Party and Soviet organizations have been dealing with the state farms. Comrade Khrushchev pointed out that the Leningrad Province Committee has incomparably better opportunities than any other Party committee. There were sufficient *aktivists* and specialists here who are capable of helping in these matters. But the province committee has not bothered itself with such a task and is now reaping the fruits of its superficial guidance of agriculture" (CDSP, vii, 15, p. 13). The speech, which is critical of Stalin and opponents of the idea of a technically functional party bureaucracy, is in *S.K. v SSSR i R.S.Kh.*, ii, 103-127.

[123] The figures are in Khlebnikov, *Voprosy Ekonomiki*, No. 7, 1962, p. 50.

[124] *S.K. v SSSR i R.S.Kh.*, ii, 342.

[125] *Pravda*, May 24, 1957 (CDSP, ix, 21, pp. 7-12); and *S.K. v SSSR i R.S.Kh.*, ii, 441-461.

party group accused our cadres of practicism and utilitarianism and the desire to oppose economics to politics."[126] Hence Khrushchev in Leningrad remarked that his new slogan would drive "the more zealous defenders of capitalism" to "invent all sorts of cock-and-bull stories about this matter. They will think of something." At the opening of the All-Union Agricultural and Industrial Exhibition in Moscow on June 2, 1957, Khrushchev bluntly stated that fulfillment of the meat and dairy slogan would necessitate "great effort and material resources."[127] Bulganin noisily left the premises, together with several other dissenting leaders.[128]

The clash over investment priorities was officially disclosed after the supporters of Khrushchev managed to call the Central Committee into plenary session on June 22, 1957, for a week-long discussion that would ultimately reverse the 7-4 vote in the party Presidium for dismissal of the first secretary as a fledgling usurper and menace to hierarchical discipline. The decree of the session charged that Malenkov, Kaganovich, and Molotov had, among other things, "waged an entirely unwarranted struggle against the party's appeal—actively supported by the collective farms, provinces, and republics—to overtake the USA in per capita output of milk, butter, and meat in the next few years."[129] This raised intriguing questions: why was the struggle "unwarranted" and how had the target date of 1961 come to be changed to "the next few years"? Answers might be found in the subtexts of commentaries by those privy to the bickering which went on at the June 1957 Central Committee session, the minutes of

[126] N. G. Ignatov, *Pravda*, February 3, 1959.
[127] *S.K. v SSSR i R.S.Kh.*, II, 467.
[128] Matskevich, *Plenum I*, p. 422.
[129] *Pravda*, July 4, 1957 (CDSP, IX, 23, pp. 3ff.).

which have still not been published. A. I. Kosygin, an industrial planner with a record of lengthy service in the consumer goods industries who entered the realigned party Presidium as a non-voting member, briefed Moscow City party officials on July 2, 1957. The opposition had contended that Khrushchev's new slogan presaged a transfer of resources from heavy engineering to agricultural machine-building, but, according to Kosygin, nothing of the sort would happen: "The group sought to contrast the rate of development of agriculture to the rate of development of heavy industry. But everyone is well aware that successes in agriculture do not at all mean that heavy industry should develop more slowly in this connection. The party always has been and always will be concerned for the preponderant development of heavy industry. It never has and never will deviate from this line."[130]

A. M. Rumyantsev, the chief editor of *Kommunist*, who like Ostrovityanov was formerly in the vanguard of neo-Stalinism and gained his post late in 1955, maintained that the anti-Khrushchev group regarded the meat and dairy slogan as negating the principle that "our country must overtake and surpass the advanced capitalist countries economically, first of all in the production of steel and other varieties of heavy industrial goods, and then in agricultural products as well. Any other formulation of the problem in their opinion is Right opportunism." Rumyantsev too overlooked the 1961 date for realizing the slogan and implausibly assured his readers that it would be achieved without any *perekachka*, or "pumping in," of resources from heavy engineering to agriculture.[131] The subsequent confluence of events leads to the con-

[130] *Ibid.* (CDSP, ix, 24, pp. 3ff.).
[131] *Kommunist*, No. 11, 1957, p. 19.

clusion that these statements were meant to rationalize the backtracking which Khrushchev had to undertake during the June 1957 Plenum in order to ensure the support of influential champions of heavy engineering like Marshal Zhukov, Kozlov, and Suslov, who were all named full members of the new party Presidium. The reappointment of Bulganin to the Presidium was in these circumstances real substantiation that a "government of national unity," instead of a Khrushchev court, had emerged to dominate the political scene.

CHAPTER III

MTS CHANGE: A JOB HALF-DONE
(1958)

AFTER THE purge of Malenkov and Molotov, the fulfillment of Khrushchev's policy ambitions depended on his skill in reducing the influence of dubious allies. There is no way of telling who initiated the purge of Zhukov, whose independent behavior raised a threat to party control of the army. The "conservative" party leader Suslov in any event played an important part in the termination of that affair. The power of Suslov, in turn, was rapidly diminished through expansion of the Central Committee Secretariat with newcomers whose subsequent behavior indicated their readiness to follow the innovating tendencies of the senior secretary. F. R. Kozlov, the other "conservative" chieftain, was shunted to the sidelines of government in the Russian Federation. Only after these organizational gambits of December 1957 did Khrushchev feel strong enough to intervene on the affirmative side in a public debate on the appropriateness of selling MTS machinery to kolkhozes. But even then one of his campaign talks was not published, suggesting that he still lacked a durable majority in the party Presidium.

The Central Committee was still Khrushchev's mainstay and its February 1958 plenary session issued a statement of principle approving the machinery transfers. A plebiscite similar to that on the disputed reorganization of industrial management was planned on the basis of Khrushchev's "Theses" in regard to the transfers and conversion of MTS into state-run repair shops and sales outlets. At the same time, Khrushchev expressed his opinion on a new system of agricultural administration in a memorandum addressed to the Central Committee or its Presidium. This document, unlike several others of its kind, has not been published. The contents presumably would be embarrassing to Khrushchev, for in mid-1958 the policy of strengthening the administrative power of the Ministries of Agriculture on the Union-republic level was implemented in the face of his long-standing opposition.

Khrushchev, therefore, won the struggle to reinforce the economic base of the kolkhoz structure. But his effort to devise a less centralized pattern of farm management was impeded. Just how heavy the dead weight of the past lay on the thinking of the bureaucratic elite was also apparent at the Central Committee session in December 1958. Khrushchev's proposals on rural reconstruction and interkolkhoz repair shops were flatly rejected.

THE GROUNDWORK

The procedure for policy change which was observed in 1953-1954 in connection with the decision on virgin lands had three aspects. Firstly, on an organizational level, the hostile ministerial bureaucracy was fractured and Khrushchev's supporter Korniyets introduced; the sympathies of the party caucus in Leningrad were swayed from Malenkov to Khrushchev. Secondly, overt propaganda was employed to create a favorable climate of opinion for the new agricultural line (the *Pravda* articles of Stepanyan and Belyayev, and Shepilov's lead article). Thirdly, a proposal was formally made in the party Presidium and interested personnel were brought into the discussion.

Similar procedure was followed once Khrushchev, in the quest for efficiency, took up the cause of selling heavy machinery to kolkhozes and thereby opened a Pandora's box of economic, administrative, and ideological dilemmas. The verbal behavior of Suslov and Kozlov during the course of the reform were to mark them as opponents of its rapid pace and decentralist execution, if not essence.

Suslov was the more formidable of the pair in view of the important role he played in major developments at the close of 1957. He delivered the keynote report at the Central Committee session held on October 29, 1957, to authorize the removal of Zhukov from the party Presidium and leadership of the Defense Ministry. This fact, however, was concealed from the public until 1961, apparently at the request of the first secretary, in order to prevent Suslov from acquiring the reputation of foremost defender of the prerogatives of the party bureaucracy against the encroachment of military or state interests.[1] Suslov also was a prime negotiator at the Moscow Conference of Communist Bloc powers on November 14-16, 1957, which adopted a Declaration embodying a number of anti-American and anti-"revisionist" formulas inserted upon the demand of the Chinese Communist del-

[1] Zhukov's release from the Defense Ministry was announced in *Pravda*, October 27, 1957. The *Pravda* leader of October 28, 1957, was entitled "Unshakable Unity of Party and People." The decree of the plenary session was published in *Pravda* on November 3, 1957, and the precise date of the session is noted in *KPSS—Spravochnik*, p. 306. Suslov's role at the plenary session is noted in S. S. Khromov, *Bor'ba KPSS za Pretvoreniye v Zhizn' Reshenii XX-ogo S"yezda Partii (1956-1958)* (CPSU Struggle for Implementation of Decisions of the 20th party Congress [1956-1958]), Moscow University Publishers, signed for printing on May 26, 1961. This disclosure was repeated at the 22nd party Congress by F. I. Golikov, chief of the Main Political Administration for the Soviet Army and Navy (*Pravda*, October 30, 1961).

egation.[2] Since Khrushchev's own "revisionist" intentions in domestic policy were shortly to prove to be interconnected with an effort to achieve some kind of limited accommodation with the United States, he was obliged to take steps to circumscribe the influence of inner-party militants like Suslov.

Both Suslov and Kozlov were overrun in an organizational realignment which Khrushchev evidently negotiated and which was sanctioned at the Central Committee meeting of December 16-17, 1957. Three leaders without records of independent achievement were recruited into the party Secretariat: N. G. Ignatov, A. I. Kirichenko, and N. A. Mukhitdinov.[3] Their duties, respectively, would be in the spheres of agricultural supervision, personnel appointment, and propaganda. Kozlov had to bide his time in the inferior post of RSFSR premier.[4] The broader sense of these arrangements was to guard Khrushchev against a recurrence of the coup situation of June 1957 in the party Presidium. Of 15 Presidium members, 10 were secretaries, and each one of these— except for Suslov—might have been expected to resist any attempt to overthrow the administration of the first secretary.[5] The organizational prerequisites were established for Khrushchev's intervention in a public discussion of MTS-kolkhoz relations.

[2] Suslov reported on the Bloc Conference at the CPSU Central Committee session in December 1957. On the drafting of the Declaration, see the text of the article on the origin and growth of the Sino-Soviet dispute published on September 6, 1963, by the Chinese Communist party organs *People's Daily* and *Red Flag*, as distributed by the Chinese Communist press agency, in *New York Times*, September 14, 1963.

[3] *Pravda*, December 19, 1957.

[4] *Ibid.*, December 20, 1957.

[5] The members of the effective organs of government after

Vinnichenko, the prescient friend of Ukrainian politicians, began the public discussion in November 1957 in the literary magazine *October*.[6] His observations were based on visits to kolkhozes in the southern regions and talks with Sanina and Venzher. The local experiments in placing MTS tractor brigades at the disposal of kolkhoz officials were alleged to have resulted in more responsible usage and maintenance of the machinery and higher crop yields. These experiments had been facilitated by a number of unpublicized directives of the USSR Council

---

the December 1957 Central Committee session were:

PRESIDIUM, CC CPSU	SECRETARIAT, CC CPSU
Full Members	
1. Aristov	1. Aristov
2. Belyayev	
3. Brezhnev	2. Brezhnev
4. Bulganin	
5. Furtseva	3. Furtseva
6. Ignatov	4. Ignatov
7. Khrushchev	5. Khrushchev
8. Kirichenko	6. Kirichenko
9. Kozlov	
10. Kuusinen	7. Kuusinen
11. Mikoyan	
12. Mukhitdinov	8. Mukhitdinov
13. Shvernik	
14. Suslov	9. Suslov
15. Voroshilov	

Candidate Members

1. Kalnberzins
2. Kirilenko
3. Korotchenko
4. Kosygin
5. Mazurov
6. Mzhavanadze
7. Pervukhin
8. Pospelov . . . . 10. Pospelov

[6] "Time Does Not Wait (Notes of a Journalist)," *Oktyabr'*, No. 11, 1957, pp. 205-223.

of Ministers and RSFSR Ministry of Agriculture. The Council had ordered the Main Administration for Agricultural Supply (*Glavsel'snab*) to sell to kolkhozes small-powered plow tractors and the Ministry had approved of kolkhoz chairmen serving as MTS directors and receiving payment only from their farms. The MTS chief engineer might be named deputy kolkhoz chairman but remain on the state payroll. Kolkhoz technicians were authorized to perform the duties of the MTS chief agronomist and zootechnician, whose posts would be abolished. Under the kolkhoz's agronomist, its foremen (brigadiers) might head the joint MTS-kolkhoz tractor-field work units. There remained separate MTS and kolkhoz bookkeepers. In general, MTS would become subordinate to kolkhozes and the state would economize through staff reductions. The only problem which Vinnichenko saw was to supply the jointly run MTS and kolkhoz motor pools with spare parts and lubricants at equal prices. As for the propriety of selling heavy equipment to kolkhozes, he interpreted the cited order of the USSR Council of Ministers to mean that "the argument about whether or not the means of production can be sold to the kolkhozes had already been solved by life itself." To his empirical way of thinking, there were no obstacles to selling or renting MTS equipment to the kolkhozes and to transforming MTS into Technical Repair Stations (RTS) for the supply and repair of kolkhoz-administered machinery.

"Time Does Not Wait" was an appropriate rubric for the article by Vinnichenko, but not for others on the subject which followed in the same magazine.[7] K. Orlovskiy, a successful kolkhoz chairman in Byelorussia,

[7] No. 12, 1957, pp. 176-191.

thought that only richer farms might purchase MTS equipment, and only on the basis of two- or three-year installments. A district party leader was content with having kolkhoz chairmen act as MTS directors and rejected the sales proposal. Another kolkhoz chairman was hesitant because fuel and spare parts would be too expensive if acquired at "commercial" rather than state prices, as he anticipated would be the case. A third chairman doubted if within two or three years very many kolkhozes would be prepared to satisfy their own technical needs. Besides, Vinnichenko had left unanswered these questions: Who would conduct major and minor repairs of tractors and combines? Should MTS become repair enterprises or ought the kolkhozes to build large repair shops? What would become of payments-in-kind for MTS services? Through what channels were the farms to obtain new tractors and combines? Who would follow technological developments? How would machine operators be paid? In view of this wide margin of uncertainty, the chief editor of *October* confined his summary to the cautious comment that readers had agreed the discussion was "timely and necessary."[8]

Within the power structure, hesitation was also considerable. RSFSR Minister of Agriculture Benediktov conceded that MTS administrative overhead costs were high, averaging about one-fifth of expenditures. The means to lower costs was to continue to merge the MTS and kolkhoz leaderships. One district merger had in a year's time reduced by 30-40 per cent the state's outlay for a quintal of produce which the kolkhozes offered as payment-in-kind. Any new proposals for improving MTS-kolkhoz relations should be examined and dis-

[8] F. Panferov, *Literaturnaya Gazeta*, December 28, 1957.

cussed; some might be tested, the results generalized, and better forms arrived at.[9] Other specialists were equally skeptical about any radical change of the MTS system. A search of the files of the All-Union Scientific Research Institute for Agricultural Economics would reveal that

. . . the materials of the session of the academic council held on the eve of the MTS reorganization contains the answer, "We do not have such conditions," to the question of whether or not there are at present the necessary economic and other conditions for the mass sale of tractors and complex machines held by the MTS. Further on it says: "It would be incorrect at present to relinquish the present forms of direct production ties among the MTS and kolkhozes," and "the sale to kolkhozes of tractors and complex machines cannot be economically justified as one of the ways of improving mutual relations among MTS and kolkhozes under present conditions; it not only will not hasten the tempo of development of agricultural production, but in several cases will be a hindrance to the development of productive forces."[10]

Khrushchev's position was clarified at a meeting of the Central Committee of the Communist party of the Ukraine held on December 26, 1957. He spoke of the matter as one which "we" had not yet discussed, but on which a preliminary exchange of opinions had occurred. MTS had once performed valuable political and organi-

[9] *Kommunist*, No. 18, 1957, pp. 45-58.
[10] V. Yefimov, K. Karpov, and Ye. Lazutkin, *Sovetskaya Rossiya*, December 20, 1959. On "certain skeptics" in the Ukraine Ministry of Agriculture, see K. Grigor'ev, *Literaturnaya Gazeta*, February 1, 1958. Also I. I. Kuz'min on the Institute of Economics of the USSR Academy of Sciences, *Pravda*, February 5, 1959.

zational functions, he declared, but kolkhozes were now economically stronger and their personnel better qualified. The main task ahead was to reduce production costs and further stimulate the initiative of farm managers. Under the MTS system, grain which the state received from kolkhozes as payment-in-kind was at least twice as expensive as that procured from state farms. The reason lay in the irrational utilization of machinery by MTS and their inflated overhead costs. Often, kolkhoz chairmen and MTS directors harmfully quarreled over the placement of equipment and the directors sought to acquire as many different types of machines as possible, albeit some were not really needed. "Consequently," Khrushchev asked, "is it not time to sell the MTS machinery to some kolkhozes?" A voice replied: "Correct!" Khrushchev evidently sensed that this did not represent acclamation and, perhaps on the basis of the Presidial exchanges which he noted, tried to soothe anxious minds: "It is possible that doubts will arise among some people: how, then, will the state supply itself with agricultural products through the kolkhozes?" Khrushchev lightly dismissed such apprehensions and assured his audience that arrangements would be made for kolkhozes to pay for machines and fuel. "I think that we shall come to an agreement on this question" was his attitude. As for the future of MTS, Khrushchev restated Vinnichenko's opinion that, after the transfers, MTS would repair kolkhozes' machinery on a contractual basis. He added that certain machines would remain in state hands and the MTS would rent them out; kolkhozes would not ask for superfluous machinery and this would amount to "a sort of ruble control" of their activity.[11] The nonpublication of these re-

[11] "One Master for Machinery and Soil," *S.K. v SSSR i R.S.Kh.*, II, 496-501.

marks at the time apparently signified sharp disagreement in the party Presidium.

About two weeks later, Osad'ko, who in 1956 had misgivings about putting too much cash in rural hands, attacked the sales proposal in a serial publication of Moscow University. He stressed the Marxian teaching that modern instruments of labor are of a public nature and can rationally be utilized in the public interest only under state control and in accordance with a state economic plan. If machinery was transferred to the kolkhozes, he argued, it would become the property of separate groups and inevitably be used to the detriment of society as a whole. The distribution of machinery on a cash basis would also be inequitable since only rich farms would be able to acquire it. Technologically, harm would be inflicted, as the kolkhozes would not be inclined to replace equipment which had not become obsolete. Osad'ko also mistrusted the ability of district party leaders to ensure the production obedience of kolkhozes: MTS were the *state*'s economic form of control over the activity of each kolkhoz.[12]

Khrushchev Forces the Issue

By mid-January 1958, Khrushchev had rallied sufficient strength to press home the attack on anti-peasant extremists. The reformist philosopher P. N. Fedoseyev, whom Suslov had once baited, argued for policy flexibility in *Pravda* of January 17, 1958. Like Stepanyan on the eve of the showdown over Khrushchev's new lands proposal, Fedoseyev stressed the necessity to resolve in good time

---

[12] M. P. Osad'ko, *Vestnik Moskovskogo Universiteta, Seriya Ekonomiki, Filosofii, Prava* (Herald of Moscow University: Economics, Philosophy and Law Series), No. 4, 1958 (approved for printing, January 11).

the discordances in the home economy. "Only meta-physicians," he polemicized, "can fail to observe or even deny the presence of contradictions under socialism. Under socialism, too, the new is born and conquers in a struggle against the antiquated. Only dogmatists and con-servatives, who cling to the old, can fear contradictions and difficulties in the development of socialist society." Fedoseyev refuted the contention of acute hostility be-tween the towns and villages and said in gibe that "inno-vators and certain conservatives can be and really are to be found among various groups of the population." This statement was backed up a day later by an announcement that the "conservative" Benediktov had been expelled from the RSFSR Ministry of Agriculture.[13]

Khrushchev broached the controversial issue of ma-chinery transfers to kolkhozes in a speech to a conference of agricultural workers in Minsk which *Pravda* ran on January 25, 1958. He again enumerated as MTS defi-ciencies the exorbitant cost of payments-in-kind to the state, which resulted from high upkeep charges, the kol-khozes' need to bargain with MTS on the placement of tractors, and the MTS directors' uncritical acceptance of indiscriminately distributed machinery, which tied up hundred of millions of rubles of state funds. Waste and inefficiency would be reduced by selling to the kol-khozes tractors, cultivators, seeders, and soil-cultivating appliances (combines and harvesters were excluded). The machines would become kolkhoz property and so the farms would have to assume the full cost and pay the salaries of machine operators. MTS would become cen-tralized repair stations and sell spare parts and machinery

[13] Benediktov was identified as deputy chairman of the RSFSR State Planning Committee in *Pravda*, January 18, 1958. He was named ambassador to India in 1959 (*Pravda*, April 22, 1959).

to the kolkhozes. The question had recently been discussed at a conference of district party secretaries, kolkhoz chairmen, and MTS directors held in central party headquarters. "All the comrades," Khrushchev reported, "thought that this question demands a timely solution." But, "certain officials" had asked by way of objection to the change: "If the machines were transferred to the kolkhozes, would the amount of products turned over to the state for its disposal not diminish?" Khrushchev once more shrugged aside these reservations and maintained that the state could only benefit from the inevitable increases in productivity. Moreover, as the costs of production dropped and the prices of produce placed at the state's disposal became lower, the government in turn would reduce the prices of goods for sale to the public. This, of course, meant no rise in procurement prices and Khrushchev assured his hearers that the machinery sales would not lead to an increase in the cost of goods delivered to the state. He also pledged that the change would be gradual, with wealthier farms buying machinery in 1958 and weaker ones continuing to rely on the MTS for two or three years. (On both counts, procurement prices and the rate of the changeover, Khrushchev would eventually reverse himself.) The MTS change would be executed like the hotly disputed pruning of the Moscow industrial apparatus in 1957. "Perhaps," said Khrushchev, "a plenary session of the party Central Committee should be convened; if the session approves, we may proceed as we did with the reorganization of industrial management—publish theses for nation-wide discussion, then convene a session of the USSR Supreme Soviet; for, I repeat, reorganization of the work of the MTS is one of the fundamental problems of further development of our agriculture."

Khrushchev concurrently bid for an early East-West heads-of-government meeting, which showed again that some kind of limited *détente* was a corollary of his reformist internal policy. While Soviet propagandists hastened to acclaim this overture, official reaction to the proposal for MTS sales was not forthcoming until January 31, 1958, and it was spotty. On the one hand, the chairman of the Orël Region Soviet Executive Committee told the RSFSR Supreme Soviet that Khrushchev's proposal had to be put into practice "as soon as possible."[14] On the other hand, F. R. Kozlov advised that "Change of the mutual relations between MTS and kolkhozes is not a simple matter and, before these mutual relations are altered, it is essential to discuss this from all sides."[15] These conflicting statements are open to varying interpretations. It might be said that Kozlov was displaying a caution not unlike that which Khrushchev had shown a week earlier while the soviet official was independently voicing local eagerness. But subsequent events do not favor an analysis of that kind. Firstly, at least two newspapers soon urged the rapid transfer of machinery to all the kolkhozes and a third, *Izvestiya*, reported the actual sale of an MTS and repair shop to a kolkhoz.[16] Secondly, Khrushchev would recommend to the Central Committee session of February 25-26, 1958, that, without waiting for the final setting of prices, it was possible immediately to sell tractors and other machines to kolkhozes that were able to buy and make rational use of them; the kolkhozes could make their payments when the prices were settled. Khrushchev also asked that installment payments be ar-

---

[14] I. N. Filatov, *Pravda*, January 31, 1958.

[15] *Pravda*, January 31, 1958.

[16] Cf. *Kommunist Tadzhikistana* (Organ of the Communist Party of Tadzhikistan), February 5, 1958; *Literaturnaya Gazeta*, February 25, 1958; and *Izvestiya*, February 7, 1958.

ranged to expedite matters.[17] It is most likely that Khrushchev all along had wished to implement the change as rapidly as possible, but chose initially to play the gradualist while his propaganda squads created the appearance of a popular groundswell in favor of dispatch. The impetuous nature of Khrushchev was highly evident in the 1953-1957 period. In the words of a character in F. I. Panferov's novel *In the Name of the Young*:

> "You cannot keep up with him; as soon as you introduce one thing, Nikita Sergeyevich comes up with something else, something new and inspiring. He keeps everyone on his toes," said Akim Morev, fully understanding that all the proposals of the CPSU Central Committee first secretary are not the result of wild fantasy, but are born of the irresistible course of Soviet reality. *One must make haste to succeed*, and to succeed, one must perceive, even in its most embryonic stages, seeds of that which is new in order to eliminate that which is old, that which is hindering the irresistible course of life (italics added).[18]

Khrushchev was not entirely successful in his pursuit of hasty action. The decree of the February 1958 Plenum gave blanket approval to his "Theses," but, as a kolkhoz chairman alertly noted, it did not specifically mention installment buying for weak farms.[19] As this text-

[17] "On Further Development of Kolkhoz System and Reorganizing MTS"—Theses of Report by N. S. Khrushchev at USSR Supreme Soviet Session, *Pravda*, March 1, 1958 (CDSP, x, 9, pp. 5-13, 40).

[18] *Oktyabr'*, No. 8, 1960, p. 13.

[19] Cf. "On Further Development of Kolkhoz System and Reorganizing the Machine and Tractor Stations," *Pravda*, February 28, 1958 (CDSP, x, 9, pp. 3-4); and *Sovetskaya Rossiya*, March 1, 1958.

ual lapse suggested upper-level dissension over the pace of the change, so another revealed differences over procedure. The "Theses" expressed disagreement with "some people" who "think that the central agencies should work out the procedure for the sale of machinery, determine the periods for carrying out this work in each zone, and quickly begin and end it." More to Khrushchev's taste were price commissions in local government offices. This decentralizing tendency was also reflected in the decision of the plenary session to schedule the Third All-Union Congress of Collective Farmers for early in 1959 in order to examine farm problems and amend the Model Kolkhoz Statutes.

COLLECTIVE OR STATE FARMS?

The doctrinal implications of the MTS shift were extremely important for neo-Stalinists wedded to the idea of transforming the collective farm peasantry into state wage-earners. Khrushchev in his "Theses" acknowledged the vitality of these elements when he obliquely recalled his disputes with Malenkov and Molotov:

> Some comrades, primarily among the economists, held that with reorganization of the MTS a vagueness would arise in regard to certain theoretical questions—in particular, the question of the two forms of ownership. They proceeded from the premise that the transition to communism requires the comprehensive strengthening of public ownership and raising kolkhoz cooperative property to the level of public property, and they voiced the fear that the sale of machinery to the kolkhozes might weaken public ownership. The question was also raised as to which form of socialist agriculture

127

is the more progressive, collective or state farming. In view of the fact that the state farm is based on public ownership, some comrades asked: should not the kolkhozes be converted to the sovkhoz form of economy?

Khrushchev retorted that while public property is the highest form of property, Lenin had never contrasted it with cooperative property and even had stressed that both may serve the general cause. But the usual canonical reference to chapter and verse in Lenin's *Works* did not follow. Khrushchev evidently expected his hearers to take it for granted that communism would be reached through the strengthening of both state and kolkhoz property—which again showed his empiricist orientation.

The decree of the February 1958 Central Committee Plenum was noncommittal about the doctrinal perplexities of the MTS change, but for purposes of political respectability a heavy volume of apologetics was called forth from Khrushchev's theorists.[20] Their example was followed by three of the four Central Committee secre-

[20] Cf. K. Ostrovityanov, *Pravda*, March 3, 1958; M. Krayev, *Sovetskaya Rossiya*, March 5, 1958; M. Mitin, *Pravda*, March 6, 1958; N. Ostroverkh, *Pravda Ukrainy*, March 6, 1958; *Kommunist*, No. 4, 1958, p. 8; A. Baulin, *Izvestiya*, March 20, 1958; *Voprosy Ekonomiki*, No. 3, 1958, pp. 9-10; I. Malyshev, *Pravda*, March 24, 1958; I. Glotov, *Kommunist*, No. 5, 1958, p. 53; and L. Leont'ev, *Pravda*, April 7, 1958. The ecclesiastical flavor of the debate is conveyed by A. V. Bolgov: "Some economists considered that the sale of machinery of MTS to kolkhozes would contradict the known proposition of Engels, expressed in his letter to Bebel, dated January 20, 1886, that in organizing cooperatives it is essential that society—consequently, in the initial period [of communism], the state—retain for itself ownership of the means of production and, thereby, not allow the private interests of a cooperative society to prevail over the interests of society at large" (P.S. Buyanov, A. A. Karavayev, and N. A. Kulagin, eds., *Novyy Etap v Razvitii Kolkhoznogo Stroya* [New Stage in Development of Kolkhoz System], Moscow, 1959, p. 95).

taries who discharged ideological functions. Mukhitdinov declared in his speech for the USSR Supreme
Soviet elections that the verdict of the February 1958
Plenum was of "enormous theoretical, political, and economic importance" and served as "a model of the creative
application of Marxism-Leninism."[21] O. V. Kuusinen in
his pre-electoral speech assailed the "dogma" that the
shift of tractors to kolkhozes would create obstacles on
the road to communism, and he averred that the change
was part of "the course toward greater attraction of the
toiling masses to active participation in the development
of the economy and administration of the state."[22] P. N.
Pospelov for his part maintained that it would be improper to regard the MTS reorganization as a strictly
organizational measure which had only practical importance; it was of "enormous political and theoretical significance."[23] Mukhitdinov again acted as a herald of innovation when he told a local farm rally that the documents
enabling the change meant important alterations in the
theory, as well as the practice, of economic organization.[24] The fourth secretary involved with propaganda
activities treated the doctrinal riddle as Bulganin had the
virgin lands proposal—silently.

Suslov told a public meeting: "The gradual reorganization of the Machine and Tractor Stations, the transfer
of their machines to the kolkhozes, and the transition to a
new form of production-technical servicing of the kolkhozes signify a new stage in the development of socialist
agriculture, will lead to a more rational utilization of

[21] *Pravda*, March 11, 1958.
[22] *Ibid.*, March 13, 1958.
[23] *Ibid.*, March 14, 1958.
[24] *Ibid.*, April 26, 1958.

machinery, and raise labor productivity to an extent which we can now hardly imagine."[25] He restated this position a few weeks later at farm award ceremonies in Bukovina.[26] His persistent stress on gradualism was acutely at variance with practice: kolkhozes did almost three-quarters of the 1958 spring field work with their own tractors.[27] In the meantime, Pospelov, as noted, had deplored a strictly organizational approach to the change and Presidium candidate member Ya. E. Kalnberzins, party boss of Latvia, had thus denounced an Oppositionist whispering campaign:

> Some pseudo-critics are trying to spread doubt about this decision taken by the party, claiming that it supposedly contradicts Leninism. "How," they ask, "shall we reach communism if we strengthen cooperative property?" Nonetheless, the decisions of the February Plenum in no sense conflict with Leninism. All-state property, which includes factories, plants, mines, state farms, subterranean wealth, etc., is the basis of the national economy and its power. Cooperative property, which comprises only a small percentage in relation to state property, has always been utilized in the interest of building socialism. Both forms of property can exist as well in the period of building communism.
>
> Other pseudo-critics have exclaimed: "It is not clear to us whether under communism there will be only kolkhozes or sovkhozes." They also were shown that both forms—kolkhozes and sovkhozes—are good for

[25] *Pravda*, March 12, 1958.
[26] *Ibid.*, April 30, 1958.
[27] Buyanov *et al.*, *op. cit.*, pp. 18-19.

the successful management of agriculture, that with both it is possible to attain communism.[28]

Khrushchev's report to the USSR Supreme Soviet on the outcome of the nation-wide discussion of the MTS change also claimed for the measure "great theoretical, truly programmatic importance."[29] The refusal of Suslov to admit the theoretical legitimacy of transferring machinery to the kolkhozes was, therefore, a display of recalcitrance.

Administering the New System

The abolition of MTS meant removal of the façade behind which district party secretaries had regulated the kolkhoz production process since late in 1953. Khrushchev remarked in his speech of May 22, 1957, that the leadership was considering the problem of staff reduction in the districts and would deal with it after the reorganization of industrial management was completed. A few months later, K. T. Mazurov, party leader of Byelorussia and candidate member of the party Presidium, who by educational training is a transport technician, complained that many kolkhoz chairmen and district officials were making agrotechnical decisions either without consulting experts or contrary to their advice.[30] D. S. Polyanskiy, party leader of the Kuban, himself the graduate of an agricultural institute, objected to the close involvement of district party secretaries in farm management and proposed that they instead concentrate on the formulation

[28] *Pravda*, March 13, 1958.
[29] "On Further Developing Kolkhoz System and Reorganizing MTS," *Pravda*, March 28, 1958 (CDSP, x, 13, pp. 5-18).
[30] *Kommunist*, No. 11, 1957, pp. 77ff.

of long-range economic tasks and political education.[31] Soon, party instructor groups for MTS zones were abolished to promote the initiative and autonomy of primary party organizations in the farms and among the kolkhoz technicians.[32] Whether Khrushchev had entirely soured on the idea of an exceptional status for the district party men is obscure. His "Theses" deal ambivalently with farm administration, stating at one point: "With reorganization of the MTS, party and soviet organizations will naturally focus their attention on direct guidance of the kolkhozes that have their own tractors and farm machinery, on giving these farms practical assistance in organizing work in a new way." At another, notice is served that "Whereas formerly many questions pertaining to the production work of the kolkhozes were decided at the MTS, now the district executive committees will have to handle these matters directly. Work must be continued to improve the structure of district Soviet agencies." Khrushchev invited an exchange of opinions on the most desirable structure for district soviets.

In the press discussion, managerial alternatives were offered by authoritarians, liberalizers, and centrists. The first urged recreation of district agricultural administrations and even direct operational leadership of kolkhozes by the regional agricultural administrations.[33] At the other

[31] *Ibid.*, No. 16, 1957, pp. 45ff.

[32] *Partiynaya Zhizn'*, No. 23, 1957, pp. 3ff.

[33] Agricultural departments under district executive committees are proposed in *Pravda*, January 31, 1958 (regional executive committee chairman); *Izvestiya*, March 5, 1958 (district committee party secretary); *Izvestiya*, March 6, 1958 (kolkhoz chairman), *Izvestiya*, March 7, 1958 (district committee party secretary), and *Pravda*, March 16, 1958 (regional executive committee chairman). A. Shkol'nikov, first secretary of Voronezh Region's CPSU Committee, wrote in *Pravda* of March 24, 1958: "In reorganizing the work of the MTS, it is essential to create condi-

extreme were the partisans of a kolkhoz federation. They urged a pyramid of locally elected kolkhoz councils building up to a USSR Central Council of Kolkhozes, which was reminiscent of the All-Union Kolkhoz Center, a short-lived body created on approval of the November 1929 CPSU(B) Central Committee session. The federation would administer the kolkhozes' planning, technical supplies, centralized marketing of surpluses and, foremost, help the weak farms by arranging for the pooling of scarce resources. Like the MTS change itself, the federation would encourage a display of local initiative, enhance the sense of responsibility, and cut bureaucratic overhead costs. Hope was abroad that the Central Council might be formed at the Third All-Union Congress of Collective Farmers.[34] Opponents of the Union, on the other hand, charged that it would undermine state control, hinder the proper combination of kolkhoz and state interests, obstruct the regional agricultural administrations, and disorient party and state officials.[35] The rapidity of nation-wide publication of these views is suggestive of the favor which they enjoyed at the highest

---

tions whereby the regional agricultural administrations guide the kolkhozes directly, without intermediary instances." See the rebuttal of A. Grigor'ev, *Izvestiya*, March 27, 1958.

[34] The kolkhoz unionist viewpoint is expressed in *Izvestiya*, March 5, 1958 (kolkhoz chairman); *Leninskoye Znamya*, March 8, 1958 (kolkhoz chairman); *Pravda*, March 8, 1958 (kolkhoz chairman); *Izvestiya*, March 13, 1958 (MTS worker); *Kommunist*, No. 4 (March 15), 1958, pp. 42-44 (agricultural economist and economic geographer); and *Literaturnaya Gazeta*, March 25, 1958 (Academician S. G. Strumilin).

[35] Cf. *Izvestiya*, March 7, 1958 (district committee party secretary); *Pravda*, March 11, 1958 (kolkhoz chairman); *Izvestiya*, March 16, 1958 (regional executive committee chairman); *Izvestiya*, March 22, 1958 (district committee party secretary and district executive committee chairman); and *Izvestiya*, March 28, 1958.

133

level. Midway between were the advocates of inspector groups under the district soviet executive committees. The groups were conceived as thinly staffed bodies of experts (including an agronomist, zootechnician, mechanic and electrification engineer, veterinarian, and land-use specialist) who would tour the farms along with the committee's chairman. This arrangement would ensure wider participation in management.[36]

At the session of the USSR Supreme Soviet which followed the public debate, Khrushchev enumerated the various proposals and called for more discussion. Most delegates spoke in favor of the inspectorates.[37] Noting the majority choice, Khrushchev, who in the course of this session displaced Bulganin as chairman of the USSR Council of Ministers, dryly commented: "Evidently, this will be correct at the present stage. The role of district organizations in the guidance of kolkhozes will now increase still more. The establishment of inspector groups in the districts will facilitate a deeper study and more successful solution of the problems of kolkhoz life." The chances are that Khrushchev was then intrigued by the idea of a kolkhoz federation, of which district party secretaries might serve as the core. During the course of the MTS discussion he had commented on the federation proposal in a memorandum to the Central Committee (Presidium?) and, following an exchange of opinions in the Committee (Presidium?), a decision was reached "not to create special agencies of the Kolkhoz Center type

[36] Cf. *Izvestiya*, March 14, 1958 (district executive committee chairman); and Matskevich, *Pravda*, March 20, 1958.

[37] Cf. D. S. Polyanskiy, *Izvestiya*, March 29, 1958; N. F. Ignatov (Moscow Region Executive Comittee chairman); *Izvestiya*, March 30, 1958; and I. R. Razzakov (first secretary, Central Committee, C.P. of Kirgiziya), *Izvestiya*, March 30, 1958.

yet."[38] The absence of this memorandum in the collection of Khrushchev's papers on agriculture which was published in 1962-1964 tends to heighten the suspicion that he responded positively to the calls for a kolkhoz union. The establishment of farm inspectorates did not in any event lead to an increased role for district agencies. Sometime later in 1958 the inspectorates were subordinated to the regional agricultural administrations.[39] As such, inspectorates were often distracted from on-the-spot organizing by a large number of requests for various sorts of statistical data.[40] This recentralization of agricultural management under state auspices was not publicly associated with Khrushchev and evidently reflected other influences at work in the leadership.

LIBERALIZERS IN THE GUISE OF CENTRISTS

A notable loose end of the MTS change was the future disposition of kolkhoz payments-in-kind for the Stations' services. Khrushchev in January 1958 had excluded the possibility of increasing the cost of farm produce which the state obtained from kolkhozes. His "Theses" seemed to provide for the retaining of payments-in-kind under RTS: "The farm products which until now came from the kolkhozes as payment-in-kind for MTS work will now be received by the state directly from kolkhozes for machinery, spare parts, fuel, fertilizers, etc." Consistent with this, the deputy chief editor of *Izvestiya* assumed that "Even after the MTS reorganization, the state will

---

[38] *Pravda*, December 29, 1959.

[39] G. P. Tikhonov, ed., *Voprosy Kolkhoznogo Prava* (Problems of Kolkhoz Law), Leningrad, 1961, pp. 24, 43.

[40] Cf. "Free Inspection Groups from Bureaucracy," *Izvestiya*, July 15, 1958; and "Paper Whirlpool," *Izvestiya*, September 30, 1958.

organize its mutual relations with the kolkhozes so that an ever-increasing portion of kolkhoz products will come under state control, bypassing the sphere of commodity turnover."[41] The editor scarcely could have imagined that he was expressing what in time would be parodied as "the opinion that natural relations in the kolkhozes are supposedly always more progressive than money-goods relations. The argument was that insofar as under communism there will be no money-goods relations, any sort of natural relations in the kolkhozes are 'nearer to communism' than money-goods relations."[42]

But an underlying financial complication was brought to the surface during the public discussion. Khrushchev hinted as much in his March 27, 1958, address to the USSR Supreme Soviet: "Some comrades raise the question of the form of procurements which we will arrive at as a result of the MTS reorganization. They ask whether we shall retain payment-in-kind by kolkhozes for spare parts, fuel, and other services of the RTS or whether the state will buy these products at prevailing prices. Evidently, we should not adopt a decision on this question now." Thousands of weak kolkhozes would surely have found themselves in grave economic difficulty if the state did not buy the products. Khrushchev may have realized this from the start and have dissembled all along in order to deter new accusations of "Right opportunism," which must arise in any Communist state whenever economic concessions to the peasantry are contemplated. Such considerations of inner-party prestige may also help to explain the simultaneous vitriolic attacks of Khrushchev's propagandists on the Yugoslavs' "revisionistic" new party

[41] A. G. Baulin, *Izvestiya*, March 20, 1958.
[42] L. Gatovskiy, *Kommunist*, No. 1, 1959, p. 75.

program and his Bloc allies' belated execution of Imry Nagy. One of his personal sources of trouble over fiscal questions at the time may be deduced from the speech which Kozlov made in April 1958 during the campaign for the elections to the USSR Supreme Soviet. He uniquely pointed out: "In order that our agriculture will surely continue to climb and the population receive more foodstuffs, we must *not for a minute* forget that the cornerstone of all branches of our economy has been, is, and will be heavy industry" (italics added).[43]

As a decision was being reached on the payments-in-kind dilemma, Khrushchev moved to discredit political conservatism, thus jockeying to assume the kind of "centristic"—neither "Right" nor "Left"—position which Communist politicians always pretend to hold. V. M. Churayev, a former associate of Khrushchev in the Ukraine who was then in charge of personnel work in the Central Committee's Russian Federation Bureau, composed a booklet on party solidarity which criticized the defunct group of Malenkov and Molotov for clinging to outmoded beliefs and urged political flexibility.[44] A. B. Aristov and L. I. Brezhnev (Central Committee secretaries and Presidium members), speaking at local farm-award ceremonies held a few weeks later, attacked Khrushchev's former rivals for neglect of popular needs and ideological bankruptcy.[45] A decree then issued in the name of the Central Committee, either by its Presidium

[43] *Pravda*, April 24, 1958. Other leaders referred to heavy industry as the economy's "leading force" or "basis," not "cornerstone," and none used the term "not for a minute." See the speeches of Ignatov, Suslov, Kirichenko, Brezhnev, and Furtseva, in *Pravda*, April 26 and 30, May 14, 18, and 21, 1958, respectively.

[44] *O Edinstve Partii* (On Party Unity), Moscow, 1958 (approved for publication on April 30).

[45] *Pravda*, May 17 and 18, 1958.

or Secretariat, retracted as unwarranted a number of criticisms of Soviet composers which had appeared in a Committee decree of February 10, 1948, and in 1951 *Pravda*
editorials. Stalin was reproached for "subjectivism" in
evaluating the arts and Molotov, Malenkov, and Beriya
were claimed to have abetted his crime.[46] This decree,
adopted on the initiative of Khrushchev,[47] was supposedly
intended to "enhance the ideological and artistic level of
Soviet music," "further rally the creative intelligentsia on
the basis of communist ideology," and "strengthen the
ties of art with the life of the people." One need not share
the Communists' assumption of universal causal interdependence in order to consider this explanation far-fetched
in view of the leadership's preoccupation at that time
with the issue of farm prices. It does seem "more than
coincidental" that most of the figures besmirched in the
May 1958 decree had at various times opposed Khrushchev on agricultural policy. The party leader therefore
may have been trying to associate with Stalinism the opponents of exclusively cash transactions between the government and kolkhozes. Specifically, the May 1958 decree
appears to have been aimed at diminishing the personal
prestige of the member of the party Presidium who both
regarded the latest socio-economic experiment with tepid
enthusiasm and had actively taken part in Stalin's postwar
campaign to regiment the musicians. At a conference on
musical affairs held in party headquarters in January 1948,
Zhdanov, Stalin's ideological whip, was assisted by
Suslov.[48]

[46] "On Rectifying Errors in Evaluation of the Operas 'Great
Friendship,' 'Bogdan Khmelnitskiy,' and 'With All One's Heart,'"
Central Committee Decree of May 28, 1958, *Pravda*, June 8, 1958.
[47] B. Ryurikov, *Literaturnaya Gazeta*, January 4, 1962.
[48] See *Bol'shevik*, No. 6, 1948, p. 62.

The ultimate decision on the payments-in-kind issue was so consequential as to have required a Central Committee session for purposes of ratification and explanation. The Plenum of June 17-18, 1958, heard and approved Khrushchev's proposals for cash transactions between RTS and kolkhozes, sizable increases in state prices for farm products, and abolition of the levy-type compulsory deliveries in favor of a system of planned state purchases.[49] This political victory of Khrushchev found organizational expression in the election to candidate membership in the party Presidium of N. V. Podgornyy, a food industry engineer who had worked under Khrushchev in the Ukraine and now headed the regional party organization, and D. S. Polyanskiy, who in April 1958 had assumed the post of RSFSR premier as Kozlov became a first deputy chairman of the USSR Council of Ministers.[50] Podgornyy and Polyanskiy were soon to join the movement for a kolkhoz federation. Meanwhile, Khrushchev initiated his followers in the art of *ochkovtiratel'stvo*, or "window-dressing" (literally: to throw dust in someone's eyes). He claimed that the kolkhozes were making better use of their newly obtained machinery than had been the case under MTS. Leningrad "researchers" estimated that in their province the total amount of soft plowing per tractor declined from 261 hectares in 1957 to 229 hectares in 1958, and that the number of "labor days" per tractor dropped from 117 in 1957 to 105 in the following year.[51]

[49] Khrushchev's report, "On Abolishing Compulsory Deliveries and Payments-in-Kind for MTS Work and on New System, Prices, and Terms for Procurement of Agricultural Products," is in *Pravda*, June 21, 1958; the plenary session's decree of the same name is in *Pravda*, June 20, 1958. The appropriate decree of the USSR Council of Ministers is in *Pravda*, July 1, 1958.

[50] *Pravda*, June 19, 1958.

[51] A. I. Klyuyev, *Vestnik Leningradskogo Universiteta* (Herald

The short-term disruptive aspect of Khrushchevian haste in pursuit of increased productivity over the long run had to be concealed, lest undue hesitation arise over future bold schemes, several of which were in the making.

JUNE-DECEMBER 1958

The enactment of pro-peasant economic legislation provided a suitable atmosphere for the extension of campaigning in behalf of autonomy measures which were in tune with Khrushchev's basic policy. The advocates of kolkhoz unions (*soyuzy*) or associations (*ob"yedineniya*) which would exercise jurisdiction beyond the district level voiced their demands chiefly in economic terms and were not of one mind on all aspects of the desired reform. Academician Strumilin emphasized the underprivileged financial status of kolkhozes vis-á-vis state industrial enterprises (almost 15 times more investment capital was made available per industrial worker than per able-bodied kolkhoznik). He concluded that large-scale kolkhoz associations were needed to ensure the pooling of scarce farm resources for the rational organization and use of the growing number of interkolkhoz electric-power stations, irrigational systems, and anti-soil erosion projects.[52] A nation-wide association might establish in-

---

of Leningrad University), No. 11, 1961, p. 33. The 1957 data is based on the work of all MTS in Leningrad Region; the 1958 figures concern tractor pools in 78 kolkhozes of the region. On stoppages and faulty maintenance, see *Zarya Vostoka*, April 29, 1958; *Leninskoye Znamya*, May 6, 13, and 22, 1958; *Bakinskiy Rabochiy*, May 14, 1958; *Sovetskaya Litva*, June 1, 1958; and *Sovetskaya Estoniya*, June 20, 1958.

[52] In the Ukraine there were about 100 interkolkhoz electric-power stations, one serving 228 farms, while 600 interkolkhoz building organizations, sustained by almost 70 per cent of the area's farms, had in 1957 constructed 400 large livestock structures,

surance funds to aid farms located in regions often affected by natural calamities. It also would redistribute kolkhoz wealth to the advantage of farms which were economically weak owing to poor soil conditions. Strumilin looked toward Kolkhoz Centers in the republic capitals and provincial seats to discharge the functions of material-technical supply of kolkhozes and centralized sale of their above-quota products. He favorably mentioned Vinnichenko's efforts prior to the MTS change and, in the spirit of that innovator, observed: "Once 'A' has been stated, 'B' as well will be stated. Such is the logic of history. And one can only hope that the road from 'A' to 'B' will be traversed in the shortest time possible."[53]

Vinnichenko returned Strumilin's compliment a month later in another of his rural trip reports carried by the literary journal *October*. He reaffirmed that an All-Union Association would be capable of establishing a social security system for the weak kolkhozes, thereby emulating the practice on richer farms, and added that the formation of interkolkhoz guaranteed insurance funds in a nation-wide union would enable the weak kolkhozes as well to shift over to an exclusively monetary system of wage payments. Vinnichenko implicitly extolled the virtues of the profit motive when he contended that the creation of big interkolkhoz enterprises, such as meat-processing plants, within a union system, would enable

---

356 production buildings, 80 recreation centers, and over 500 private homes, all at costs below those of state enterprises (P. Golubkov and V. Ovchinnikova, *Voprosy Ekonomiki*, No. 12, 1958, p. 89; this source usefully summarizes decrees and official statements on the question). But in the RSFSR only 10 per cent of the kolkhozes paid dues to maintain the 400 interkolkhoz organizations of all types (D. Polyanskiy, *Kommunist*, No. 3, 1959, p. 35).

[53] *Voprosy Ekonomiki*, No. 5 (May), 1958, pp. 33-45.

the accumulation of large funds, a considerable portion of which could be used to aid the poorer farms. Such units would also experience an upturn once procurement plans were issued from above for a district union as a whole. The district union would apportion such plans by kolkhoz, taking into consideration the peculiarities of each farm, and this would facilitate specialization, enabling weak farms to develop their economies in line with their capabilities. True, the change would reduce by at least one-third the staffs of agricultural ministries and regional agricultural administrations (the hope of Khrushchev). But it would not detach kolkhozes from the state, as feared by "hopeless dogmatists," who "over the course of many years have placed kolkhozes in opposition to state property." Vinnichenko replied to the neo-Stalinists that kolkhoz unions would ease the task of state control, create more favorable conditions for unifying the production of city and village, and politically strengthen the "worker-peasant alliance." Apropos of production unification, Vinnichenko set forth as an objective of his decentralist school of thought the merger of regional kolkhoz unions and councils of the national economy (sovnarkhozes) into a single system for directing the economy.[54]

About the same time, challenging views were presented at the USSR Academy of Sciences' conference on socio-economic affairs. G. T. Kovalevskiy, an economist from Byelorussia, opposed Strumilin's writing on the kolkhoz union. He in effect confirmed Vinnichenko's characterization of the "hopeless dogmatists" by prefacing his anti-union sally with the remark that the kolkhozes were destined to become government-operated enterprises.

[54] *Oktyabr'*, No. 6, 1958, pp. 119-138.

Kovalevskiy reminded the conference that kolkhozes were located adjacent to state farms and adduced that the creation of regional kolkhoz unions would lead to the existence of two parallel systems for the administration of agriculture—state bodies for sovkhoz direction and co-operative bodies to run kolkhozes—which would "complicate and make more expensive the system of agricultural management."[55] Thus, an economic objection of questionable merit was appended to the political and administrative ones arrayed against the union proposal during the public discussion of the MTS change.

Shadings of opinion soon appeared in the unionists' own ranks. The pragmatic economist Venzher agreed with Strumilin that a broader cooperative association was essential to satisfy the managerial requirements of inter-kolkhoz enterprises, improve the planning of kolkhoz production, organize the sale of farm surpluses (especially perishable commodities) and, in the future, take charge of the supply and repair of farm machinery. But he did not share Strumilin's belief in the efficacy of profit-sharing as a means of resolving the problem of the weak farm. Venzher thought that this problem could be solved only in a national economic context, suggesting that the structure of government-fixed purchasing prices was defective.[56] Another unionist, who forthrightly demanded abolition of the Ministry of Agriculture in his locality, rejected the proposal to recreate a USSR Kolkhoz Center. Khrushchev's industrial management reorganization, he

[55] *Voprosy Stroitel'stva Kommunizma v SSSR. Materialy Nauchnoy Sessii Otdelenii Obshchestvennykh Nauk Akademii Nauk SSSR* (Problems of Building Communism in the USSR. Materials of a Scholars' Meeting of the Department of Social Sciences of the USSR Academy of Sciences), Moscow, 1959, p. 343.

[56] *Voprosy Ekonomiki*, No. 8, 1958, pp. 122-123.

said, had supposedly demonstrated the advantages of decentralized administration.[57] Meanwhile, in the pages of
October, an agronomist and district party secretary
clashed on the issue. The Siberian technician shrank
from the prospect of unions lest they jeopardize the
sovkhoz system, while the Ukrainian party functionary
supported them on the grounds of the irresponsible conduct of regional agricultural administrations.[58]

The rural reconstruction plan which Khrushchev had
fought for in 1950-1951 was now revived and argued for
in terms of equalitarianism and practicality. An economist from Kazakhstan told the social sciences conference held in the Academy of Sciences shortly after
the Central Committee meeting in June:

> I think that the idea of agro-cities is correct and that
> it represents a contribution to the theory of Marxism-
> Leninism. Really, what is bad about the idea of the grad-
> ual conversion of our villages into agro-cities in the
> course of the transition to communism? We not only
> dream but also prove scientifically that under the total
> victory of communism there will be no classes and
> class differences in society, that under communism
> there will reign the precept "from each according to
> his ability, to each according to his needs." Why not in-
> clude here the prospects for the development of our
> villages?
>
> I think that in the future our villages will develop
> and consolidate. Perhaps the time will come when some
> current-day districts will be one big agricultural pro-
> duction association with a single cultural center. But

[57] Kh. Khaskhayan, *Kommunist* (Organ of the Communist Party
of Armenia), December 8, 1958.
[58] Cf. M. Baranov and P. Rukavets, *Oktyabr'*, No. 10, 1958, pp.
166ff.

this will not be a village of the current type. It will be a new kind of village, essentially a rural town, an agro-city.[59]

Ostrovityanov, director of the Academy's Social Sciences Department, who had recently performed as Khrushchev's spokesman on the theoretical side of the MTS change, seconded these remarks at the close of the conference.[60] The lead article in *Izvestiya* of August 17, 1958, dealt with rural reconstruction, reproducing a fragment of Khrushchev's controversial speech of 1951 but omitting mention of "kolkhoz settlements," which suggested that the idea was still upsetting in certain quarters. But the article which a kolkhoz chairman wrote for *Leninskoye Znamya*, daily of the Moscow Regional Party Committee, and which was featured on page one of the issue for December 12, 1958, was entitled "We Need Agro-Cities." The question had to be raised, since populated points often were located far from the central farmstead and that caused great loss of funds.

CENTRAL COMMITTEE SESSION OF DECEMBER 15-19, 1958

One of the many grievances which Ovechkin had articulated after the death of Stalin was the conspiratorial handling of party work, which he succinctly described as "the discussion in secret conclave of problems that should be solved together with the people."[61] The change-

---

[59] *Voprosy Stroitel'stva Kommunizma v SSSR*, p. 283.

[60] "The idea of agro-cities must hold an important place among the measures for eliminating the essential differences between town and country and ensuring conditions for the raising of kolkhoz-cooperative property to the level of all-people's property" (*ibid.*, p. 427).

[61] See J. M.'s "From Soviet Publications—A New Definition of Alignments Within the Party," *Soviet Studies*, Vol. VI, pp. 77-91.

resistant forces with whom Khrushchev grappled in the
1953-1957 period were especially desirous of muting the
great issues of policy, and indeed suppressed a number of
the reformist utterances of the first secretary, whose natural interest it was to broaden the arena of conflict.[62] The
passing of Stalin's closest associates from the political
scene enabled Khrushchev to provide the general public
with sufficient information to appraise it of the character
of the latest movement of opinion in the upper stratum,
even if it was still denied an effective voice in the
decision-making process. More than demogogy seems to
have been involved. The political purpose evidently was
to foster the creation of some kind of "public opinion"
which might eventually help to swing the official consensus in the direction of radical reform. This new tendency
began in earnest at the Central Committee's plenary session on agriculture in December 1958. For the first time in
decades, the press carried day-to-day reportage of the
speeches made on the floor of the gathering, and several
hundred non-members of the Committee took part in the
open proceedings. The decisions, as usual, were reached
in private at expanded meetings of the party Presidium,
but the active issues were made objects of common
knowledge.

Khrushchev's keynote report was a grand review of

[62] The chronicled events of the early post-Stalin period tend
to bear out the charge that "Only the anti-party group, which
had become detached from the people, and whose ringleaders
had stained themselves by the persecution of many honest people,
could see danger in the further democratization of all aspects of
the life of Soviet society. A fear of the masses—this sickness of
intriguers—was demonstrated in all the work of the factionaries,
who were accustomed to the secretive, anti-democratic discussion
and decision of the most important problems" (*Kommunist*, No.
18, 1961, p. 13).

agricultural progress since 1953 and included the usual
seminar in new production techniques. The leader re-
joiced over the record grain harvest of 8.6 billion poods
(3.5 billion in state purchases) and was able to claim that
productivity had in general risen, thanks to greater inputs
and material rewards and, until recently, less centralized
management.[63] In this regard, it is worth noting that the
economist Khlebnikov estimates that total farm production rose 51 per cent, or 8.5 per cent annually, from 1953
to 1958 and offers the figures shown in Table 1 on per
capita farm output in percentage to the 1928 situation.

TABLE 1

	1953	1958
Gross Agricultural Production	107	147
inclusive of:		
tillage	115	162
livestock	98	131

SOURCE: Khlebnikov, *Voprosy Ekonomiki*, No. 7, 1962, p. 49.

Khlebnikov attributes the rise to improved technical outfitting and stressing of the material incentive principle.
He also estimates that in 1958 collective farmers received
in cash and produce for their labor in the socialized sector almost double in retail price value their equivalent
earnings in 1953. The raising of incentives resulted in a
doubling of the efficiency of capital investment: in terms
of 1958 prices, the 1951-1953 increment of gross production in kolkhozes was 32 rubles per 100 rubles of capital
investment of farms and MTS; during 1954-1958 the
same increment was 65 rubles.[64] True, in an indetermin-

[63] *Pravda*, December 16, 1958.
[64] *Voprosy Ekonomiki*, No. 7, 1962, p. 49.

able number of weak kolkhozes the payment for a "labor day" still did not exceed the Stalin-period iron ration of a kilogram of grain and 2 or 3 rubles, as pointed out by the advocates of wealth-redistributing kolkhoz unions.[65] But these interkolkhoz disparities do not detract from the importance of the production gains outlined in Khrushchev's report.

The party leader, however, did not rest on his oars but advanced several characteristic proposals to encourage self-reliance and renovation in the villages. A few months before, he had told farm officials in Smolensk that he was thinking of Central Committee discussion of the problem of kolkhozes that refused for reasons of economy to buy machinery and chose to deal with remaining MTS.[66] Khrushchev reported to the plenary session that over 55,000 kolkhozes, or 81 per cent, had purchased machinery and about 80 per cent of the MTS had been reorganized into RTS. He condemned "dependent tendencies" in kolkhozes still served by MTS and called for "proper discussion" of the question. Khrushchev also stated that various kolkhoz chairmen were of the opinion that the RTS tended to concentrate on jobs which were of the greatest advantage to themselves as economically self-sustaining units, and that it would be better for the kolkhozes to switch over to self-service, leaving to RTS the sale of machinery, fuel, and spare parts. Khrushchev thought that this proposal should be heeded, but rhetorically inquired if it would not be better for the kolkhozes

[65] Cf. Strumilin, *Voprosy Ekonomiki*, No. 5, 1958, p. 34; D. Polyanskiy, *Kommunist*, No. 3, 1959, p. 34; and I. Vinnichenko, *Nash Sovremennik*, No. 4, 1959, pp. 174ff.

[66] *Pravda*, August 24, 1958. N. Mukhitdinov in *Sovetskaya Kirgiziya*, September 11, 1958, censured local kolkhozes for avoiding the purchase of machinery.

to refrain from building their own repair shops and instead pool their funds to build interkolkhoz shops on a cooperative basis. He added: "This does not mean, of course, that we should immediately launch a campaign to sell the workshops. Here we must rationally and economically assess the expediency of such a measure in each separate case." Khrushchev likewise assumed the guise of moderation by avoiding use of the terms "agro-cities" and "kolkhoz settlements" when treating the subject of bridging the cultural gap between cities and villages:

> Sturdy production buildings, well-appointed residences, clubs, schools and boarding schools, libraries, communal services establishments, good roads, electricity, radio, television, cinema—such are the realistic features of the Soviet village of the not remote future. Thanks to the widespread application of technology in agricultural production and the maturing of personnel, the nature of the collective farmers' labor will more and more approximate that of industrial workers, and living conditions in the rural areas, in connection with the development of culture, will differ little from those of the socialist city. Our land is surely embarking on the practical solution of a most important problem of building communism—overcoming the existing differences between town and country.

Khrushchev deemed it inopportune to present forthrightly to the Central Committee his own recommendations to abolish existing MTS, create interkolkhoz repair shops, and build kolkhoz settlements. That he personally favored these measures is clear from the plenary speech of N. Belyayev, who had raised the trial balloon in regard to virgin lands in 1953 and since become party leader in Kazakhstan. Belyayev declared:

> Comrades! in the report of Nikita Sergeyevich, the problem of kolkhoz organization has been clarified from Leninist theoretical positions. The party pays special attention to the fortunes of the kolkhoz system because this is a matter which concerns an entire social class, namely, the Soviet peasantry, and the further consolidation of the worker and peasant alliance. But theory is presented in the report not like chapters from a textbook, but closely linked with practice, and it is a rich generalization of experience. . . . The Central Committee Plenum will support unanimously the proposals advanced by Nikita Sergeyevich Khrushchev for reorganizing the MTS which still exist, the creation of interkolkhoz repair shops, the building of kolkhoz settlements, and other advanced problems [the nature of which I am unable to establish—S.P.]. They are fully animate, ripe, and entirely in accord with the boldness and scope of our party's plans for the transition to communism.[67]

A study of the published transcript of the December 1958 Plenum reveals no actual debate on any of the issues compactly defined in Belyayev's speech. This debate must have transpired in the closed meetings of the 69-man "editorial" commission formally elected at the fourth of the Plenum's eight sittings. Khrushchev chaired this body, which was comprised of the entire party Presidium (22 members and candidate members, whose names precede all others in the listing of commission

[67] *Plenum I*, p. 105.

members in the minutes), the Union-republic party first secretaries (14, inclusive of 5 members or candidate members of the party Presidium), 16 individuals indentifiable as regional party first secretaries, a few party and state officials resident in Moscow, and a handful of farm practitioners.[68] One day after this *ad hoc* body was formed, Khrushchev requested members of the Plenum to examine a draft resolution which had been circulated and submit comments to the chiefs of the Central Committee Sections for Agriculture in the Union Republics and Russian Federation, who would study them and inform the commission.[69] On the final day of the session, P. A. Satyukov, chief editor of *Pravda*, reported on the activities of the commission. This report enumerates amendments of the draft resolution but, like the draft itself, is not in the public transcript, which states only that the revised draft was adopted unanimously as the plenary session's decree.[70]

The draft resolution and Satyukov's report were cloaked in secrecy to make less obtrusive the divisions on the interkolkhoz repair shops and kolkhoz settlements. For while the Plenum's decree authorizes rapid completion of the MTS change, it contains not a word about the shops or settlements. Khrushchev might have gained some measure of satisfaction on the settlements: at some unknown time in 1958, the Central Committee letter of

[68] *Ibid.*, p. 260, lists 68 names. At the next session the Siberian agronomist Mal'tsev was elected to the commission on the proposal of an anonymous figure. Lysenko was also elected at the urging of some unknown person. But Khrushchev is identified as the sponsor of V. I. Polyakov, who at the time of writing is Central Committee secretary and chairman of the Committee's Bureau for Agriculture in the Union Republics.

[69] *Ibid.*, p. 304.

[70] *Ibid.*, pp. 468-469.

1951 which had outlawed his agro-cities plan was invalidated.[71] But the lack of endorsement of the plan in the decree of the plenary session was a reversal for Khrushchev. The logic of numerical representation in the "editorial" commission and earlier statements by regional party leader Mazurov and USSR Minister of Agriculture Matskevich in behalf of a RTS-repair monopoly[72] suggest that the passions behind the differences of opinion transcended the boundaries of apparatus loyalty. Not a few party bosses must have joined up with ministerial forces to block steps which would increase the autonomy of kolkhozes and threaten a slackening of production effort in the communal sector. Mazurov and Matskevich a few years later would again agree publicly on the necessity of enhancing the administrative fiat of the USSR Ministry of Agriculture (see Chapter V). In 1958 their authoritarian viewpoint prevailed; in 1960 it was rebuffed.

As Khrushchev and his followers had generated anti-"conservative" propaganda in April-May 1958 with a view toward discrediting and isolating the bureacratic elements opposed to their conciliatory solution of the payments-in-kind dilemma, so at the December 1958 Central Committee session they reopened the casebook on the Malenkov-Molotov faction, at least partly in the hope of similarly discrediting opponents of the unbinding of kolkhozes. But the implicit demands made for the expulsion of Malenkov and Molotov from the ranks of the Communist party were inconclusive. The adversaries of inter-

[71] The TASS version of L. F. Il'ichëv's speech to the 22nd party Congress dates the annulment to 1958 (*Sovetskaya Rossiya*, October 25, 1961). The *Pravda* version of October 26, 1961, does not mention the year.

[72] Cf. *Sovetskaya Belorussiya*, July 26, 1958; and *Kommunist*, No. 12, 1958, p. 29.

kolkhoz repair shops and kolkhoz settlements not only strained to withhold from Khrushchev the fearsome right to conduct party purges, but refused to bring into final disrepute the symbols of authoritarian centralist control of the peasantry.

CHAPTER IV

DEADLOCK OVER THE KOLKHOZ FEDERATION AND OTHER ISSUES (1959)

THE INCIPIENT dissolution in 1959 of the anti-"conservative" front which Khrushchev had put together in December 1957 was an outcome of his encouragement of radical reform. Khrushchev's optimistic assessments of the internal cohesion of the regime and of the world situation provided the proper setting for new proposals aimed at loosening central controls and stimulating initiative at the grass roots. The immediate goal in agriculture was creation of the nation-wide kolkhoz union, which Vinnichenko now depicted as the harbinger of a far-reaching transformation of the whole system of economic management into something resembling a syndicalist pyramid. A token of the feeling at the opposite end of the spectrum of political opinion in the ruling group was the renewed demand to solve the problem of the many economically weak kolkhozes by merging them with state farms. Once more, the historical division of competing groups into "Right" and "Left" made itself known.

More balance in policy and personal power became the order of the day once differences in the party Presidium were thrashed out in the Central Committee. The supreme caucus rejected the extremist plans of both the agricultural apparatus of the party Secretariat, which was dominated by the reform group of Khrushchev, and the Ministry of Agriculture, which remained a hotbed of the authoritarian centralist mentality. The preponderance of executive power vested in Khrushchev as a result of the personnel shifts of December 1957 was somewhat redressed. The Ukrainian interloper Kirichenko was forced to withdraw from his ranking position in the Secretariat and amends had to be made for the purges of Russian Federation officials which had occurred under his auspices. The "conservatives" Suslov and Kozlov, whose interests were gravely impaired in the reorganization of December 1957 and who evidently fought Khrushchev's new decentralization measures, were grudgingly appeased. Suslov was given a share in the leadership of party control activities that verified agricultural performance, and Kozlov was allowed to pick the successor to Belyayev, Khrushchev's follower in charge of Kazakhstan until innerparty tensions came to a head at the December 1959 Central Committee session.

Defending the Cooperative Principle

Short of specifically endorsing the controversial proposal for a kolkhoz federation, Khrushchev in the first half of 1959 did everything conceivable to promote its acceptance. A special party Congress was held in January-February 1959 to ratify the new Seven-Year Economic Plan and hear Khrushchev's personal report on developmental trends within the society.[1] Khrushchev declared that the country was embarking on a new phase of its history, which he called "the period of the full-scale building of communism." State regulation of public affairs would diminish and an enhanced role be granted to public organizations like soviets, trade unions, and the Young

[1] The report is in *Pravda*, January 28, 1959.

Communist League. The ruling Communist party would itself have to be freed of bureaucratic encumbrances. Khrushchev buttressed this thesis by claiming that the regime had achieved the utmost in political consolidation ("the total and irrevocable victory of socialism in the USSR"). Thus, he invalidated one of the foremost talking points against wider participation by rank-and-file workers in the management of economic affairs. For example, a year and a half earlier, during the public discussion of the industrial management change, a proposal had been made for the election of factory directors at worker meetings. M. Sakov, an editor of *Kommunist*, criticized those behind the proposal as "opportunists" who contemplated "making a demogogic play for the nonparty masses or their enticement." Sakov charged that if a system of producers' self-administration was created, "the election, which the working class would enter into in a politically unorganized manner, could be used by *class-hostile forces* to the detriment of the interests of the workers and all toilers" (italics added).[2] Significantly, Sakov was not included in the new editorial board of *Kommunist* which was formed just prior to Khrushchev's announcement of the regime's definitive consolidation. The new board was expected to air more regularly "new, vital questions posed by experience and practice."[3]

Khrushchev in his 21st Congress discourse on agriculture reendorsed interkolkhoz production ties and maintained that the joint construction projects would require "the more systematic coordination of the efforts of sev-

[2] *Kommunist*, No. 8 (June), 1957, pp. 10ff.
[3] The Central Committee decree of January 9, 1959, criticizing the editorial board of *Kommunist* and approving a new one is in *Spravochnik Partiynogo Rabotnika* (Handbook of the Party Official), Moscow, 1959, pp. 534-537.

eral kolkhozes." He was more explicit on the related subject of the merger of collective and state farms into an integral communist property. He held that property forms
depend on the nature and level of productive forces and
that the kolkhoz system fully accorded with the level and
developmental needs of agriculture's productive forces.
For a long time to come, he said, the kolkhoz-cooperative
form of productive relations would serve to strengthen
the productive forces. These remarks triggered an intensive propaganda campaign against the forced merger of
kolkhozes and sovkhozes.

Vinnichenko tried to convince his readers that the kolkhoz system was economically more viable than state-run
farming. He cited a study of conditions in Stavropol'
Territory which purportedly showed that the daily wages
in any slightly reinforced kolkhoz exceeded those in a
sovkhoz; that as a cooperative enterprise the kolkhoz had
the possibility of conducting exchange operations and
with its available cash could pay higher prices and so
resolve problems of capital investment and material-
technical supply more simply and quickly than the sovkhoz; that sovkhoz work norms when fixed by the ministry were either exaggerated or minimized, which led to
frequent evasion; that the piece work system used on
sovkhozes was not dependent on output or work results;
and that sovkhoz directors were almost entirely deprived
of managerial initiative. Vinnichenko maintained that the
peasants who had once looked upon the sovkhoz as a
well-ordered "estate" of the ministry had become disil-
lusioned and did not "feel close" to it. He hinted that the
conversion of kolkhozes into sovkhozes was determined
in the RSFSR Ministry of Agriculture upon the petition
of local leaders. In this same article, Vinnichenko out-

lined a federative structure for managing industry and agriculture:

> In a word, if we are to speak about prospects, then obviously there will be two converging processes. On the one hand, unification of separate kolkhozes into a united, democratically governed, kolkhoz-cooperative system which would include sovkhozes modified in a corresponding fashion; on the other hand, further democratization of administration of production for industry and construction, on the basis of maximum utilization of the thorough, creative independent labor of all members of production collectives united in trade unions. And there is no doubt at all that the completion of these two processes will lead in the final analysis to a merger of all forms of organizations and enterprises under the over-all command of sovnarkhozes into the same *unified, proletarian-governed cooperative* of which Vladimir Il'ich Lenin dreamed so fondly at the dawn of the Soviet era.
>
> Yes, yes, everything is coming to this (italics added).[4]

The press and radio campaign against nationalization of kolkhoz property brought to light the reasoning of the authoritarians who desired to organize the entire peasantry in sovkhozes. M. Bronshteyn, Candidate of Economic Sciences, upholding the kolkhoz form in *Sovetskaya Estoniya* (organ of the Communist Party of Estonia), on May 21, 1959, acknowledged as among its organizational deficiencies the fact that the manpower force in the communal sector of kolkhozes had a smaller work load than in state enterprises and much of the collective farmer's labor was spent on his small personal

---

[4] *Nash Sovremennik*, No. 4, 1959, pp. 174-192.

allotment. Moreover, it was more difficult to concentrate and redistribute resources in the kolkhoz than in the command-managed state sector.

Khrushchev further assisted the unionist cause in May and June of 1959. At a farm rally in Kiev he caricatured officials of the Ministry of Agriculture as retrograders who were nostalgic about the time they had to visit some particular kolkhoz and count the number of destroyed weevils. Khrushchev urged that the USSR and Union-republic Ministries of Agriculture be stripped of their right to distribute chemical fertilizers and spare parts to kolkhozes and that commercial organizations assume this function. As in 1956, he contended that agricultural agencies had to become organizers of production, perhaps merged with experimental establishments, so that their technically qualified staff members could serve as instructors of farm personnel.[5] Khrushchev restated these views in the preface to his speech at the June 1959 Central Committee session, which dealt with questions of industrial management. He asserted that bureaucratism was the reason for the existence of backward farms, and inveighed against overadministration with aid of the proverb, "The child with seven nurses is not watched." He also appeared willing to resume the policy of land expansion: "Perhaps thought should be given to exploiting new lands in the Amur Region and other regions of the Far East. Let the secretaries of regional party committees and chairmen of regional executive committees think about this and then make their suggestions."[6]

PREPARING FOR THE DECEMBER PLENUM

Pravda on July 14, 1959, reported that the Central Com-

[5] *Pravda*, May 12, 1959.
[6] *Ibid.*, July 2, 1959.

mittee, evidently the Presidium,[7] had decided to convene a regular plenary session of the Committee in November or December. The precise date of the meeting was to be announced later. The agenda consisted of a number of production questions, the economic problem of "strengthening the public sector of kolkhozes and raising the material welfare of collective farmers," and the managerial task of "strengthening kolkhozes and sovkhozes with personnel." Union-republic leaders were to report on these matters and a discussion would follow. In actuality, the main business of the meeting proved to have been foreshadowed by Khrushchev's remarks at the June Plenum. As noted, he wished to put an end to bureaucratic methods of leadership, improve the terms of trade for agriculture, and plow up additional massifs of virgin soil. This required a vast press campaign to discredit the leaders of Ministries of Agriculture and the "conservative" viewpoint on administrative and agrotechnical policy as well as to whip up support for appropriate changes.

Soviet history knows of more than one instance of a direct link between officially expressed concern about bureaucratic malfeasance and conflict in the upper stratum. A prominent anti-Stalinist of the 1920's claimed that

[7] The Presidium's "status symbols" had since come into prominence at the expense of Khrushchev's. In the lead article of *Kommunist*, No. 9 (June), 1959, Khrushchev was referred to as first, rather than First, secretary (p. 7). In the next issue of the same magazine, S. Chervonenko noted that "The CPSU Central Committee Presidium every day shows itself to be a model of the Leninist work style," and Sh. Rashidov attributed the expansion of local rights to (a) the CPSU Central Committee, (b) the C.C. Presidium, and (c) personally, Comrade N. S. Khrushchev (No. 10, 1959, pp. 34 and 44). This was a remarkable departure from the singling-out of Khrushchev at and immediately after the 21st Special party Congress.

"charges of moral turpitude were sometimes fastened on those whom it was desired to discredit on political grounds."[8] During the Great Purge, ousted heads of the Young Communist League, men and women bewildered over the increasing despotism of the Stalin regime, were formally accused of "concealing the morally corrupt, the drunkards, the elements hostile to Party and Komsomol, the doubledealing elements."[9] This weapon of political struggle has not become obsolete. It was utilized by G. Yenyutin, chairman of the Soviet Control Commission in the USSR Council of Ministers and a former member of the Ukrainian apparatus, in *Izvestiya* on August 14, 1959. Yenyutin's agents had discovered that funds were being squandered in the USSR Ministry of Agriculture. Certain officials had improved their personal cottages and garden areas at a cost to the state of 1.3 million (old) rubles. Some ministerial employees, exploiting their official positions, had acquired ready-made frames and various building materials at cut-rate prices in subordinate enterprises. The chief of the Finance Administration bought a set of parts for a two-apartment cottage from one timber trust at a price 9,000 (old) rubles below retail cost. The chief of the Economics Administration was primarily concerned that a road be extended to his garden section and at state expense. Major abuses were uncovered at the former All-Union Agricultural Exhibition. Scarce building materials were systematically squandered there, and more than one million (old) rubles' worth of them sold to various organizations and private persons. Other "discoveries" of bureaucratic malpractice in the Ministry

[8] See E. H. Carr, *A History of Soviet Russia: Socialism in One Country, 1924-1926*, New York, 1960, II, 217.
[9] *Komsomol'skaya Pravda*, November 20, 1938.

would be made during subsequent conflict over its administrative prerogatives (see Chapter V).

Like Khrushchev at the Kiev farm rally, several officials proposed that the RTS network of the USSR Ministry of Agriculture be relieved of its function as outlet for the sale of machines and fuel to kolkhozes. The main grievance was that RTS, like the abolished MTS, had inflated staffs with high administrative overhead costs and, as profit-making "middlemen" between kolkhozes and ministerial supply agencies, their warehouse and transport surcharges at times raised sales prices by as much as 13-20 per cent. Most of the complainants advocated the transfer of RTS commercial functions to various state trading organizations, but L. Florent'yev, first secretary of the Kostroma Regional Party Committee and Candidate of Economic Sciences, desired the fusion of these organizations into a single, centralized supply organ.[10] Plans for such an organ in Latvia, where all RTS had discontinued their sales work by December 1, 1959, were announced on the eve of the Central Committee Plenum.[11]

While Florent'yev believed that RTS should be retained for capital repair work, others went all out for the interkolkhoz repair shops. T. Ul'dzhabayev, first secretary of the C.P. Tadzhikistan, a staunch decentralizer in

[10] Cf. *Sovetskaya Rossiya*, October 15, 1959 (comptroller of a group of checkers in the RSFSR Soviet Control Commission); November 25, 1959 (RSFSR Supreme Soviet Deputy); December 20, 1959 (survey of readers' letters); and Florent'yev, *Kommunist*, No. 18, 1959, pp. 31ff.

[11] *Sovetskaya Latviya*, December 4, 1959. The sale of equipment and fuel to kolkhozes would be conducted by a Main Administration of Agricultural Trade under the republic Council of Ministers. RTS in the area were renamed Machine and Soil Improvement Stations (MMS).

the area of industrial management, declared in *Pravda* of November 15, 1959, that economically strong kolkhozes could transfer entirely to technical self-service. Ul'dzha-bayev would report to the December Plenum that all RTS in Tadzhikistan were abolished, and a subsequent article in the regional press commended interkolkhoz repair shops as the successors of RTS.[12] This expressed Khrushchev's thinking on the matter, since on the eve of the plenary session Belyayev's clarification of his earlier remarks was repeated: "Life engenders ever-new forms of production cooperation of the kolkhozes. So, in connection with the transfer of all farm machinery to the artels [kolkhozes], the question arose of organizing an interkolkhoz repair base. At the December 1958 Central Committee Plenum, Comrade N. S. Khrushchev advised the kolkhozes to join their resources and, on the basis of shares, to buy or build interkolkhoz repair shops."[13] On balance, the pre-Plenum articles in favor of downgrading or abolishing RTS heavily outnumbered those defending it on technological grounds.[14]

[12] Cf. *Pravda*, December 24, 1959; and *Kommunist Tadzhikistana*, February 4, 1960. In *Izvestiya* of June 4, 1959, Ul'dzhabayev reported that branch administrations and a greater number of trusts had been eliminated in the Tadzhikistan Sovnarkhoz, and the management of enterprises entrusted to branch divisions which, according to the sovnarkhoz chairman, meant direct management without intermediate links and reduced staff salaries (*Pravda*, June 27, 1960). Repair workshops in each kolkhoz were favored also in *Pravda Ukrainy*, August 26, 1959 (kolkhoz chairman) and October 2, 1959 (district party secretary); in *Komsomol'skaya Pravda*, October 13, 1959 (chief engineer of the Rostov Regional Agricultural Administration) and December 15, 1959 (RTS chief engineer); and in *Pravda*, November 11, 1959 (kolkhoz chairman).

[13] L. Braginskiy, *Kommunist*, No. 17, 1959, p. 23.

[14] Pro-RTS materials are in *Pravda Ukrainy*, November 12, 1959 (local economist) and November 15, 1959 (kolkhoz chairman?); and in *Komsomol'skaya Pravda*, December 15, 1959

The kolkhoz union was a different proposition. The unionist cause does not appear to have been espoused forthrightly from late in the spring until early November, when the Central Committee Plenum was scheduled for December 22, 1959.[15] Then, only the press in the Ukraine and Kirgiziya featured articles which outlined the familiar pros and cons of the issue.[16] The central press ran only material which tacitly upheld the federative scheme. I. Glotov, an economist who in 1958 had summarized for *Kommunist* the discussion of ideological aspects of the MTS change, wrote in *Sovetskaya Rossiya* on September 2, 1959, that any change of the structure of agricultural administration which might follow Khrushchev's remarks at the June Plenum would probably affect the district kolkhoz unions, whose activities hinted at "*forms of leadership of kolkhoz production from below*" (italics added). The same point was made by one L. Braginskiy in an article on interkolkhoz relations which appeared in the issue of *Kommunist* sent to the press on November 30, 1959. Braginskiy depicted the interkolkhoz building societies as "molding themselves into a certain new system of leadership for kolkhozes" which would be "a peculiar sort of kolkhoz union." Once such a body came into existence, "the managerial autonomy of kolkhozes will be unlimited."[17]

(deputy chief of the Stavropol' Territory Agricultural Administration).

[15] *Pravda*, November 11, 1959.

[16] Cf. *Pravda Ukrainy*, November 13, 1959 (kolkhoz chairman M. Kovalenko, an acquaintance of Vinnichenko), and December 15, 1959 (staff correspondent); and *Sovetskaya Kirgiziya*, November 28, 1959 (kolkhoz chairman)—all in favor of unions beyond the district level; and a district party secretary's objection in *Pravda Ukrainy*, December 19, 1959.

[17] No. 17, 1959, pp. 21-28.

The article by V. Ivanov, V. Pchelin, and M. Sakov, "Growth of the Role of the Party in the Building of Communism,"[18] was a propaganda adjunct to Braginskiy's survey of interkolkhoz activites. Ivanov, an expert on literary affairs, was appointed to the editorial board of *Kommunist* in January 1959 when it was realigned to encourage fresh thought on current problems. Pchelin, not an editor, but a specialist in the work of public organizations, is most likely to have favored the union proposal.[19] Sakov, on the other hand, is identifiable as an exponent of the "conservative" viewpoint.[20] His return to the editorial board of *Kommunist* in August 1959 complemented signs of rising tension in the hierarchy (to be discussed below). The collaboration of these diverse personalities evidently followed an agreement of party leaders about the tolerable limits of subtext propaganda in the central press in behalf of the kolkhoz federation. The passage most favorable to the scheme read:

Under present-day conditions an ever-greater number of new forms and methods of work are developing. These forms meet the requirements of the new period. There is consistent execution of the party's course toward a more flexible and total use of objective laws

[18] *Ibid.*, pp. 3-21.

[19] In a 1960 review of booklets on new civic bodies, Pchelin regretted the authors' neglect of "the growth of public self-expression in the management of kolkhoz affairs" (*Kommunist*, No. 16, 1960, pp. 120-121).

[20] Sakov, as noted, wrote the *Kommunist* article of June 1957 against workers' self-rule. He was chosen to praise the virtues of heavy industry in *Kommunist*, No. 12 (August), 1961, at a time of high-level argument on the question of resource allocation. His article on political economy in *Politicheskoye Samoobrazovaniye*, No. 9, 1962, ignores the errors of Stalin and so is greatly at variance with similar pieces in other Soviet journals of the day.

and precepts of socialism in all fields of public life and toward the *maximum development of the masses' self-expression in the building of communism.* . . .

The period of the full-scale building of communism is characterized by a new level, a new quality of leadership by the party in literally all fields of our economic life. In the stage of inadequate development of social production, when we felt an acute need for both material resources and skilled personnel, the direct intervention of the leading organs of the party into all details of the operative management of the economy was at times inevitable. "Earlier," N. S. Khrushchev has noted, "in our country there predominated the management of industry and agriculture by means of injunction." Under present-day conditions such interference, *petty tutelage, and regulation of economic life are superfluous and can even retard the movement forward.* The decisive intervention of party organizations is needed where it is essential to clear a path for all that is advanced and progressive, where the elements of conservatism and inertness are still strong and the new is having difficulty in smashing through the bureaucratic obstructions. Communists cannot remain mere observers of such phenomena in either small or big matters (italics added).

Khrushchev personally entered the kolkhoz-union debate in early December. The newspaper *Izvestiya*, edited by his son-in-law, reported on December 11, 1959, that the party leader had spoken with a kolkhoz chairman while stopping over in L'vov enroute to Moscow from the Hungarian party Congress. "Nikita Sergeyevich noted," the report states, "that he had familiarized himself with the memorandum of the first secretary of the C.P. Ukraine Central Committee, N. V. Podgornyy, on interkolkhoz unions and remarked that this question merited study and discussion." Podgornyy's speech at the forthcoming Central Committee session leaves no doubt that his memorandum described the district unions in glowing terms and recommended the establishment of a USSR kolkhoz federation. Khrushchev's approval of Podgornyy's viewpoint is indicated by the phrase "this question merited study and discussion." In December 1957 he had said of his own proposal to sell heavy machines to kolkhozes: "This question merits attention," and he did the same a year later with respect to interkolkhoz repair shops. The bureaucratic elite was thereby notified of Khruschev's opinion in a manner calculated to safeguard his personal prestige should unsurmountable opposition arise.

The pre-Plenum arrangements were rounded out by the circulation of materials favorable to the cultivation of new lands. An open letter to the Kazakhstan leadership (Belyayev) offering congratulations for agricultural successes in the past year was run in *Pravda* on December 19, 1959, above the signature of the CPSU Central Committee. This letter evidently was drafted in the Committee's Secretariat, perhaps by Kirichenko, Khrushchev's alter ego. The first secretary-premier must have approved of the letter in view of the many channels of information about agricultural performance which were open to him (including the Central Committee Section Chief for Agriculture in the Union Republics, the USSR Ministry of Agriculture, and his personal secretary—the agronomist Shevchenko). Another note of jubilation was struck in the lead article of the issue of *Kommunist* approved for printing on December 18, 1959. There had been a "good" harvest of grain in the country at large despite unfavorable weather conditions in a number of regions.[21] N. Anisimov's article in the same issue, "Assimilation of Virgin Lands Is a Big Reserve for Greater Output of Agricultural Products,"[22] acclaimed the fiscal soundness of the new lands venture over the past five years (state profits of 103.7 million rubles), alleged that in 1959 farms on the new lands "achieved fresh successes in raising the economic efficiency of production," and advocated the exploitation of virgin soil tracts in Eastern Siberia.

Khrushchev might not have phrased so cautiously his June 1959 proposal to increase the cultivated area were it not for reservations on the matter among some of his colleagues. The wish to isolate such vacillators evidently prompted renewed criticism of the agrotechnical conservatism of Malenkov and Molotov on the eve of the December 1959 Plenum. The effort of Anisimov was notably defensive: "The assimilation of virgin and fallow lands under conditions of a planned and socialist economy is one of the forms of intensification of agricultural production. The anti-party group, which opposed the party's line, asserted that this measure is a mere expansion of plowland, an extensive means of developing the economy." A more aggressive posture was assumed by the authors of an article in *Kazakhstanskaya Pravda* of December 18, 1959, which heavily criticized the 11-month-old locally published brochure, *Struggle of the Party Organization of Kazakhstan for Assimilation of Virgin Lands*. The pamphleteer was implicitly charged with failure to acknowledge Khrushchev's distinctive contribution

[21] No. 18, 1959, p. 5.
[22] *Ibid.*, pp. 10-19.

to agriculture's recovery in the post-Stalin period and displaying lack of enthusiasm about the loosening of state controls over the farms. Most unfortunately, he had ignored "the secret and open opponents of the virgin lands project."[23]

DANGER SIGNS

While the Khrushchev group strenuously agitated for adoption of its proposals, there were indications of indecision and acrimony in the leadership. The curious absence of forthright propaganda for kolkhoz unions in the central press just prior to the December Plenum has been mentioned and is explicable in terms of a censorship agreement made in the party Presidium upon the insistence of authoritarian centralists. Still another token of hesitation was the failure to execute the directive of the February 1958 Central Committee Plenum and convene the Third All-Union Congress of Collective Farmers. Had this meeting occurred, the integrity of the kolkhoz form might have been ensured and the number of sovkhozes not have increased in 1959 by as many as 492, some of these having been organized on the basis of weak kolkhozes.[24]

[23] I. Shamshatov, the criticized pamphleteer, was enrolled at the Institute of Party History in Alma-Ata. The Institute had assigned him the theme for his dissertation and recommended that the work be published. According to the review, Shamshatov dated to 1929 the policy of utilizing virgin soil and so confused two different historical periods, viz., the beginning of collectivization (Stalinist) and the present "new stage" (Khrushchevian). Also, the charge ran, "To show the exclusively important role of party measures in developing agriculture, the author takes the reader back to 1947." Shamshatov had mentioned only casually the "historic" September 1953 Central Committee Plenum and "even then he gives a low evaluation of its importance."

[24] *Narodnoye Khozyaystvo SSSR v 1959 Godu* (USSR National Economy in 1959), Moscow, 1960, p. 307. This source gives the

Most important was the latest series of personnel changes. Kirichenko, along with Khrushchev's other dependents, Aristov and Churayev, supervised a plenary session of the Moscow Regional Party Committee held on March 2, 1959, which relieved I. V. Kapitonov of his duties as first secretary and member of the Regional Committee's Bureau. N. F. Ignatov, chairman of the Regional Soviet Executive Committee, was also released from the party Committee's Bureau and later removed from his government post.[25] Both victims of the purge were soon charged with moral turpitude and professional incompetence:

> Serious mistakes in work were permitted by Comrade Kapitonov, former first secretary of the Moscow Regional Soviet Executive Committee. The incorrect, unparty relations which had arisen between them took up much time, to the detriment of business, and could not but influence the level of leadership of industry and agriculture in the province. They did not raise questions sharply, in a principled and party-like manner, and did not display the necessary demandingness toward personnel in the matter of implementing tasks in economic and cultural construction which were assigned by the party. As a result of this, the reserves of kolkhozes and sovkhozes were far from completely used, particularly reserves for a further rise in animal husbandry; and socialist pledges assumed by several

---

number of all types of sovkhozes at the end of 1958 as 6,002 and the number at the end of 1959 as 6,496. The number of all types of kolkhozes at the end of 1958 was 69,100 and at the end of 1959 was 54,600. The respective figures for purely agricultural kolkhozes are 67,700 and 53,400.

[25] *Pravda*, March 3, 1959.

170

districts, kolkhozes, and sovkhozes were not fulfilled. . . .

[The party] rids itself of those who do not cope
with assigned tasks, lag behind life, and do not justify
the trust shown them by party organizations.[26]

Notwithstanding this denigration, *Pravda* announced on
September 23, 1959, that Kapitonov had been installed as
first secretary of the Ivanovo Regional Party Commit-
tee. The fortunes of Kapitonov's "unparty" confederate,
N. F. Ignatov, hinged on the outcome of the impending
Central Committee meeting.

The surprising rehabilitation of Kapitonov was followed
by a spasm in the Latvian body politic. Kalnberzins, candidate member of the CPSU Central Committee Presidium, in November was dismissed as first secretary, C.P.
Latvia, and awarded the sinecure of chairman of the Presidium of the Latvian SSR Supreme Soviet.[27] This action
was the culmination of a political scandal which had
broken out in Latvia a few months earlier. Ye. K. Berklav
was deprived of the regional premiership in July 1959
and taxed with the heresy of demanding rejection of enlarging railroad-car building and diesel building plants,
and favoring an increase of capital investments in the
light and food industries.[28] The affair did not end there.

[26] *Partiynaya Zhizn'*, No. 8, 1959, pp. 9ff. A Reuters dispatch
of March 10, 1959, reports a Moscow rumor to the effect that
Kapitonov and N. F. Ignatov were involved in a movement at
the 21st Congress to halt the criticism of Malenkov and Molotov.
Some credence might be lent to this by Kapitonov's speech of
February 20, 1959, at an RSFSR Supreme Soviet electoral rally.
He noted that the 21st Congress marked the "full and final" con-
demnation of the Malenkov-Molotov group (*Sovetskaya Rossiya*,
February 21, 1959).

[27] *Sovetskaya Latviya*, November 26 and 28, 1959.

[28] Cf. *ibid.*, July 16, 1959; and V. Latsis (Berklav's successor)
in *Partiynaya Zhizn'*, No. 16, 1959, pp. 15ff.

In October 1959, one Ya. Bumber, corresponding member of the Latvian Academy of Sciences, resumed the attack on "Right opportunism" in an article which asserted that the party had conducted "and is conducting" an uncompromising struggle against efforts to overturn the conventional pattern of resource allocation.[29] While Bumber restricted himself to the question of industrial growth rates, his usage of the pejorative term "Right opportunist" is not likely to have set well with Kalnberzins. It will be recalled that during the public discussion of the MTS change he had taunted its "Leftist" critics. Kalnberzins had also initiated a local press discussion of the RTS outlook shortly after Khrushchev's May 1959 proposal to deprive RTS of their sales functions. Kalnberzins' successor was A. Ya. Pel'she, an Old Bolshevik, who had served in the Soviet secret police from 1920 to 1940 and held a diploma from the Institute of Red Professors. This authoritarian career background is reflected in Pel'she's speech at the November 1959 meeting of the Latvian C.P. Central Committee. Pel'she demanded an intensified mental drill of student youth, emphasizing that "peaceful co-existence" signified a battle of rival ideologies and that "every day" the imperialist states made more persistent attempts to carry this battle into Soviet territory.[30] This vigilance theme is recurrent in the public papers of Suslov, which also underscore the importance of maintaining the capital goods bias in national economy plans. Suslov evidently conducted the intrigue which led to the demise of Kalnberzins.

THE COCKPIT

The December 1959 Central Committee Plenum began

[29] *Sovetskaya Latviya*, October 2, 1959.
[30] *Ibid.*, November 26, 1959.

and proceeded under a cloud of uncertainty. A year before, Khrushchev opened the agricultural plenary with a comprehensive report, indirectly proposing a number of measures (which his retainer Belyayev overconfidently associated with the party leader's name), and a draft resolution was speedily made available to the participants, who were encouraged to submit comments. Now Khrushchev spoke last and his remarks were in the nature of a personal speech, not a report—which evidently is compiled jointly in the party Presidium; a draft resolution was not circulated until the last moment. The entire course of events at the meeting suggests that these procedural variations were expressive of a total deadlock in the party Presidium on the questions of the kolkhoz federation, terms of trade for agriculture, and the expediency of cultivating virgin soil in remote areas. The Central Committee, or a section of it, was expected to resolve these disputes.

Polyanskiy, candidate member of the party Presidium and Russian federation premier, had backed the inter-kolkhoz associations earlier in the year.[31] At the opening session of the December 1959 Plenum, he advanced the kolkhoz federation proposal under the watchwords of Khrushchev's "new period"—viz., "democratization" (decentralization) and "creative initiative" (permitting operational decision-making at lower levels):

The tasks of the further upturn of agriculture demand a certain change in the operational forms of leadership of kolkhozes in favor of further democratization. Many kolkhoz leaders and local party and soviet officials are expressing opinions about the expediency of creating kolkhoz agencies or unions—district, region, and

[31] *Kommunist*, No. 3, 1959, p. 35.

republic—elected at conferences of kolkhoz representatives. It is presumed that under this arrangement the
agencies will assume functions of operative management of kolkhozes, strengthening of interkolkhoz ties,
and organization of joint projects, will solve questions
of material-technical supply of kolkhozes, and will give
aid to economically weak kolkhozes. They will create
cash-and-kind kolkhoz funds. This will permit them to
organize the joint construction of enterprises for proc-
essing agricultural products, new schools, hospitals,
homes for the aged, and kolkhoz sanitoriums, to examine and resolve the question of pensions, and to implement several other measures. Without doubt, the new
system of kolkhoz leadership will permit an intensification of creative initiative on the part of kolkhozniks.

If there is a positive decision of this question, it will
be necessary to reorganize the work of the Ministry of
Agriculture and its agencies and to reduce them sub-
stantially.

All this can only be of advantage. . . .[32]
Polyanskiy was seconded by Podgornyy, party Presidium
candidate member and first secretary, C.P. Ukraine, and
Belyayev, party Presidium member and first secretary,
C.P. Kazakhstan, who both addressed the opening session
of the plenary session, and by A. I. Kirilenko, party
Presidium candidate member and first secretary of the
Sverdlovsk Regional Party Committee, who spoke on
the second day of the four-day meeting.[33] Podgornyy

[32] *Plenum Tsentral'nogo Komiteta Kommunisticheskoy Partii
Sovetskogo Soyuza, 22-25 dekabrya 1959 goda, stenograficheskiy
otchët* (Plenum of the Central Committee of the Communist Party
of the Soviet Union, December 22-25, 1959, Minutes), Moscow
1960, pp. 32-33 (source cited hereafter as *Plenum II*).
[33] *Ibid.*, pp. 61, 87, and 189.

and Kirilenko were associates of Khrushchev in the Ukraine and, as the party leader would intimate at this plenary session, Belyayev was his personal friend. None of the three is apt to have spoken for the kolkhoz federation without Khrushchev's approval. That Polyanskiy, Podgornyy, and Belyayev also repeated Khrushchev's demand that RTS be divested of trading functions further suggests that they were acting according to the requirements of group discipline.

The drive for a kolkhoz federation abruptly halted on the second day of the meeting. V. P. Mzhavanadze, party Presidium candidate member and first secretary, C.P. Georgia, on the third day tacitly rebuked Khrushchev's group for its anti-RTS inclination and implied that here it was seeking to revise agricultural terms of trade in a manner detrimental to industrial interests: "In solving the problems concerning the fate of RTS, concerning the organization of repairs and the sale of equipment to the kolkhozes, and concerning prices for spare parts and chemical fertilizers, we must proceed from state interests and from interest in developing our industry and agriculture. Premature conclusions and decisions can cause only harm to our general cause."[34]

That evening, a commission of 90 persons was formed to draft a resolution. This increase of 21 over the number of individuals appointed to the "editorial" commission of the December 1958 Plenum is explicable in terms of Lenin's directive for the management of inner-party conflict: ". . . V. I. Lenin stressed *the need to safeguard the unity of the party, create a stable Central Committee, able to avert a division of the party*. With this in mind, V. I. Lenin proposed foremost to increase the number of

[34] *Ibid.*, pp. 229-230.

175

Central Committee members so as to raise its authority, improve the work of the apparatus and 'prevent the conflicts of small parts of the Central Committee from assuming undue importance for the destinies of the party.' "[35] Khrushchev was named chairman of the commission, as in 1958, but no longer would the stenographic record list the names of other Presidium members and candidate members before those of the other commissioners. In strictly alphabetical order are the names (after Chairman Khrushchev's) of 21 party Presidium members and candidate members, 14 Union-republic party first secretaries (including 4 party Presidium members and candidate members), 15 identifiable regional party secretaries, and a number of central party and state functionaries and agricultural workers.[36] Once more, the lion's share of representation went to senior figures of the party bureaucracy.

Only if that bureaucracy is regarded as nonhomogeneous in the ideological sense can one understand the eccentric behavior of USSR Minister of Agriculture Matskevich, who spoke toward the close of overt debate at the session. Obviously with the full approval of party leaders at the highest level, Matskevich directly challenged the viewpoint of one party Presidium member and three Presidium candidate members on the question of kolkhoz unions. His main caveat was that adoption of the proposal would impede the process of unifying kolkhozes and sovkhozes. Indeed, Matskevich even advocated the merger of economically weak kolkhozes with strong kolkhozes and sovkhozes. This, of course, was sharply at odds with the viewpoint which Khrushchev had ex-

[35] Ponomarëv *et al.*, *op. cit.*, p. 362.
[36] *Plenum II*, pp. 312-313.

pressed at the 21st party Congress and subsequent admonitions in propaganda media. Matskevich further demonstrated his newly won independence and authoritarian tendencies by requesting that coordination of the activities of district kolkhoz unions be entrusted to councils under the Regional Agricultural Administrations. He conceded that in some districts it was appropriate to sell RTS to interkolkhoz associations but in general thought it necessary to strengthen their repair bases, and he kept silent about Khrushchev's proposal to free RTS of commercial duties. These opinions were stated initially in a ministerial note on agricultural administration which was written on instruction of the Central Committee (Presidium or Secretariat) and circulated among Committee members.[37]

When public debate closed on the morning of December 25, Kozlov, the presiding officer, announced a recess until 4 P.M. and requested the 90 commissioners to remain in the hall.[38] That evening, Suslov, acting as presiding officer, gave the floor to Khrushchev.[39] The party leader had not a word to say about the commission, but its deliberations had fundamentally altered his outward position. Polyanskiy, Podgornyy, Belyayev, and Kirilenko were left in the lurch as Khrushchev suddenly agreed with his ministerial foes that the Kolkhoz Center should not be created; interkolkhoz organizations should be restricted to the district level; and only certain RTS ought to be

[37] *Pravda*, December 26, 1959.
[38] *Plenum II*, p. 375. The previous sessions were chaired by Khrushchev, Brezhnev, Ignatov, Furtseva, and Mukhitdinov, all Central Committee secretaries. The presiding officers in December 1958 were Suslov, Aristov, Ignatov, and Brezhnev, all Committee secretaries.
[39] *Ibid.*, p. 376. Khrushchev's speech is in *Pravda*, December 29, 1959.

converted into interkolkhoz repair shops. Moreover, Khrushchev entirely dropped his recommendation to free RTS of their trading operations. Belyayev would probably have settled for that, since Khrushchev next pounced on him for allegedly concealing flagrant mismanagement practices in Kazakhstan. Khrushchev in effect damned as fraudulent the pre-Plenum encomiums to Kazakhstan in *Pravda* and *Kommunist*. He cited Ministry of Agriculture data to the effect that when the harvest was gathered in Kazakhstan, 32,000 combines and 11,000 reapers were idle because of stoppages and a shortage of operators. Over 1.6 million hectares of grain was unreaped when the first, premature snow arrived and the harvesting which was resumed afterward proved useless. Khrushchev admitted that he himself was "exaggerating the situation somewhat," but claimed that this was proper and gave this contrived explanation: "Friendship is friendship, but work is work. The people say, 'You are my brother, but truth is my mother.' If we do not tell he truth here at the Plenum to you, Comrades Belyayev and Kunayev, then they will not tell it to you in Kazakhstan; they will applaud you. You will say that there was a Central Comittee Plenum and everything went well. In reality, things are bad, very bad." The preceding speeches of Belyayev and D. A. Kunayev, the Kazakhstan premier, suggest that Khrushchev in actuality was performing the embarrassing ritual of self-criticism. Both regional leaders had seen fit to admit that Kazakhstan had fallen short of its grain target by 94 million poods.[40] Some top leaders, however, were determined not to let the matter rest there, and insisted that the Khrushchev group atone for its latest feat of "window-dressing."

[40] Cf. *Plenum II*, pp. 71 and 206.

After Khrushchev had bathed himself in the purifying waters of Bolshevik self-criticism, the meeting's draft decree was circulated. G. A. Denisov, Central Committee Section Chief for Agriculture in the Union Republics, reported on the draft and it was adopted by acclamation.[41] The decree assigned the party Presidium the task of studying and reviewing the questions of interkolkhoz associations and reform of the Ministries of Agriculture. It was mute about the future of RTS, sharply criticized the leaders of Kazakhstan for being remiss, and skirted the issue of virgin soil potential in Eastern Siberia. The proposal of Matskevich to merge economically weak kolkhozes with nearby sovkhozes was not, however, authorized.[42] The standoff was pointedly summarized in Khrushchev's remarks on the December Plenum at the agricultural conference of East European Communist parties in February 1960: "I must tell you that when we prepared for this plenary session, our agricultural agencies—the Central Committee Agricultural Sections for the Union-Republics and RSFSR and Ministry of Agriculture—worked out fairly broad proposals for the development of all branches of agriculture in the Soviet Union. We rejected these proposals."[43]

FACTIONAL LOSSES AND GAINS

The December 1959 Central Committee session turned out quite differently than its managers had intended. The "conservative" administrative and agrotechnical policies which had been under preliminary fire were ultimately victorious. There would not be terms of trade more ad-

[41] *Ibid.*, pp. 421-422. Denisov's report is unpublished.
[42] *Pravda*, December 27, 1959.
[43] *S.K. v SSSR i R.S.Kh.*, IV, 109.

vantageous to agriculture, nor a kolkhoz federation, nor a new surge of "extensive" cultivation. The Plenum's managers were Khrushchev and Kirichenko. Just as they had sought to discredit their ministerial opponents on grounds of moral turpitude, so were they themselves discredited for "window-dressing" the situation in Kazakhstan. That faulty exercise was apparently designed to sustain the reputation of Belyayev and obscure the difficulties of farming in the borderlands. While Khrushchev's own position as chief executive was secure, he had no choice other than to deal with Kirichenko and Belyayev in the manner often employed when a Soviet boss's authority is undermined but his patronage still strong: transfer to another post. Kirichenko left Moscow to become first secretary of the Rostov Regional Party Committee.[44] Belyayev was released from the party leadership of Kazakhstan and compensated with the party first secretaryship of Stavropol' Territory.[45] Khrushchev's continued intimacy with Belyayev was demonstrated when the latter was awarded a medal for "outstanding services to the state."[46]

Other personnel shifts indicated that territorial jobs were still distributed on the basis of negotiation in the party Presidium rather than secretarial fiat. Just after Kirichenko was demoted, N. F. Ignatov, whose dismissal he had policed in March and who later was condemned for having engaged in "unparty" dealings, was appointed first secretary of the Orël Regional Party Committee.[47]

[44] *Ibid.*, January 13, 1960. Aristov supervised the investiture.
[45] Cf. *Kazakhstanskaya Pravda*, January 21, 1960 (Brezhnev supervising); and *Pravda*, January 29, 1960 (Pospelov supervising).
[46] *Pravda*, January 17, 1960.
[47] *Sovetskaya Rossiya*, January 14, 1960 (M. T. Yefremov, Party Organs Section Chief for the RSFSR, attended the meeting that restored Ignatov to power).

Although not a member of the Central Committee Secretariat, Kozlov was now sufficiently influential to nominate candidates for important office. Belyayev's replacement as first secretary in Kazakhstan was Kunayev, a native of the region, and as such probably no more powerful than the new Great Russian second secretary. Kunayev indeed paid homage to this figure, N. N. Rodionov, whose professional training and career background linked him with Kozlov. At the party meeting which formally empowered them to rule the area, Kunayev spoke of Rodionov as "an experienced party official, a metallurgical engineer, a pupil of the Leningrad party organization which is strong in its revolutionary traditions, a former member of the Bureau of the Leningrad Regional Party Committee, and former first secretary of the Leningrad City Party Committee."[48] Kunayev himself was a graduate of the Moscow Institute of Non-Ferrous Metals and a mining engineer. One of the first official acts of the new regime in Kazakhstan was to lift out of obscurity Malenkov's former henchman, A. I. Kozlov, and appoint him republic minister of state farms.[49] Kunayev later expressed disagreement with Khrushchev's notorious preference for administrative compactness in the localities.[50] Khrushchev would eventually personally criticize Kunayev for his handling of agriculture in Kazakhstan and degrade both him and Rodionov.

The fortunes of Suslov also rose after the inconclusive business of the December 1959 Plenum. On the symbolic level, he was advanced to "eminent party figure" in a conventional listing of wartime political heroes which had previously included only Khrushchev and Voroshilov

[48] *Kazakhstanskaya Pravda*, January 22, 1960.
[49] *Ibid.*, January 26, 1960.
[50] See *S.K. v SSSR i R.S.Kh.*, iv, 168-169.

among the current members of the party Presidium.[51] Organizationally, Suslov became directly involved in agricultural operations, albeit as technically ill-equipped as members of the "anti-party group" who were sometimes criticized for their impertinent meddling in farm affairs. Suslov in March 1960 interviewed the participants of a seminar conference of the heads of agricultural sections of regional party committees held in Moscow.[52]

The diminution of Khrushchev's political capital as a result of the fiasco at the December 1959 Plenum was best expressed in the unveiling of a hitherto unpublished quotation from Lenin's papers. The acknowledged leader of the party asked the diplomat Joffe to keep in mind that his preeminence did not ensure against setback on "really important questions": "You are mistaken when you repeat constantly that I am the Central Committee. Such a thing can be written only by someone who is under great nervous strain and is overworked. The old Central Committee (1919-1920) defeated me on one of the really important questions, as you know from the discussion. There were a number of instances when I was in the minority on questions relating to organizational and personal affairs. You yourself, when you were a member of the Central Committee, saw examples of that many times. Why be so nervous as to write such a *totally impossible, totally impossible* [*sic*] phrase as one which holds that I am the Central Committee? This is a sign of overwork."[53] Lenin's record of accomplishment, however,

---

[51] Cf. *Partiynaya Zhizn'*, No. 4, 1960; and Ponomarëv *et al.*, *op. cit.*, p. 526.

[52] *Pravda*, March 17, 1960.

[53] *Kommunist*, No. 1 (January 11), 1960, pp. 33-34. It is noteworthy that Khrushchev's title was rendered as *first*, rather than *First*, secretary in *ibid.*, No. 2, 1960, pp. 55ff.

immeasurably surpassed that of Khrushchev, for whom the time factor was habitually a matter of primary importance. Whether he would make his mark as a great ruler in the tradition of Lenin and Stalin or go down as a mere transitional figure depended upon his ability to achieve rapid victories of policy and organization. Viewed from that perspective, the events of late 1959 constituted a thwarting of Khrushchev's deepest ambition.

CHAPTER V

NEO-STALINISM
IN THE FOREGROUND
(1960-1961)

As THE result of conflict over the entire trend of internal and foreign policy, a landmark in the politics of the post-Stalin era was reached on May 4, 1960. A Central Committee plenary session formally overturned the organizational arrangements of December 1957 which had ensured Khrushchev's domination of the party Secretariat, the most important administrative body of the regime. Five individuals whose speeches and career records indicated personal loyalty to Khrushchev were released from the Secretariat. A sixth would shortly leave it and be formally discharged at the July 1960 Central Committee session. The beneficiaries of these changes were the "conservatives" Kozlov and Suslov, who had been isolated in the maneuvering of December 1957. Kozlov at last entered the Secretariat and with Suslov confronted in that organ the weakened reform group of Khrushchev. Other personnel shifts in the party Presidium and territorial apparatus further demonstrated Khrushchev's vulnerability at the time.

The agropolitical developments which followed the great reorganization of May 1960 indicate that it had rendered indistinct the lines of authority between the Presidium and Secretariat. Administrative initiatives of a regressive character which had serious implications for basic policy were now mounted, evidently in the

Secretariat. Khrushchev's concept of the technically functional party bureaucracy was subverted. The USSR Minister of Agriculture was provided a tribune from which to demand greater executive rights for his agency. Ministries of state farms were created on the Union-republic level to guide the increasing number of sov-khozes, many formed on the basis of economically weak kolkhozes. The confiscatory spirit of Stalin's Three-Year Plan of Animal Husbandry was abroad in the form of large-scale transfers of cows from the private to the socialized sector. Moreover, a gesture of reconciliation was made to partisans of the grassland system. A befitting accompaniment to these events was the enlargement of Stalin's historical image.

Khrushchev in no sense condoned this backtracking and in the autumn of 1960 resorted to his familiar tactic of seeking a new consensus through appeal to the broader party forum. The propaganda groundwork was laid for an inner-party referendum on problems of agriculture; a relevant memorandum which Khrushchev submitted to the party Presidium filtered down to basic party units; various press articles urged the decentralization of farm management; and new rounds of bargaining commenced at party headquarters. As a consequence, Khrushchev made certain headway. Ministries of Agriculture were reduced to scientific-research foundations and their most vocal spokesman was posted to Kazakhstan. The local technicians were granted some voice in the ordering of farm machinery. Agricultural and consumer goods branches of the economy were allocated resources obtained from the overfulfillment of industrial plans in 1959 and 1960. Terms of trade for kolkhozes were improved and tax and credit conditions liberalized. Also, Khrushchev's basic principle of party functionalism was reasserted.

The neo-Stalinist onslaught was checked, but Khrushchev's victory was hardly clear-cut. In spite of his strong warning about the dire effect of neglecting the fiscal needs of agriculture, dissentient notes were audible in the speeches of Kozlov and Suslov, and the scale of national priorities remained weighted in the direction of capital goods. The new organ for distributing farm machinery was encumbered with bureaucratic obstacles which were not of Khrushchev's making and compromise candidates emerged in the latest reshuffle of senior personnel. The contending groups now prepared for tests of strength at a regular party Congress, and the nature of their latest quarrels over agrarian policy helps to explain why the question of "destalinization" would loom so large on the agenda of that gathering.

KHRUSHCHEV VERSUS THE MINISTRY

The first secretary in March-April 1960 tried to diminish the administrative power of Ministries of Agriculture, undermine the authority of USSR Minister of Agriculture Matskevich, and reduce his propaganda capability. The 3,500 RTS which the ministries controlled were deprived of their sales and supply functions.[1] Khrushchev had recommended this course of action in May and December 1959, but collective judgment was reserved. The sale of new equipment to kolkhozes and sovkhozes in the Russian Federation became a function

[1] The number of RTS on January 1, 1960, is given in *Narodnoye Khozyaystvo SSSR v 1959 Godu*, p. 307, which adds that RTS were being reorganized into machine repair shops (*masterskiye*); the Ukase of March 16, 1960, is in *Vedomosti Verkhovnogo Soveta SSSR* (Gazette of the USSR Supreme Soviet), March 24, 1960.

of two state trading agencies (RSFSR Main Administration for Vehicle and Tractor Supply and Sales, and RSFSR Administration for Agricultural Supply). By the end of May 1960, these were merged into an RSFSR Administration for Farm Machinery Trade under the RSFSR State Planning Committee.[2] None of these bureaucratic superstructures was to the liking of Khrushchev. Yet back in 1956 he had called for a supply system whereby machinery would be sent to MTS and sovkhozes exclusively on the order of junior-grade technicians.[3] At the end of 1960, Khrushchev was to propose the creation of a nation-wide supply association to solicit the advice of local consultants; about one year later, he questioned the need for any intermediary between farms and agricultural machinery plants.

Khrushchev wielded his influence to discredit the reputations of ministerial opponents and reduce their opinion-shaping potential. Matskevich and Benediktov's replacement as RSFSR Minister of Agriculture, S. V. Kal'chenko, were criticized in the newspaper *Trud* (Labor) on April 1, 1960, for their failure to attend the Fourth Congress of the Trade Union of Workers and Employees in Agriculture and Procurement. Matskevich in particular was attacked. Many delegates to the Congress were "quite surprised" by his absence, implying that he had become "detached from the masses," as the saying went about Khrushchev's rivals of an earlier day. Shortly thereafter, the newspaper *Sel'skoye Khozyaystvo* (Agriculture), published by the USSR Ministry of Agriculture and Central Council of the Trade Union of

[2] V. Mikhaylov, *Leninskoye Znamya*, May 26, 1960.
[3] See his Kazakhstan speech of July 28, 1956, in *S.K. v SSSR i R.S.Kh.*, II, 261.

Workers and Employees of Agriculture and Procurement, was "reorganized" and issued under the title of *Sel'skaya Zhizn'* (Rural Life) as an organ of the CPSU Central Committee.[4] The publishing changes redounded to the benefit of the Committee's Secretariat, which since June 1957 had been the coordinating center of bureaucratic activity. An enhanced role for the Secretariat in agricultural management had been portended by a seminar conference of the agricultural section chiefs of Union-republic party committees held in central party headquarters on March 10-16, 1960. The seminar resembled those of 1953-1954 insofar as the participants were lectured on agrotechnical as well as party organizational subjects.[5] In keeping with this secular trend, propagandists legitimated day-to-day party control over the economy. Some extolled Khrushchev's choice of an expanded Central Committee Secretariat, averring that this accorded with "the rise in the leading role of the party in the building of communism and the tasks of increasing the political and organizational role of central party bodies and collectivity in their work."[6] Others criticized "some revisionistic elements" and "certain comrades" who deplored Khrushchev's choice of a utilitarian yardstick to gauge the effectiveness of political

[4] *Pravda*, April 3, 1960. On April 16, 1960, *Pravda* reported that *Promyshlenno-Ekonomicheskaya Gazeta* (Industrial-Economic Newspaper), an organ of the State Scientific and Technical Committee of the USSR Council of Ministers, had been "reorganized" and as of May 1960 would be published as a newspaper of the Central Committee under the title *Ekonomicheskaya Gazeta* (Economics Newspaper).

[5] *Ibid.*, March 16 and 17, 1960.

[6] *Velikoye Torzhestvo Idey Leninizma* (Great Triumph of the Ideas of Leninism), Anthology of the CPSU Central Committee's Academy of Social Sciences, Moscow (signed for printing on March 29, 1960).

cadres and his notorious contempt of a generalist approach to full-time party work.[7]

Supplementing these conventional signs of friction in the leadership were incantations for party unity which cannot be wholly explained in terms of prophylaxis against Peiping's rising criticism of Khrushchev for seeking accommodation with the United States. The Old Bolshevik historian A. P. Kuchkin wrote in *Pravda* of April 20, 1960: "Lenin taught that the party must devote exceptional attention to its unity, which is based on the principles of Marxism, and guard this unity as the apple of its eye. The unity of the party is the decisive condition for the strength and invincibility of the dictatorship of the working class and Soviet system. It is ensured by discipline, which must be iron-clad and the same for those who are led and for the leaders. The unity of the party and its discipline are ensured by unswerving realization of the principle of collectivity in work." One S. L. Titarenko warned in a 500-word account of Khrushchev's struggle with Malenkov and Molotov: "One cannot but reckon with the possibility of the development of relapses into anti-party actions by certain elements, especially at moments of a sharp turn in course."[8] A "sharp turn in course" supposedly had occurred in world affairs in 1959, when Khrushchev paid a good-will visit to America.[9] The reviewers of the new biography *Vladimir Il'ich Lenin* also urged cohesion in the issue of *Party Life* approved for printing on May 3, 1960:

[7] Cf. N. Lomakin, *Partiynaya Zhizn'*, No. 7, April, 1960, pp. 12-13; and V. Kirsanov, *ibid.*, No. 8, April 1960, pp. 59-62.

[8] *Voprosy Istorii KPSS*, No. 3 (April 27), 1960.

[9] *Ibid.*, No. 2 (March 4), 1960.

One can trace V. I. Lenin's struggle for unity in the party ranks from striking and convincing examples. This makes it easier to comprehend the significance of the Leninist principle of party unity. It would be a serious mistake to think that party unity does not have the same important significance under present conditions as it did during the period of its struggle for power. On the contrary, when the Communist party had come to power, its ideological and organizational unity took on an exceptional significance: it ceased to be a matter only within the party and became a very important condition for the strength and firmness of the socialist state and for the victory of socialism and communism. Lenin taught that the complex and varied problems of building communism can be successfully solved provided there is complete unity, solidarity, and firm, conscious discipline in the party ranks. From this it becomes all the more clear that the decisive measures which the party took against the anti-party group of Malenkov, Kaganovich, Molotov, Bulganin, and Shepilov, who would have wrecked this principle of unity, were completely inevitable and absolutely necessary. Just as always, our party even in this instance acted in the Lenin manner.[10]

As Soviet commentators remarked about a speech in behalf of Western integration which Mr. Harold Macmillan made in 1961: "If the British prime minister appeals for unity in such dramatic tones, it would seem that such unity is lacking."[11]

[10] *Partiynaya Zhizn'*, No. 9, 1960, p. 23.
[11] V. Gantman and S. Mikoyan, *Kommunist*, No. 10, 1961, pp. 94-95.

ADVENT OF NEO-STALINISM

The substantive nature of a few of the recent heated exchanges in the party Presidium was revealed in Khrushchev's speech of May 5, 1960, at the USSR Supreme Soviet session.[12] "Some comrades" had presented challenging views on price and tax policy, investment priorities, and the advisability of protesting to Washington about an alleged U-2 overflight of April 9, 1960. Divergence over such matters and the U-2 incident of May 1 evidently was partly responsible for the great reorganization of the leadership which was decreed on May 4, 1960, at a plenary session of the party Central Committee.[13] The changes more than equalized the hitherto one-sided configuration of forces in the Committee's Secretariat. One-half of that body's members whose public statements and pattern of career development indicated loyalty to Khrushchev were released (Aristov, Ignatov, Furtseva, Pospelov and, retroactively, Kirichenko). Brezhnev, still another of Khrushchev's followers, was released from the Secretariat about this time in connection with appointment as chairman of the Presidium of the USSR Supreme Soviet and the formalities took place at the next Committee meeting in July.[14] This left as Khrushchev's associates in the Secretariat the non-Russian Mukhitdinov and 79-year-old Kuusinen, neither of whom could hope to command a following in the bureaucracies. The recruitment of Kozlov into the Secretariat was thus rendered all the more impressive. A Khrushchev-Kozlov-Suslov "troika" had

[12] *Pravda*, May 6, 1960.
[13] The plenary's "Information Bulletin" is in *ibid.*, May 5, 1960.
[14] *Ibid.*, July 17, 1960.

emerged as the interpreter of general policy and served as prototype of the collegial arrangement which Soviet diplomatists shortly proposed for the directorship of current affairs in the United Nations.

Annulment of the verdict of Khrushchev's victory Plenum in December 1957 entailed the removal of Belyayev and Kirichenko from the party Presidium. Both were soon deprived of the regional party jobs which their protector, the first secretary, had generously bestowed on them a few months before.[15] Kirichenko's successor was A. B. Basov, who would in doctrinaire fashion urge the curtailment of private activities in farming when Khrushchev opposed it.[16] In time, the Great Russian Basov had to make way for another Ukrainian.[17] Other supporters of Khrushchev, Podgornyy and Polyanskiy, were raised to full membership in the Presidium in May 1960. Podgornyy, however, remained at work in Kiev, where party officials were notified that "collegiality" was "the highest principle of party leadership."[18] The third candidate promoted to full membership in the Presidium was Kosygin. His sympathies for former colleagues in light industry was tempered by a relatively cautious approach to administrative forms and his increased influence helps to explain the semi-recentralization of industrial management in June 1960.[19]

[15] See *ibid.*, June 16 and 26, 1960.
[16] Cf. *Plenum Tsentral'nogo Komiteta Kommunisticheskoy Partii Sovetskogo Soyuza, 5-9 marta 1962 goda, stenograficheskiy otchët* (Plenum of the Central Committee of the Communist Party of the Soviet Union, March 5-9, 1962, Minutes), Moscow, 1962, p. 322 (source cited hereafter as *Plenum IV*); and *S.K. v SSSR i R.S.Kh.*, VII, 24.
[17] See Chapter VI.
[18] *Kommunist Ukrainy* (Communist of the Ukraine), No. 6 (June), 1960, p. 45.
[19] See Wolfgang Leonhard, *The Kremlin Since Stalin*, New York, 1962, p. 370.

Kozlov and Suslov used the Secretariat as a vantage point from which to strike at Khrushchev's utilitarian and conciliatory policies. The misguided "comrades" recently criticized for opposing a technological orientation in party work were now proved correct. The chiefs of Central Committee Agricultural Sections for the Union Republics and RSFSR were dismissed, and no one was reassigned to the task of prodding ministerial chair-warmers.[20] Party officials in agriculture and industry were instructed to divest themselves of narrowly productive interests.[21] Mass indoctrination and tracking down of ideological nonconformists became primary objects of party concern.[22]

The path was clear for Matskevich to repudiate

[20] G. A. Denisov, who was first identified as head of the C.C. Section for Agriculture in the Union Republics in August 1959, was named ambassador to Bulgaria (*ibid.*, May 25, 1960), and G. I. Vorob'yëv, identified as head of the Agricultural Section for the RSFSR of the CPSU Central Committee in April 1959, was appointed first secretary of the Krasnodar Territory Party Committee (*ibid.*, June 10, 1960).

[21] On agriculture, see *Partiynaya Zhizn'*, No. 13, 1960, pp. 6-7. An editorial devoted to the July 1960 Central Committee Plenum on industrial affairs instructed party officials: "It is necessary to eliminate decisively every case of replacement of managerial organizations and their leaders and petty interference in their work. Each person must do his own work" (*ibid.*, No. 14, 1960, p. 6).

[22] Cf. P. Sysoyev's attack on "anti-popular and decadent tendencies" in art, *Partiynaya Zhizn'*, No. 14, 1960, p. 30; "Better Satisfy the Ideological Demands of Communists and Non-Party People," *ibid.*, No. 16, 1960, pp. 4-7; L. Alekseyev, "We Are Enhancing the Role of the Press in the Communist Character Training of the Toilers," *ibid.*, No. 17, 1960, pp. 8-14; "Rear the New Man, the Man of Communism" (an editorial article devoted to the September 6-9, 1960, conference of ideological functionaries in central party headquarters), *ibid.*, No. 18, 1960, pp. 3-7; N. Gadzhiyev's reference to Suslov's criticism of nationalistic deviations in the cultural field, *ibid.*, No. 20, 1960, p. 12; and "Study Marxism-Leninism, Master the Communist World Outlook," *Kommunist*, No. 13, 1960, pp. 3-9.

Khrushchev's outlook on ministerial functions and reassert his own, which bore a close resemblance to that of Malenkov. Matskevich delivered the keynote address at an All-Union Conference of Agricultural Specialists held in Moscow from June 14 to June 17, 1960.[23] He pitted against Khrushchev's program to stimulate initiative in the localities an authoritarian centralist plan for managing agriculture. According to it, the boundaries of some districts would expand as the means of transportation and communication developed. Consequently, party and soviet agencies in the rural districts should have only skeleton staffs and the center of managerial gravity rest in the territorial capitals. Regional agricultural administrations would then be masters of the production process. They would be top-heavy bodies comprised of trusts for sovkhozes, RTS, supply, and the production and purchase of building materials, and last of all run an experimental station. Khrushchev since the mid-1950's had conceived of the Agricultural Ministries as first and foremost the propagandists of improved farming techniques.

Academician Lysenko too sensed a shift in the political winds and, as in 1947-1948, 1950, and 1954, he cast his lot with the leadership group which he considered to be ascendant. Now it happened to be the Kozlov-Suslov bloc. The academician began an inspection tour of the eastern regions in June 1960. Early in the following month, he spoke at a conference of agricultural officials in northern Kazakhstan. On August 5, *Pravda* devoted ten newspaper columns to Lysenko's speech, which attacked A. I. Barayev of the Institute of Agricultural Sciences of Kazakhstan for thinking that late sowing of grain in the

[23] The speech is in *Pravda*, June 15, 1960.

east was advisable. Lysenko was supported by a number of agronomists in the Kunayev-Rodionov organ *Kazakhstanskaya Pravda* on August 26, 1960. They also charged that Barayev was wrong in favoring the widespread use of cultivation without plowing. All this added up to criticism of Khrushchev's technical acolyte Mal'tsev, whose method of working the eastern soil had been denounced in scientific quarters on the eve of the abortive coup staged in the party Presidium three years before.[24] As will be seen, the Khrushchevites would soon respond vigorously to Lysenko's challenge on this "question of principle."

The doctrinaires were also determined to press forward with enserfment of the rural population through the massive conversions of kolkhozes into sovkhozes. Since the RSFSR Ministry of Agriculture handled local requests for such conversions in the largest of the republics, it had to be put in the charge of someone favorably disposed to a tightening of the screws. Kal'chenko was dislodged from the top of the Ministry and replaced by G. L. Smirnov, former deputy chief of the Agricultural Section in the Central Committee Bureau for RSFSR Affairs.[25] Smirnov would be ousted from his new post in about six months' time, when the practice of indiscriminate farm conversions was no longer in vogue.[26] Khrushchev in 1961-1962 was all for the substitution of sovkhozes for kolkhozes around the main cities and in

[24] Khrushchev acclaimed Mal'stev's system as one of international importance in a speech of July 28, 1956, in *S.K. v SSSR i R.S.Kh.*, II, 261. On the criticism of Mal'tsev's method in the *Journal of the Academy of Sciences* in 1957, see R. Conquest, *Power and Policy in the USSR: The Study of Soviet Dynastics*, New York, 1961, p. 238.

[25] *Pravda*, June 15, 1960.

[26] *Sovetskaya Rossiya*, January 27, 1961.

virgin land areas. But during 1960 the number of sovkhozes rose by almost 1,000 and the number of agricultural kolkhozes decreased by as many as 8,500.[27] The partisans of massive conversions alleged a complete lack of compulsion in the voting by some collective farmers to petition Moscow for the merger of their property and goods with those of a local sovkhoz.[28] The claim was obviously false, in view of the subsequent criticism of the many forcible instances of expropriation of cows in the peasants' supplementary allotments during 1960.[29]

The political importance of the kolkhoz-sovkhoz dispute occasioned the article by B. Ukraintsev which *Kommunist* ran "for purposes of discussion."[30] Ukraintsev, deputy chief editor of *Problems of Philosophy,* scholastically argued the viewpoint that the conversion of backward kolkhozes into sovkhozes would facilitate their economic upturn: "Communist public property opens ever-greater horizons to the further communalization of productive forces and such communalization will aid the uninterrupted improvement of public property, distribution, and the management of production

[27] At the close of 1960 there were 44,900 agricultural kolkhozes and 7,386 sovkhozes (*Narodnoye Khozyaystvo SSSR v 1961 Godu* [USSR National Economy in 1961], Moscow, 1962, p. 291; and *S.K. v SSSR i R.S.Kh.,* v, 344).

[28] See V. Velichko, *Sel'skaya Zhizn',* September 16, 17, and 18, 1960.

[29] See B. S. Ukraintsev, A. S. Koval'chuk, and V. P. Chertkov, *Dialektika Pererastaniya Sotsializma v Kommunism. Osobennosti Deystviya Osnovnykh Zakonov Dialektiki v Razvitii Sotsializma* (Dialectic of the Growing of Socialism into Communism. Peculiarities of Action of Basic Laws of the Dialectic in Development of Socialism), Moscow, 1963, p. 291. The reformist ideological functionary Ts. A. Stepanyan edited this book.

[30] "Problems of the Dialectic of the Growth of Socialism into Communism," No. 13 (September 10), 1960, pp. 61-73.

and all other affairs of society." Ukraintsev, furthermore, extolled the working class's unremitting "struggle" with the peasantry as a means toward "reeducation" of the latter. Still another reactionary measure directly attributable to the changed composition of the party Secretariat was the closing down of the magazine *Fertilizer and Yield*. That publication was once banned under Stalin and did not resume activity until 1956, when Khrushchev was generally in the ascendant.[31] As the "conservative" party leaders attacked on various sectors of the policy front, they invested the Stalin symbol with a new propriety. Stalin was now revered as one of the "pioneers of Russian Marxism."[32]

The Empiricist Response

Khrushchev's method of handling his alignment's differences with the Chinese Communists in 1960 over the strategy and tactics of the world Communist movement paralleled his approach to simultaneous quarrels with other Soviet leaders over domestic agricultural problems. In both cases, he affirmed his determination to uphold his personal opinions while offering to parley. Mao Tsetung and his lieutenants, who were merely identified as "people," were criticized for rejecting Khrushchev's article of faith about the noninevitability of world war, but allowance was made for "struggle of opinions" in the Communist movement as well as "creative deliberations, discussions, and arguments."[33] This, of course, was the prelude to Sino-Soviet bargaining at the November 1960

[31] See *Pravda*, September 12, 1963.

[32] V. Ivanov, *Kommunist*, No. 14, 1960, p. 97.

[33] Cf. A. Butenko and V. Pchelin, *Kommunist*, No. 12 (August 23), 1960, p. 11; and A. Bovin, *ibid.*, No. 14 (October 1), 1960, p. 47.

Conference of Representatives of the 81 Communist and Worker Parties. Internally, too, account was taken of political dissension at the highest level. A propagandist warned in an anthology of the CPSU Central Committee's Higher Party School, approved for printing on August 30, 1960:

> ... it would be profoundly erroneous to think that we are absolutely guaranteed against the appearance in our midst of certain groups and persons who are not in agreement with the party's line. In such a mass-type party as the CPSU there can be people who are insufficiently staunch in matters of principle, weakly tempered politically, and capable of displaying political instability. One may also find such people who approach questions of internal and foreign policy as sectarians and dogmatists and who uncritically interpret Marxism-Leninism.[34]

Ye. Bugayev, head of the Propaganda Sector of the Central Committee's Section for Propaganda and Agitation for the Union Republics, in a two-part article in the party study journal[35] alluded to mistaken conceptions of the party as a strictly educational agency, and the feasibility of massive conversion of kolkhozes into sovkhozes. But controversies might be resolved in party debate:

> Are freedom of opinion and freedom of discussion in matters of party policy necessary in the party? Of

[34] S. A. Smirnov in *O Nekotorykh Problemakh Stroitel'stva Kommunizma v Svete Resheniy XXI-ogo S"yezda KPSS* (On Some Problems of Building Communism in Light of the Decisions of the 21st CPSU Congress), Moscow, 1960.

[35] *Politicheskoye Samoobrazovaniye*, No. 9 (September), 1960, pp. 33-37, and No. 10 (October), 1960, pp. 43-50.

course they are. Lenin always fought for the development of independence and creative initiative among local party organizations and all Communists. Any large question put before the party demands discussion. The wider the circle of participants, the greater the chances that the discussion will be comprehensive and fruitful. In this way, various and often divergent points of view will inevitably be expressed. This is completely natural. The staunchest Leninists can variously judge different aspects of the problem under discussion on the strength of the differences in their degree of political preparation, knowledge, and experience.

The striking correlation of these pronouncements on inter- and inner-party relations constitutes one of the various scraps of purely circumstantial evidence which belie the notion of Khrushchev as unchallenged leader of Soviet policy. There is no reason to believe that the "groups and persons" in the CPSU who disagreed with Khrushchev and had to be overcome in discussion were of lesser station than the outside "people" (Mao) who contested his viewpoint on a series of policy issues which required settlement by negotiation within the ranks of world Communism.

The issue of the journal which carried Bugayev's advocacy of broad inner-party discussion was passed for the press on August 27, 1960. Shortly thereafter, on October 29, 1960, Khrushchev submitted a memorandum on agriculture to the party Presidium.[36] The document called attention to scarcities in meat and dairy products

[36] "Against Placidity, Complacence, and Conceit over the First Successes in the Development of Agriculture," *S.K. v SSSR i R.S.Kh.*, iv, 162-186.

and an insufficiency of fodder for livestock. It proclaimed in some alarm that "If the needed measures are not taken, we may revert to the situation which existed in 1953." A proposal was made to channel into agriculture the funds and resources accumulated from the overfulfillment of industrial plans, which it was estimated would total over 90 billion rubles by 1965. Secondly, Khrushchev implied that funds earmarked for other branches of the economy should be diverted into agriculture; he stated that it had been erroneous to reduce state investment in agriculture. While the memorandum refers only to the decline of inputs in sovkhozes to the 1956-1957 level, the economist Khlebnikov points out that in 1960 state and kolkhoz investments amounted to 5.2 billion rubles, or 15.3 per cent of total inputs in the national economy, which was the lowest ratio since 1953, when the figure was 13.7 per cent.[37] Khrushchev also gave the cue for renewed hazing of Matskevich. The minister was charged with erroneously advising the June conference of agricultural specialists that all sovkhoz divisions should be concentrated in a central farmstead and with failing to execute an assignment to present draft regulations on the structure of a sovkhoz.

But the party leader requested that decisions not be adopted until the Central Committee's next meeting on agriculture, which *Pravda* of October 29, 1960, announced would open on December 13. A defensive bit of rhetoric follows in Khrushchev's letter to his associates: "It may be asked: Then why do I write this memorandum?" He went on to explain that when he had left for the United States on September 10, 1960, to attend the 15th U.N. General Assembly session, he suggested to

[37] *Voprosy Ekonomiki*, No. 7, 1962, p. 50.

Presidium members that a conference be held in party headquarters to deal with preparations for the next Central Committee meeting. The solitary purpose of this conference as represented in Khrushchev's letter was exhortative: "Obviously, someone should administer a good shaking up for the defects in agricultural leadership in certain republics, territories, and regions. Then these questions must be handled specifically in the central committees of Union-republic parties and in councils of ministers." Kozlov evidently was chosen to prod the remiss local bosses; at a secret conference held in party headquarters at the end of October 1960 he criticized the Tadzhik party first secretary for obtaining small yields of green mass corn.[38] The predecisional conference was really intended to set the stage for an inner-party referendum on the meaningful subjects of the disposition of industry's fiscal and material surpluses, the raising of agricultural inputs, and the destiny of the Ministries of Agriculture. Such referendums are provided for by the party Rules, "if within the Central Committee of the Communist party of the Soviet Union there is not a sufficiently firm majority on the most important questions of party policy," or "if, in spite of the presence of a firm majority in the Central Committee which holds a definite viewpoint, the Central Committee nevertheless considers it essential to verify the correctness of its policy by means of discussion within the party." A party historian would amplify this point a short time later:

...V. I. Lenin never made decisions unilaterally, despite his high position and the enormous authority of a chief. He always convinced the majority of the

[38] T. Ul'dzhabayev, *Pravda*, January 15, 1961 (CDSP, XIII, 6, pp. 5-7).

Central Committee of the correctness of his opinion. V. I. Lenin fought for the execution of the charted line only when it had been approved by the Central Committee and had become a party decision. *But if he met with the insurmountable resistance of Central Committee members, he appealed to the masses and brought disputed questions to them for the purpose of discussion.* In the struggle for party unity, V. I. Lenin relied on the support of Communists and the working class (italics added).[39]

The party referendum was indirectly mentioned in the *Pravda* lead article of November 21, 1960, which told of meetings throughout the country that were discussing "pressing problems of agricultural production." Khrushchev's letter to the party Presidium formed the basis of these talks.[40] On the surface, the debate raged over agrotechnical and managerial policy. Khrushchev's personal secretary, the agronomist Shevchenko, in a series of articles in *Pravda*, November 17-19, 1960, stated that his recent tour of the eastern lands had convinced him that Lysenko's most recent prey in the scientific community, Barayev, was correct. Lysenko was not mentioned, but Ovechkin hastened to denigrate one of the

[39] A. M. Kopteva, *Iz Istorii Bor'by V. I. Lenina Za Edinstvo Partii* (From the History of V. I. Lenin's Struggle for Party Unity), Moscow, (July 11) 1961, p. 91.

[40] Cf. D. S. Polyanskiy, *Pravda*, January 12, 1961 (CDSP, xiii, 1, pp. 15-23); N. V. Podgornyy, *ibid.*, January 12, 1961 (CDSP, xiii, 2, pp. 3-9, 24); and I. R. Razzakov, Ya. N. Zarobyan, B. Ovezov, and F. S. Goryachev in *Plenum Tsentral'nogo Komiteta Kommunisticheskoy Partii Sovetskogo Soyuza, 10-18 yanvarya 1961 goda, stenograficheskiy otchët* (Plenum of the Central Committee of the Communist Party of the Soviet Union, January 10-18, 1961, Minutes), Moscow, 1961, pp. 218-219, 234, 256, and 318 (source cited hereafter as *Plenum III*).

academician's political cronies. Only a few weeks earlier, someone who had accompanied Lysenko on his inspection tour of the east reported on the latter's impression of the first secretary of the Omsk Regional Party Committee: "The academician saw in him a champion of everything new and advanced and a person with much knowledge about Siberia. During the conversation he approved with a word or gesture everything valuable and useful, and with examples from his experience he reaffirmed what Lysenko had spoken about so convincingly."[41] Ovechkin contradicted this appraisal in *Sel'skaya Zhizn'* on November 23-24, 1960. He declared that the fields in Omsk were choked with weeds and the farming leadership was stereotyped. Moreover, baseless rumors were circulated in Omsk that Mal'tsev's practices were harmful. Ovechkin forthrightly cited Khrushchev's support of Mal'tsev and cast doubt on the agrotechnical expertise of Matskevich and RSFSR Minister of Agriculture Smirnov. On the heels of this accusation came the familiar one of moral turpitude: directors of the USSR Ministry of Agriculture had connived in the persecution of on Old Bolshevik subordinate who was inconvenient to them.[42]

Matskevich's beleaguered cause was taken up by party Presidium candidate Mazurov, who had sided with the minister at the December 1958 Central Committee Plenum. Mazurov wrote in *Pravda* on December 11, 1960: "It is necessary to enhance the role of agricultural agencies of all levels. The duties of the USSR Ministry of Agriculture, republic ministries, Regional Agricultural Administrations, and district inspectorates

[41] N. Kosolapov, *Sel'skaya Zhizn'*, September 30, 1960.
[42] *Literaturnaya Gazeta*, November 29, 1960.

have to be stipulated more precisely. I think that the agricultural agencies have been wrongfully deprived of their long-standing functions of planning agricultural production, planning output and allocation of machinery and supplies."[43] In reply to Mazurov, a Siberian agronomist addressed an open letter to the party Central Committee which quaintly began: "Dear Nikita Sergeyevich! I wish to be frank and to talk with you as with a father in whom his children believe." The agronomist dismissed the June conference of farm bureaucrats as worthless, since it left unsettled the questions of the power invested in agronomists, a shift to a rational system of cultivation, and farm specialization. Khrushchev was implored to reestablish the more flexible managerial regime which had existed prior to the anomalous recentralization of 1958: "Make it so that life in the countryside is on the same happy upswing as in the years 1954-1957, following the September [1953] and January [1955] plenary sessions of the Party Central Committee. Inspire this living stream again."[44] Meanwhile, the Central Committee session which was scheduled to open on December 13, 1960, was postponed until sometime in January 1961.[45] There is reason to believe that the postponement was arranged about the third week in November, at the time of renewed attack on Matskevich.[46]

The nation-wide plenary session might have been

---

[43] The State Planning Committees evidently took up the planning of farm output in 1958 or 1959. See Khrushchev in *Pravda*, January 21, 1961 (CDSP, xiii, 7, pp. 3-10; xiii, 8, pp. 10-23).

[44] I. Osharov, *Sel'skaya Zhizn'*, December 20, 1960 (CDSP, xii, 51, pp. 24-25).

[45] *Pravda*, December 9, 1960.

[46] The Armenian party daily *Kommunist* on November 23, 1960, announced that the local Central Committee Plenum had been postponed from December 6 to January 1961.

delayed because party leaders were engrossed in the work of the three-week-long Conference of the 81 Communist and Worker Parties. But in view of Mazurov's article it is just as probable that the hesitation was a byproduct of unresolved differences in their midst. A stocktaking of the results of the inner-party debate on controversial aspects of Khrushchev's memorandum occurred at the party Presidium meeting held before the USSR Supreme Soviet session opened on December 20, 1960, and at subsequent conferences in party headquarters which examined the fate of the USSR Ministry of Agriculture and heard Khrushchev deliver several emotional speeches.[47] The outcome of these transactions was revealed in part on December 27 and 30, 1960. The USSR Council of Ministers met on December 24 under the chairmanship of Khrushchev, and the premier, along with other cabinet members, recommended that assets gained from the overfulfillment of industrial plans during the past two years be utilized in agriculture and light industry.[48] The acceptance of this proposal aided recipients to the tune of 11.3 billion rubles.[49] About a week later, Matskevich was dismissed as USSR Minister of Agriculture and replaced by M. A. Ol'shanskiy, an agricultural scientist, which foreshadowed the ministry's conversion to a scientific-research establishment, avowedly on the initiative of Khrushchev.[50] The basic instruments of

[47] The closed gatherings and Khrushchev's speeches are mentioned by Mzhavanadze and Ul'dzhabayev in *Plenum III*, pp. 149, 150, and 220.

[48] *Pravda*, December 27, 1960.

[49] A. Vishnyakov, *Politicheskoye Samoobrazovaniye*, No. 2, 1963, p. 30.

[50] *Pravda*, December 30, 1960, and Ovezov, *Plenum III*, p. 258. The decree reorganizing the Ministry is in *Pravda*, February 21, 1961 (CDSP, XIII, 8, pp. 3-6).

agricultural administration from January 1961 to March 1962 were subsequently identified as follows: "The party district committees and district soviet executive committees decide all problems of the operative leadership of agriculture and control the fulfillment of plans"; "All worries about the leadership of kolkhozes have lain chiefly on the shoulders of the party apparatus."[51]

In the party caucuses of December 1960, Khrushchev further secured a mandate to improve the terms of trade for agriculture and liberalize tax and credit conditions for kolkhozes. A party and government decree of early January 1961 reduced as of February 1, 1961, the prices of spare parts for tractors, motor vehicles, farm machinery, and gasoline; exempted from income tax before the end of the Seven-Year Plan 80 per cent of all taxable income from the sale of meat, livestock, poultry, eggs, milk, and dairy products; lowered long-term and short-term credit rates; and granted kolkhozes an extension of five years on their liabilities for state bank loans and of five to ten years on payments for the machinery, premises, and equipment of the former MTS which they had acquired.[52] The enactment of these measures was expected to reduce kolkhoz and kolkhozniks' expenses by about 887 million rubles annually.[53]

Khrushchev was less successful in his effort to decentralize the system of supplying farms with machinery and chemical fertilizer. Contrary to the hopes which he had expressed in 1956 and on the eve of the MTS

[51] F. D. Kulakov and L. Ya. Florent'yev, respectively, in *Plenum IV*, pp. 334 and 342-343.
[52] Pel'she, *Pravda*, January 14, 1961 (CDSP, XIII, 5, pp. 8-10).
[53] Khrushchev, *ibid.*, January 21, 1961 (CDSP, XIII, 7, pp. 3-10; XIII, 8, pp. 10-23).

change, equipment was still sent to the districts on the basis of lists drawn up centrally by the USSR Ministry of Agriculture or USSR State Planning Committee. These lists had failed to take into account the farms' actual needs and as a result some districts received equipment that they could not put to practical use while others were in need of the same items. Khrushchev thought that an All-Union Farm Machinery Association might receive supply requests from the farms and, in accordance with them, place orders with industry through the USSR State Planning Committee for the production of given types of equipment. The FMA might have a central board "operating on a democratic basis" with territorial representatives on its staff. The main administrative bodies would be in the provinces and supervise district branches composed of farm leaders which also would take charge of RTS.[54] This organizational structure is reminiscent of certain features of the kolkhoz federation plan, but the party and government decree of February 1961 which set up the new farm machinery agency endowed it with the bureaucratic trappings of a state committee of the USSR Council of Ministers.[55] P. S. Kuchumov, USSR Deputy Minister of Agriculture, 1954-1961, was named chairman of the committee. Khrushchev was not entirely responsible for bureaucratic perversion of the "association" idea. About a year later he would encourage giving thought to the problem of reducing excess overhead costs by having agricultural machinery plants accept orders di-

[54] See Section IX, "On the Work of Agricultural Agencies and the Development of Agricultural Science," in the "Theses" of Khrushchev's speech to the January 1961 CPSU Central Committee Plenum, *S.K. v SSSR i R.S.Kh.*, IV, 255ff.

[55] See *Pravda*, February 21, 1961 (CDSP, XIII, 8, p. 6).

rectly from client farms instead of through the planner intermediaries.[56] "Certain leading officials" of the USSR State Planning Committee who objected to FMA participation in distributing orders for agricultural machinery among industrial enterprises[57] apparently scored a few points with the help of Kosygin.

Most important, Khrushchev was rebuffed on the issue of agriculture's position on the scale of national priorities. In spite of his complaint about the relatively diminished financing of sovkhozes during the past few years, agricultural investment as a percentage of total investment was decreased in 1961 by 2 per cent when compared with the 1956 figure.[58] On the other hand, overt defense expenditures rose by 2.3 billion rubles and, for the first time since 1955, increased in proportion to total government spending.[59]

CONTINUED APPEAL TO THE PARTY

Khrushchev used the January 1961 Central Committee session on agriculture to shape a new consensus of elite opinion in behalf of greater inputs in agriculture and increased material incentives to peasants. The fight was waged against leaders who were relatively more austerity-minded and disturbed over the implications of Khrushchev's inchoate welfare program for industrial expansion and social values. The opposition was comprised of heavy engineering partisans who were caricatured as ridden with "fears of a growth of 'the bourgeois

[56] *Ibid.*, March 6, 1962.

[57] G. I. Volkov, deputy chairman of the USSR FMA, *Sovetskoye Gosudarstvo i Pravo*, No. 10, 1961, pp. 116-125.

[58] I. Buzdalov, *Voprosy Ekonomiki*, No. 1, 1963, p. 71.

[59] "Sovetskiy Voyennyy Byudzhet" (Soviet Military Budget), *Yezhednevnyi Informatsionnyi Byulleten'* (Daily Information Bulletin), Radio Liberty, Munich, No. 1627, October 30, 1963.

mentality'" and pejoratively labeled " 'theoreticians' who reckon that to focus attention on concern about people, their mode of life, and improvement of the supply of the population with goods is to display a 'consumptionist' and 'petty-bourgeois' approach to the building of communism."[60] Kozlov and Suslov led this austerity group in the hierarchy.

An outline version of the speech which Khrushchev intended to deliver at the Central Committee meeting was completed on January 5, 1961, and distributed to party organizations before the meeting opened five days later.[61] The outline included a polemic against "officials who think that agriculture now has such an abundance of machinery that it is possible to reduce the output of agricultural machines." These "officials" were instrumental in policy-making, since a number of agricultural machinery plants had recently been converted to other manufactures and the output of tractors in 15 h.p. units had dropped from 258,000 in 1957 to 252,000 in 1958 and stood at 236,000 in 1959; the number of new grain combines was 134,000 in 1957, 65,000 in 1958, and 53,000 in 1959. The presentation of these data would soon be construed as a plea to raise the state's agricultural investment.[62] Its circulation on the eve of the Central Committee session was to predetermine the mood and course of oratory in that forum. But the outline was not published at the time, as had been the case with some of

[60] See O. Yurovitskiy's defense of post-1953 welfare measures, in *Kommunist*, No. 12, 1960, p. 31; and the lead article in *ibid.*, No. 4, 1961, p. 4.

[61] The "Theses," entitled "Enhancing the Welfare of the People and Tasks of Further Increase of Production of Agricultural Products," is in *S.K. v SSSR i R.S.Kh.*, IV, 193-280.

[62] See Polyanskiy, *Pravda*, January 12, 1961 (CDSP, XIII, 1, pp. 15-23).

Khrushchev's proposals of 1957 and 1958 for various socio-economic changes. How then could a farm administrator write in *Izvestiya* of February 13, 1963: "Shortly before it [the January 1961 Central Committee Plenum], the Theses of the plenary speech of Nikita Sergeyevich Khrushchev were published in our press"? The possibility of an innocent lapse of memory can be excluded. There are no such inadvertencies when it comes to internal political procedure in Russia. It could only mean that Khrushchev had intended to publicize the outline of the speech but under the aforementioned censorship ruling had been frustrated by other party leaders (the "officials" indifferent to the technical needs of agriculture).

Khrushchev's difficulties with a segment of the party Presidium and desire to exalt the authority of the Central Committee at its expense account for the failure of the compilers of the public transcript of the January 1961 Plenum to have mentioned the Presidium as sponsor of the meeting's agenda, as was true of the verbatim accounts of the Committee's agricultural sessions of 1958 and 1959. The main protagonists in the struggle over investments are readily establishable by a comparative study of the contemporary pronouncements of Khrushchev, Kozlov and Suslov.

Khrushchev exhibited his will to raise appropriations for the technical outfitting of agriculture and create effective labor incentives for peasants on January 6, 1961, when he told over 1,300 affiliates of higher party institutes:

...I wish to say a few words about our iron and steel industry. The Seven-Year Plan is so drawn as to call for output of from 86,000,000 to 91,000,000 tons of steel in 1965. Last year we already had 65,000,000 tons. An increase of 6,000,000 tons is scheduled for 1961. This means we shall have 71,000,000 tons. If in the subsequent years of the Seven-Year Plan we get the same increase as in 1961, by the end of 1965 we could be producing 95,000,000 tons of steel. Or if in the future the steel output grows at the same rate as in the first three years of the Seven-Year Plan, it could reach from 100,000,000 to 102,000,000 tons in 1965.

Evidently, however, now we shall not pursue a policy of developing the iron and steel industry to the utmost. Evidently, we shall transfer part of the capital investments to agriculture and light industry. Communism cannot be built only by offering machines and ferrous and nonferrous metals. It is necessary for people to be able to eat well, dress well, and have housing and other material and cultural conditions.

This is not a revision of our general line but rather a sensible use of our material potentialities. When we were in an encirclement of enemies and our industry was weaker than industry in the capitalist countries, we economized on everything—even, as Lenin said, on schools. Now the situation is different: We have a powerful industry, and our armed forces have the most modern armament. Why should we deny a man what he can receive without detriment to the further development of our socialist state?[63]

On the other hand, Kozlov and Suslov praised the virtues of heavy engineering. Khrushchev long had

[63] *Pravda*, January 25, 1961 (CDSP, XIII, 3, p. 18). Cf. the report on Ovechkin's welfare propaganda in *New York Times*, January 15, 1961.

contended that the prospect of a steep rise in domestic living standards was a major irritant to foreign enemies. But Kozlov, speaking on November 6, 1960, in honor of the anniversary of the Revolution, turned the edge of this polemical sword, claiming that "The Americans are especially worried over the fact that the USSR is rapidly overtaking the United States in steel output. They have plenty of cause, we must say, for worry. In 1945 the production of steel in the Soviet Union stood at only 17 per cent of the level of American production, while in 1959 the amount of steel we turned out was 71 per cent of the volume of production in the US. And everyone knows that the volume of steel production is one of the basic indices of a country's might."[64] Suslov registered his distress at the thought of diminishing the country's industrial-military potential when he told local party officials: "The coming year will be one of further rapid development of all branches of the national economy, especially heavy metallurgy, machine-building, and electric power."[65]

The argument over resource allocation was carried into the Central Committee session of January 1961. Khrushchev ridiculed the "comrades" who had "developed an appetite for giving the country as much metal as possible." He offered a reminder to Kozlov: "It must always be kept in mind that the prosperity of the state is determined both by the supply of metal and by other indices—for instance, by the quantity of food products a man receives and consumes, by the extent to which all the requirements that go to make up a man's life are satisfied in general." Khrushchev moved a step beyond

[64] *Pravda*, November 7, 1960 (CDSP, xii, 45, pp. 9-13, 38).
[65] *Pravda Vostoka*, December 25, 1960.

his anti-Stalinist theory of 1954 that the supply and demand of consumer goods could be balanced when he requested that conditions be created in which public demand for food products and consumer goods be met in full and production always outstrip demand.[66] This new formula would recur in the speeches which Khrushchev made in the agricultural areas during the next few months.[67]

The immediate outcome of the dispute over prospects for investment was decided in the commission formed to draft the agricultural decree of the plenary session. The commission had 68 members, including 19 members and candidates of the party Presidium (Mukhitdinov's name is unlisted), 15 Union-republican party first secretaries (three of Presidium status), at least 12 regional party committee secretaries (one a Presidium candidate member), about 13 senior party and state officials, and a few district workers.[68] The commission worked in the deepest sort of privacy: the transcript mentions neither the circulation of a preliminary draft nor a report of the commision at the end of the session. Truly a model of "the secretive, anti-democratic discussion and decision of the most important problems"!

The statement of the commission was a compromise between Khrushchev on the one side and Kozlov and Suslov on the other. Khrushchev extracted an admission

[66] *Pravda*, January 21, 1961 (CDSP, xiii, 7, pp. 8-10; xiii, 8, pp. 10-23).

[67] See *S.K. v SSSR i R.S.Kh.*, iv, 380, and v, 141 and 149.

[68] *Plenum III*, pp. 605-606. As distinct from the listings of commissioners at the agricultural Plenums in 1958 and 1959, this one specifically identifies two district party committee secretaries, a sovkhoz director, and a kolkhoz chairman. The identifications presumably symbolized the enhanced importance of local personnel after the downgrading of the agricultural ministries.

that it was possible to increase greatly the capital investment which the Seven-Year Plan called for in agriculture and in industry serving it. The Central Committee (Presidium or Secretariat) and USSR Council of Ministers were asked to examine the question in the near future. Consumer goods that would build incentives were something else again. The view of the majority was that it was proper to see that supplies outstrip the public demand for agricultural products, but not for consumer goods.[69] Moreover, the dogma of preponderant development of heavy industry was reaffirmed in the lead article of *Kommunist* dealing with the January 1961 Plenum.[70]

The points which the rival leaders made in the various secret conclaves as usual found expression in bureaucratic appointments. A corollary of the decline in the ministerial element upon the insistence of Khrushchev was a return to normalcy in the agricultural departments at party headquarters. The vacancies created in the main positions of the departments were filled.[71]

The Khrushchevite Polyanskiy read to the Central Committee sessions what was essentially a factional black list of intermediate-grade leaders who had long tenure, particularly in the northwestern area, where Kozlov had many connections. Polyanskiy belittled as incompetent five first secretaries of regional party committees in the RSFSR and in due course three of them were purged.[72]

[69] The plenary session's decree on agriculture is in *Pravda*, January 20, 1961 (CDSP, xiii, 8, pp. 23-26).

[70] No. 2, 1961, p. 4.

[71] V. A. Karlov was first identified as head of the Union-Republic Agricultural Section in *Pravda*, February 1, 1961, and I. S. Pan'kin as RSFSR Agricultural Section Chief in *Sovetskaya Rossiya*, March 2, 1961.

[72] The purged secretaries were Khrushchev's one-time follower, P. I. Doronin of Smolensk (February 12, 1961), V. A. Prokof'yev of Novgorod (April 11, 1961), and M. Ya. Kannunikov of Pskov

Khrushchev evidently took the measure of Aristov, who joined his group after rising by his own wits in the Stalin era. Aristov was named ambassador to Poland and so in effect was deprived of his seat in the party Presidium and deputy chairmanship of the RSFSR Bureau.[73] Churayev, more trustworthy from Khrushchev's standpoint, was awarded a Bureau deputy chairmanship for industry.[74] The two new candidate members of the party Presidium were independents. G. I. Voronov, who also gained a deputy chairmanship for agriculture in the RSFSR Bureau, had a record of party and ministerial work dating back to 1950 and Khrushchev had once admired his expertise in sheep-breeding.[75] He would later fight for state authoritarian centralism and lose executive prerogatives in the wake of Khrushchev's great restructuring of the party in 1962. V. V. Grishin, the other new aspirant to full membership in the Presidium, had likewise established himself in the party bureaucracy without Khrushchev's acquiescence and since 1956 had been chairman of the All-Union Central Council of Trade Unions.

(April 19, 1961). Of those criticized, L. A. Florent'yev of Kostroma alone retained office and S. O. Postovalov of Kaluga was eventually recruited into the central party apparatus. Khrushchev had interjected after Polyanskiy's criticism: "It is necessary to help them understand their mistakes. Herein lies leadership. (*Stir in the hall.*)"

[73] *Pravda*, February 1, 1961.
[74] *Ibid.*, February 12, 1961.
[75] *S.K. v SSSR i R.S.Kh.*, I, 406.

CHAPTER VI

KHRUSHCHEV'S RETREAT
(1961-1963)

A CONTROVERSY over general economic and social policy erupted in the leadership once it decided to draft a new party Program, or manifesto of national goals, for the next twenty years. Khrushchev persistently called the attention of the party Presidium to the material requirements of agriculture and attempted to secure from the elite at large a commitment to amend the scale of economic priorities to the benefit of agricultural and consumer interests. He also recommended to the Presidium new steps to ensure wider public participation in agricultural management. Accordingly, Khrushchev sought to invalidate party doctrine which upheld the supremacy of heavy engineering and anti-peasant measures like the forced conversion of kolkhozes into sovkhozes, abolition of supplementary allotments, and curtailment of trade in kolkhoz marketplaces. This meant demolishing certain residual features of the ideological escarpment which Stalin had perfected to guard the structure of his exploitative policy ("preponderant development of heavy industry" and "dictatorship of the proletariat"). The wrangle over domestic policy therefore led initially to contradictory manipulation of the Stalin symbol in party literature during the summer of 1961 and was one of the major reasons for the vitriolic attack by Khrushchev's group on Stalin and neo-Stalinists at the 22nd party Congress in October 1961.

Khrushchev's losses more than offset his gains. He

did succeed in having the new party Program express recognition that the regime of anti-peasant repression known as "dictatorship of the proletariat" had been superseded by one of class harmony called a "state of the entire people." The relatively more liberal kolkhoz form of organizing the bulk of the peasantry was lauded at the expense of the sovkhoz. The principle of decentralized planning of agriculture was reasserted in the final version of the Program after having been conspicuously absent in the draft. Khrushchev also had excluded from the draft Program the conventional slogan for an all-out drive in heavy engineering. On the other hand, the claim of the draft Program about the advent of a "new period" in industrial development which would improve the welfare of the citizenry was excised from the completed text. The oligarchy rejected a proposal which contradicted Stalin's axiom that agriculture could never achieve technological parity with industry. The massive conversion of kolkhozes into sovkhozes resumed. These "conservative" victories ensured for Kozlov and Suslov a privileged position in the leadership.

In 1962 as well, the Khrushchev group strenuously agitated for democratization of farm management, greater output of scarce machinery and chemical fertilizers, and tangible incentives for peasants. On all counts, the mandate of the Central Committee was "conservative." An authoritarian centralist pattern of state management was laid down in March 1962. An increase of 1 billion rubles in state purchasing prices for the stockbreeding products of kolkhozes was effectuated through a disorienting rise of retail sales prices in towns. State inputs in agriculture no more than kept pace with the growth of the state farm sector. The ledger of production results confirmed Khrushchev's foreboding of 1960 that "If the necessary measures are not taken, we may revert to the situation which existed in 1953."

TOWARD A NEW PROSPECTUS OF COMMUNISM

In his speech of January 6, 1961, to party intellectuals, Khrushchev announced the drafting of a new party Program to replace the 1919 edition.[1] The first sitting of the Central Committee Plenum which opened on January 10, 1961, adopted a decree which called the 22nd party Congress for October 17, 1961, and approved Khrushchev as rapporteur on the draft Program.[2] The party's new platform was to be written by a committee of undisclosed composition, which later was reported to have worked under Khrushchev's chairmanship.[3] This outstanding event in the ideological life of the party afforded him an opportunity to codify his distinctive prescriptions for the repair of the Soviet system. Khrushchev's immersion in agricultural affairs at the onset of 1961 and the tone of his pronouncements indicate that he was eager to obtain programmatic sanction for badly needed measures to accelerate the technical outfitting of agriculture, increase material rewards for farm workers, and stimulate local initiative.

[1] *Kommunist*, No. 1, 1961, p. 14. The preparation of a new Program was ordered at the 20th party Congress, as at the 19th in 1952. Kuusinen has alleged that two abortive attempts to rewrite the Program were made in the 1930's (*Pravda*, October 27, 1961).

[2] "On Convocation of the Regular, 22nd CPSU Congress," *Plenum III*, pp. 4-5. The draft Program and draft party Rules were to be published.

[3] The communiqué of the June 1961 Central Committee Plenum mentions the "Program Commission" but fails to mention Khrushchev as its chairman. The only reference to Khrushchev's official role in the matter seems to have been D. Korotchenko's in *Pravda*, August 22, 1961.

According to an agreement reached in the party Presidium,[4] Khrushchev soon after the January 1961 Plenum made an extensive tour of the farming regions. In the seven-week period of January 28-March 21, 1961, he spoke at nine zonal conferences attended by over 25,000 farm officials and workers. The speeches were mostly critical, instructive, and exhortative.[5] But Khrushchev's sense of realism never left him. He repeatedly stressed the importance of an increased flow of consumer goods to raise labor productivity and, as if to vindicate a shift in investment policy, contended that the USSR had the most powerful rockets in the world and as many nuclear and thermonuclear bombs as were needed to wipe out an aggressor. This sober outlook on at least the farm problem was likewise evidenced in the memorandum of March 31, 1961, which Khrushchev submitted to the party Presidium.[6] Incantation offered no hope in the quest for greater output: "The further development of grain production, an increase in the output of specialized crops, and a sharp upturn of livestock products are possible only on the basis of equipping agriculture with up-to-date machinery." As had been the case five months earlier, certain members of the Presidium were discreetly rebuked for complacence in this matter: "At the zonal conferences, as well as in talks with the leaders of republics, territories, regions, districts, sovkhozes, and kolkhozes, I was again convinced that some of our leading officials, including officials of the State Planning Committee, have not profoundly

[4] *Plenum III*, p. 605.
[5] *S.K. v SSSR i R.S.Kh.*, iv, 379-475, and v, 5-312.
[6] "Certain Results of the Zonal Conferences on Problems of Agriculture," *ibid.*, v, 313-352.

studied the actual situation with respect to satisfying the machinery requirements of kolkhozes and sovkhozes and have drawn unjustified conclusions to the effect that agriculture is adequately equipped with machinery." The machinery shortage was universal but most acute in the eastern regions (where Khrushchev's personal prestige was at stake) and the situation had to be rectified.

Khrushchev informed his colleagues that in Kiev and at other conferences the speakers from economically weak farms had appealed for practical aid. He agreed that this was a serious problem and advised that its solution depended on the proper use of material incentives. The regional leaders, he said, must formulate a system of bonuses for labor in the weak farms. But Khrushchev did not elaborate on the "vicious circle" contradiction which was raised and implausibly refuted in the issue of *Party Life* approved for printing on April 1, 1961:

Also mistaken is the view that the application of material incentive and cost accounting is possible only on economically strong farms, while on lagging farms it becomes a "vicious circle": people must have material incentive in order to boost production and the economy, and it is necessary to boost the economy in order to give the people material incentive. Such a contradiction does indeed exist, but it can be fully solved within the framework of the collective farm system. Such contradictions, V. I. Lenin taught, "are resolved by a change in the mood of the masses, by the heroic initiative of individual groups, which against the background of such a change often plays a decisive role."[7] The kolkhoz federation had been devised as a means

[7] Ye. Lazutkin, *Partiynaya Zhizn'*, No. 7, 1961, pp. 17-24 (CDSP, XIII, 19, pp. 15-17, 28).

to bolster weak farms through a pooling of resources. Khrushchev evidently was still attracted by this prospect and in his memorandum of March 31, 1961, recommended the creation in Moscow of a Kolkhoz-Sovkhoz Center. Like the still-born Kolkhoz Center, this body too would be organized along representative lines, but instead of administering kolkhozes it would dispose of a network of inspectors to verify farmers' complaints and study new practices in the running of farms. The recommendations of the Kolkhoz-Sovkhoz Center would be transmitted to the policy-making authority. Obviously owing to the opposition of some members of the party Presidium, the Kolkhoz-Sovkhoz Center was not heard of again until the publication of the anthology of Khrushchev's agricultural policy statements of 1953-1963, which commenced about 18 months later.

Yet at the end of January Khrushchev's propagandist Bugayev rebuked past and present "conservative elements" in the upper stratum.[8] After the party leader had made his farm tour and shared impressions with other members of the Presidium, efforts continued to discredit the retrograde outlook in bureaucratic circles. An ideological functionary recalled that early in 1957 two associates had glossed over social discrepancies and so underrated the value of timely reforms.[9] L. F. Il'ichëv,

---

[8] ". . . in conditions of a socialist society, the edge of inner-party struggle is directed not against people who express the interests of some exploiter classes (which do not exist), but against conservative elements which cling to outmoded forms and methods of work, which are unable to master new and progressive tendencies and support them, against dogmatists in theory and policy, people who may embark on unprincipled factional struggle, as was the case with the anti-party group of Malenkov, Kaganovich, Molotov, Bulganin, and Shepilov" (Bugayev, *op. cit.*, p. 26).

[9] See S. F. Yeliseyev's criticism of V. P. Tugarinov's and V. P. Rozhin's article in *Voprosy Filosofii*, No. 3, 1957, in M. M.

chief of the Central Committee's Section for Propaganda and Agitation for the Union Republics, in an article for Lenin Day which *Pravda* published on April 21, 1961, stressed the importance of formulating a clear national policy to meet new problems. The main trend of this policy had to be "all-around development of the production of material benefits and an increase in the well-being of the Soviet people." Specifically, material incentive had to be provided for agricultural workers. Party members were expected to anticipate the rejection of "one or another Marxist-Leninist formula divorced from life and the dictates of the time." They were cautioned against the temptations of "people who under the guise of politics undertake niggardly actions which lead to deceit." Struggle was expected against "all that is old, backward, and conservative." A week later, the second installment of Il'ichëv's article appeared in *Pravda*

Rozental', ed., *Dialektika Razvitiya Sotsialisticheskogo Obshchestva* (Dialectic of Development of Socialist Society), Academy of Social Sciences attached to the CPSU Central Committee, Department of Philosophy, Moscow (sent to the press on April 14), 1961, pp. 4ff. Yeliseyev admonished: "Conservatism and inertness, clinging to stagnant social forms, can under socialism as well hinder—and not rarely do hinder—the determination of the moment for resolving contradictions. Conservatism is always characterized by a fear of novelty; a timid approach to novelty is intrinsic to it. 'What will happen?' The danger of conservatism also increases in connection with the fact that, in their defense of the old, the conservatives appeal to reality and maintain that development proceeds as well under the old forms. Just such inertness, metaphysical one-sidedness, and fear of novelty ('What will happen?') marked the position of the anti-party group of Molotov, Malenkov, Kaganovich, Bulganin, and Shepilov when it came time to perfect the forms of management of industry and construction. The adversaries of the charted measures referred to the fact that, even under the forms of management which had existed earlier, the economy did not stand still and plans were fulfilled. However, it is not a question of development ceasing, but of its being retarded and stymied by old practices."

and readers were conditioned for a socio-economic *povorot*, or "turning point."

Early in 1955, just after Malenkov had lost the premiership for having in part urged equal rates of growth of heavy and light industry, various "muddleheaded economists" of the same persuasion had been criticized for having acclaimed recent measures to pull up agriculture and light industry as "some kind of *povorot*."[10] The events surrounding Il'ichëv's articles suggest that he utilized the term *povorot* in conjunction with Khrushchev's intention to balance the growth rates of heavy and light industry. Such balancing, and even a temporarily increased growth rate for consumer goods, were explicitly approved by the economist I. Oleinik in a journal sent to the press on May 10, 1961.[11] Khrushchev himself would reportedly tell foreign visitors on May 20, 1961: "Now we consider our heavy industry as built. So we are not going to give it priority. Light industry and heavy industry will develop at the same pace."[12] Khrushchev's remarks were not featured in the Soviet press, but *Pravda* on May 24, 1961, ran an article by K. G. Pysin, USSR First Deputy Minister of Agriculture, which restated the party leader's novel outlook

---

[10] Cf. *Kommunist*, No. 2, 1955, pp. 14ff., and No. 3, 1955, pp. 34 and 35.

[11] "The need for preeminent growth of production of the productive means in each socialist country does not, however, exclude the possibility that certain countries, with the aim of solving certain economic tasks, can in the course of a relatively short period of time develop both subdivisions of public production [i.e., capital and consumer goods branches] at equal rates or even develop at higher rates the production of consumer goods" (*Voprosy Ekonomiki*, No. 5, 1961, p. 68). Oleinik did not acknowledge this possibility in a similar article on Bloc economies in *ibid.*, No. 9, 1959, pp. 94ff.

[12] *New York Times*, July 31, 1961.

223

on the supply and demand of both foodstuffs and consumer goods as "a most important theoretical tenet of Marxist-Leninist science." The same article unprecedentedly referred to agriculture as "the most decisive branch of the national economy."

The failure of Soviet media to report Khrushchev's "equal rates" statement of May 20, 1961, brings to mind previous instances when he had confided in strangers about policy proposals which had not been agreed upon in the leadership and were refused a public airing on the insistence of other members of the party Presidium. A furtive attack on Khrushchev's latest scheme to alter the pattern of resource allocation began about the time of Oleinik's ideological escapade. In a brochure sent to the press on May 8, 1961, one Ye. P. Gorbunov recalled that the Seven-Year Plan adopted in 1959 required annual growth rates of capital and consumer goods of 9.3 per cent and 7.3 per cent, respectively, and he tortuously contested Khrushchev's theory about the chances to create conditions in which popular demand for foodstuffs and consumer goods would be met "in full": "A coarse error of bourgeois critics is that they completely lose sight of the demands of production and this is the decisive factor which shapes social demand. The demand of production grows at a violent rate and follows technical progress, which imposes new demand on industrial products. Hence, *the satisfaction of society's demands is always relative,* must trail behind production and actively stimulate it" (italics added).[13] Gorbunov's reference to the plan directives of the 21st party Congress in-

[13] *Sovetskiye Tempy i ikh Burzhuaznye Kritiki* (Soviet Rates and Their Bourgeois Critics), "Znaniye" Series of the All-Union Society for the Dissemination of Political and Scientific Knowledge, Moscow, 1961.

sinuated that the proponents of "equal rates" were violating party standards of discipline and group decision-making, the sanctity of which would be underscored at the close of debate on the new party Program. Still another didactic exercise in anti-Khrushchevism found an outlet in the academic publication which in 1958 had served as the vehicle for opponents of the plan to reorganize MTS. *The Herald of Moscow University: Series IX, History*, approved for printing on May 17, 1961, carried V. I. Tetyushev's essay, "Party Struggle for the General Line Against the Right Deviation in the CPSU(B) in the Period between the 15th and 16th Party Congresses." It maintained that Lenin's design for the building of socialism required pursuit of "the policy of high rates of industrialization with preeminent development of branches of heavy industry"; the November 1928 Central Committee Plenum resolved "to *ensure fully* the adopted rate of development of industry in Group 'A' [heavy industry]."

The crypto-public expressions of dissent over investment policy recurred in the following weeks. A pair of theoretical economists averred in *Kommunist* that buying and selling was imcompatible with socialism and conjured up favorable memories of the suppression of economic liberalizers in the final years of Stalin's regime. An unsigned rebuttal accused these theorists of "dogmatism" for having in effect resurrected the products-exchange scheme, which envisaged a sharp curtailment of material incentives and the introduction of a rationing system. A number of unspecified officials in the state planning agencies—there was criticism of "pseudo-planners" Malenkov and Molotov early in 1957—were represented as sympathetic toward this

austerity viewpoint.[14] An important shading of difference arose on June 13, 1961, when *Pravda* and *Izvestiya*
ran versions of a speech delivered by academician M. V.
Keldysh. *Pravda* alleged that Keldysh had said: "As is
known, the harmonious development of the entire economic organism requires that the growth of heavy
industry ensure the *development* of all branches of the
economy and production of consumer goods" (italics
added). In *Izvestiya*, the second underlined word was
also "growth." The editors of *Izvestiya*, headed by
Khrushchev's son-in-law, presumably wished to assess
uniformly the merits of heavy and light industry. But on
June 15, 1961, an article in *Literaturnaya Gazeta* ascribed to Keldysh the thought that "development of
heavy industry must surpass the development of the
means of consumption." The situation underlying this
propaganda disarray was clarified for local party members, who were reapprised of Khrushchev's statement of
May 10, 1957, that "heated debates" occasionally transpired in the party Presidium.[15]

Stalin's products-exchange plan had aimed at the
eventual replacement of kolkhozes by state farms, but
the renewal of argument over this plan involved the
short-run outlook for kolkhozes as well. The aforementioned reprimand of "dogmatic" economists was indeed
accompanied by an unsigned article directed against cor-
respondents in towns of the Russian Federation who,
for technical and ideological reasons, demanded either

[14] Cf. I. Malyshev and V. Sobol', "On the Scientific Basis of
Study of the Socialist Economy," *Kommunist*, No. 8 (May 29),
1961, pp. 82-88; and "Concerning the Article of I. Malyshev and
V. Sobol'," *ibid.*, pp. 89-97.
[15] See the report of a conference on "collective leadership" held
in Tashkent with the participation of A. F. Vodolazskiy, an expert on the subject, in *Pravda Vostoka*, June 16, 1961.

the transformation of all kolkhozes into sovkhozes or abolition of the farmers' supplementary allotments.[16] A hint that the junior-grade partisans of massive conversion found backing in certain quarters of the top leadership was supplied in a Moscow Radio talk of May 23, 1961. The talk was based on an article by A. Perlovskiy, "Party Policy Expresses the People's Basic Interest," which first appeared in *Kazakhstanskaya Pravda* on April 12, 1961. The original text noted that "certain leaders *in the localities* were ready to transform all kolkhozes into sovkhozes in the near future" (italics added). The radio version merely stated that "certain leaders suggested converting all kolkhozes into sovkhozes in the near future."

Organizational maneuvering attended the incipient conflict over the draft Program. A Plenum held in Frunze on May 8-9, 1961, removed I. R. Razzakov as first secretary of the C.P. of Kirgiziya, and recalled to the disposal of the CPSU Central Committee the former secretary, V. N. Zaychikov.[17] Zaychikov had been chief of the Leningrad Komsomol under Kozlov and was installed in the Central Asian position in February 1960, or just after Rodionov, another former associate of Kozlov, became party second secretary in Kazakhstan. Zaychikov's protection had weakened, since the next post with which he was identified was a comparatively minor one.[18] Kozlov, to be sure, was absent from

---

[16] See "Correspondence with Readers—Some Economic Problems of the Kolkhoz Countryside (Survey of Letters, Notes, and Articles Sent to the Editors)," *Kommunist*, No. 8, 1961, pp. 111-120.

[17] *Pravda*, May 11, 1961.

[18] As deputy chairman of the Board of the All-Union Society for Dissemination of Political and Scientific Knowledge, in *Partiynaya Zhizn'*, No. 9 (April 29), 1963, p. 48.

the 1961 May Day festivities in the capital, reportedly convalescing from a "heart attack." On the other hand, Khrushchev's entourage benefited from recent developments behind the scenes. Z. T. Serdyuk, who had served in Khrushchev's Ukrainian bureaucracy and would verbally demonstrate his continued loyalty to the premier at the 22nd Congress, was relieved of the first secretaryship of the C.P. of Moldavia and appointed to the CPSU Party Control Committee.[19]

DISCUSSING THE PROSPECTUS

The Central Committee met on June 19, 1961, to act on drafts of the party's new Program and Rules. The official communiqué[20] states that the party Presidium had examined the draft Program submitted by a special commission and the Plenum unanimously approved it after the reading and discussion of a report by Khrushchev. The Presidium, however, did not approve the document, as it tacitly had the draft Rules, which it offered for the Plenum's consideration. Also, the Plenum heard and discussed a report on the new Rules which Kozlov delivered, but merely endorsed the draft Rules "in the main." The Presidium evidently was able to reach a compromise agreement on the draft Rules but was hopelessly split over the draft Program. A majority of the Central Committee apparently supported Khrushchev, chairman of the Program Commission, and the Committee's full assembly was duly exalted at the Presidium's expense as "the highest leading organ of the party in the period between its Congresses."[21]

[19] *Pravda*, May 30, 1961.
[20] *Ibid.*, June 20, 1961.
[21] *Kommunist*, No. 9 (July 6), 1961, p. 3.

The future bias in the regime's industrial program was one of the main issues in the struggle over the draft Program. The axiom about the preponderant development of heavy industry was dropped and a *povorot* to benefit the consumer implicitly announced: "In the new period of the Soviet Union's development, the growth and technological progress of heavy industry must ensure the expansion of consumer goods industries to meet ever more fully the requirements of the people."[22] This revolutionary formula was consistent with the mainstream of Khrushchev's thought as expressed in his utterances of the last few months. It made credible the draft's forecast that, by 1971, "The demand of all sections of the population for high-quality consumer goods—attractive clothes, footwear, and goods improving and adorning the daily life of Soviet people, such as comfortable modern furniture, up-to-date domestic goods, a wide range of goods for cultural purposes, etc.—will be amply satisfied." Furthermore, the forecast ran, "The second decade will see an abundance of material and cultural benefits for the whole population, and material prerequisites will be created to complete the transition to the communist principle of distribution according to need in the period to follow." On the other hand, the draft reaffirmed Stalin's theory of "nonessential" differences between town and country, which had legitimated a permanent lag of farm technology behind its urban counterpart. This represented a concession to urban and industrial interests, to judge from a statement of disapproval in the ensuing discussion in the press.

Khrushchev's ascendancy over the anti-peasant militants was reflected in the draft Program's sections on

[22] Supplement to *Moscow News*, No. 31 (554), August 5, 1961.

agriculture and state institutions. The kolkhoz system was recognized as an integral part of national life which had stood the test of history and conformed to the distinctive features of the peasantry, whose creative initiative had to be enhanced. Contrary to the arguments of those favoring exclusive reliance on state farms, assurances were made that kolkhoz farming did allow for the effective use of new machinery and the rational employment of manpower. Only in the long run would conditions arise for the merging of kolkhoz and state property. The other side of the same coin was the draft's assertion that the "dictatorship of the proletariat," which had functioned as a weapon of class supremacy, had become a "state of the entire people," expressive of the interests and will of the population as a whole. Nonetheless, the urban elites still retained the political edge. The working class was described as the foremost and best organized force of Soviet society and thus worthy of a leading role until communism was built.[23] A pledge of the urban oligarchs to ensure a measure of peaceful collaboration—not full reconciliation—between the traditionally hostile towns and villages was probably the most that the great domestic conciliator Khrushchev was able to bargain for.

The abstruse ritual of condemnation which is usually performed after the setback of a minority grouping in the leadership was observed after the June 1961 Plenum. The editors of *Kommunist* impugned "certain economists" who out of blindness to changes in the foreign and internal environment clung to outmoded ratios of

[23] See Ye. Panfilov, "Our Consultations—Working Class and Leadership of Society," *Sovetskaya Rossiya*, August 4, 1962, which is addressed to the question, "Why in the new phase as well must the leading role in our society remain with the working class?"

development in various branches of the economy.[24] Khrushchev soon announced that an increase in the military budgets of the NATO countries had compelled the Soviet government to increase defense expenditures by one-third in the current year.[25] This raised before the Kremlin the question of whether to invoke the clause of the draft Program which made the achievement of welfare goals contingent on a more or less stable world atmosphere. There is no evidence that Khrushchev intended to invoke the escape clause at any time during the public discussion of the draft Program, which began after the document's release on July 30, 1961. On the contrary, an editorial article in *Pravda* of August 2, 1961, interpreted the programmatic goal of overtaking the USA in per capita output by 1971 to mean a race in production indices such as foodstuffs, footwear, clothing, housing, and other consumer goods, especially consumer durables. Moreover, Khrushchev's formula about the supply and demand of both agricultural products and consumer goods was restated in the press discussion, even though the draft Program embodied the less radical variant approved at the January 1961 Plenum.[26]

Other leaders, who sought to maximize industrial-military potential and were disinterested in the short-run satisfaction of consumer demands, opportunely seized upon the rise of US-Soviet tensions in Berlin as a pretext to insist anew on unflagging conduct of the regime's traditional investment policy.

[24] No. 10 (July 6), 1961, p. 36.

[25] *Pravda,* July 9, 1961.

[26] Cf. *Ekonomicheskaya Gazeta* (Economics Newspaper), August 21, 1961, p. 13; *Molodoi Kommunist* (Young Communist), No. 8 (August 21), 1961, p. 28; *Politicheskoye Samoobrazovaniye,* No. 10 (September 26), 1961, p. 49; and *Voprosy Filosofii,* No. 10 (October 2), 1961, p. 32.

The unreconstructed Stalinist P. F. Yudin scaled down the programmatic estimate of consumer satisfaction in the issue of *Kommunist* approved for publication on August 9, 1961. He misrepresented the draft as forecasting that "total satisfaction of the needs for foodstuffs and items of primary necessity [kerosene, matches, sugar, etc.]"[27] would not occur until 1980. V. V. Grishin, writing in *Pravda* on August 14, 1961, also presented dimmer consumer prospects than those sketched in the draft Program. Grishin's union newspaper *Trud* on August 17, 1961, editorially supported "preponderant" development of heavy industry, which remained "the bedrock" for "strengthening the defense capability of our country." This hard-line position had been taken in the lead article of the Central Committee newspaper *Ekonomicheskaya Gazeta* on August 14, 1961.

While *Pravda* and *Izvestiya* were still relatively neutral on the issue of resource allocation, a neo-Stalinist majority crystallized in the editorial board of the Central Committee magazine *Party Life*. A lead article paraphrased the draft Program in a manner calculated to arouse jingoist passions:

Draft Program	*Partiynaya Zhizn'*, No. 17, August 31, 1961, p. 8.
The CPSU considers that the chief aim of its foreign policy activity is to provide peaceful conditions for the building of a communist society in the USSR and developing the	The Communist party considers that the chief aim of its foreign policy activity is to *foil the sanguinary designs of the imperialists*, provide peaceful conditions for building a com-

[27] No. 12, 1961, p. 51.

232

world socialist system, and together with the other peace-loving peoples to deliver mankind from a world war of extermination.

munist society in the USSR and developing the world socialist system, and together with all peace-loving peoples to deliver mankind from a world war of extermination (italics added).

The discussion article of one S. Figurnov, in the same issue, upheld "preponderant" development of heavy industry and advised limitation of the production race with the USA to "certain" consumer goods.[28] This conservative propaganda was topped by the advertisement of writings by Stalin and Mao.[29]

Khrushchev's unwavering determination to achieve a revolutionary change of policy to help agriculture and the consumer was expressed in the subsequent discussion article by Il'ichëv.[30] Il'ichëv restated verbatim the draft Program on the main aim of Soviet foreign policy, sustained the innovative opinion on the desirable ratio of production and consumption, and scoffed at "theoreticians" encumbered by rigid concepts of the Stalin era. Shortly, a distinction was drawn between Stalin and the "classicists" of Marxism-Leninism. I. Pustovalov, deputy editor of *Problems of Economics*, challenged the validity of the theory of eternal "nonessential" differ-

---

[28] *Partiynaya Zhizn'*, No. 17, 1961, pp. 19 and 21.

[29] Stalin's *Foundations of Leninism* was included in the periodically advertised "Little Library of Scientific Socialism" in *Partiynaya Zhizn'*, Nos. 14 (July 17), 15-16 (August 4), and 17 (August 31), 1961. Mao's *On the New Democracy* (in Russian, 1960) entered the list in No. 17, 1961.

[30] "Theory of Scientific Communism in Action," *Kommunist*, No. 13 (September 5), 1961, pp. 9-24.

ences between town and country. He argued that this restrictive tenet was alien to the works of Marx, Engels, and Lenin and was formulated initially in 1952 by Stalin.[31] The Stalin symbol was also degraded in the issue of *Kommunist* released on the eve of the 22nd party Congress.[32]

THE CONGRESS OF CONFLICT

Contrary to Khrushchev's opposition to the policy of utmost development of the iron and steel industries, a party and government decree of October 13, 1961, claimed an "acute" shortage of ferrous and nonferrous metals.[33] A day later, the Central Committee unexpectedly met and ratified an amended version of the draft Program. The altered text was to be submitted to the 22nd party Congress for examination.[34] Originally, the Congress was supposed to examine and *approve* the Draft. The improvised procedure tended to subordinate the nominally supreme Congress to the Central Committee, whose formal mandate was about to expire. This anomaly is all the more fascinating in view of the cited anti-Stalin article in the pre-Congress issue of

---

[31] "On Social Differences and Overcoming Them Under Communism," *Voprosy Ekonomiki*, No. 10 (October 7), 1961, pp. 51-60.

[32] A. Sidorov and G. Shitarëv, "Lenin and Party Congresses," No. 15 (October 12), 1961, pp. 92-101, recalls that Lenin addressed to the 12th party Congress a letter which included criticism of Stalin's "personal shortcomings."

[33] "On Regulating the Material-Technical Supply of the National Economy and Setting Norms for the Expenditure of Material Resources," *Spravochnik Partiynogo Rabotnika* (Handbook of the Party Official), Moscow, 1963, pp. 277-291.

[34] *Pravda*, October 15, 1961. Khrushchev spoke on the draft and the Central Committee Report to the Congress, which too was endorsed. The Plenum heard Kozlov speak on the draft Rules and it approved a corrected version of the latter.

Kommunist which charges that the Mensheviks and "other opportunistic groupings and currents which came after them" dismissed the party's Congress as a mere consultative body.[35] The only recorded precedent for the October 14, 1961, Central Committee session is the Committee meeting of December 15, 1925, three days before the 14th party Congress. The purpose then was to approve draft resolutions of the Politburo and secure a moratorium on existing arguments in that body.[36] In the situation of 1961, the neo-Stalinists Kozlov and Suslov desired to keep Khrushchev from bringing their disputes into the private meetings of delegation leaders which are sometimes held at party Congresses.

The verdict of the party Presidium on resource allocation was "conservative" and Khrushchev elected to overturn it. On the first days of the 22nd Congress[37] he taunted the metallurgical group and underscored the timeliness of modifying the scale of economic priorities to consumer advantage. Khrushchev spitefully tried to depict as a personal victory the provisional decision to produce from 95 to 97 "or more" million tons of steel by 1965, as opposed to the 100 million tons desired by "some people." The metallurgical group in June 1957 had resisted the circulation of Khrushchev's slogan about overtaking and surpassing the USA in per capita output of livestock products. As in May 1957, Khrushchev censured "some American journalists" who were wont to "make fun of this slogan of ours." He justified the draft Program's clause about the dawn of a "new period" in the functioning of heavy industry: "Now the

[35] Sidorov and Shitarëv, *op.cit.*, p. 93.
[36] Carr, *op.cit.*, pp. 127-128.
[37] *Pravda*, October 18 and 19, 1961.

role of heavy industry in growth of the people's well-being, as well as in the solution of problems of accumulation, is manifested in a new way. . . . In developing heavy industry, we proceed from Lenin's tenet that 'means of production are manufactured not for the mere sake of means of production, but only because more and more capital goods are needed in the branches of industry which turn out consumer goods.' "

Khrushchev's agitation was supplemented by certain other leaders' sharp attacks on the "conservatism" of the Malenkov-Molotov group.[38] The sallies of Mikoyan and Polyanskiy were especially timely. Mikoyan was critical of state farm enthusiasts and Polyanskiy recalled Molotov's opposition to the decentralization of agricultural planning, which was conspicuously omitted in the draft Program's listing of post-Stalin reform measures. But during the second week of the Congress Il'ichëv conceded defeat, in behalf of Khrushchev's group, in the quarrel over economic priorities. He suddenly denounced Malenkov's "anti-Leninist assertion that preponderant development of heavy industry is supposedly not obligatory."[39]

The negotiations which preceded this notification of a reformist setback shifted to a commission of 92 members.[40] It was to prepare a resolution on the Central Committee Report and examine corrections in and additions to the draft Program. Among the 92 members were

[38] Cf. in particular the speeches of A. I. Mikoyan and Ye. A. Furtseva, *ibid.*, October 22, 1961; D. S. Polyanskiy, *ibid.*, October 24, 1961; and A. N. Shelepin, *ibid.*, October 27, 1961. Party propagandists were later directed to study the criticisms of the "anti-party group" made at the Congress by Khrushchev, Mikoyan, Polyanskiy, and Shvernik (*Voprosy Istorii KPSS*, No. 3, 1963).

[39] *Ibid.*, October 26, 1961.

[40] *Ibid.*, October 28, 1961.

Khrushchev (chairman), 20 members and candidate members of the party Presidium (Pervukhin, a former member of the Malenkov-Molotov group was excluded), 14 Union-republic party first secretaries (three with Presidium status), 23 first secretaries of regional party committees, about a dozen central ministers, and equal number of experts in party organization and propaganda, five local government men, five hero workers, two writers, and two scientists. Over half of the commissioners were not members of the outgoing Central Committee. The commission surveyed the proposals which Congress delegates had made in speeches and letters and then adjusted the draft Program.[41]

Khrushchev won a number of concessions during the private settling of differences. The old maxim about heavy industry was kept out of the party Program. Clauses were added which approved of simplifying and reducing the structure of economic management and decentralizing agricultural planning. But the general ruling on investment policy was "conservative." The new age in the production of consumer goods was forgotten and the demands of the military establishment asserted:

Draft	*Final Text*
A first-class heavy industry, the basis for the country's technical progress and economic might, has been built up in the Soviet Union. The CPSU will continue to devote unflagging attention to the growth of	A first-class heavy industry, the basis for the country's technical progress and economic might, has been built up in the Soviet Union. The CPSU will continue to devote unflagging attention to the growth of

[41] B. N. Ponomarëv, *XXII S"yezd KPSS*, III, 198.

heavy industry, which ensures the development of the country's productive forces and defense potential. In the new period of the Soviet Union's development, the growth and technological progress of heavy industry must ensure the expansion of consumer goods industries to meet ever more fully the requirements of the people. Thus, the main task of heavy industry is to meet the needs of the country's defense in full and to satisfy the daily requirements of man, of Soviet society, better and more fully.

heavy industry and its technical progress. The main task of heavy industry is to meet the needs of the country's defense in full, and to develop those branches of the national economy producing consumer goods to meet ever more fully the requirements of the people, the daily needs of Soviet man, and to ensure the development of the country's productive forces. (*Pravda*, November 2, 1961)

Khrushchev's response to the stubbornness of external and internal enemies at the 22nd Congress was to organize an anti-Stalin demonstration. His speech against Stalin at the close of the proceedings and the ensuing removal of the despot's corpse from the tomb on Red Square were acts to dramatize the Sino-Soviet conflict and induce at home an atmosphere more congenial to the voicing of progressive sentiment. Khrushchev's simultaneous reassertion of the "collective leadership" principle was meant to indicate that he more than any other top leader was apt to honor the consensus of elite opinion if entrusted with the stewardship of the party. This demonstration was followed by organizational reflections of Khrushchev's policy defeats at the Congress. His clients Furtseva, Ignatov, Kirilenko, Mukhitdinov, and Pospelov were dropped from the Presidium. Mukhitdinov also lost his place in the Secretariat. The configuration of forces in the new Presidium appeared to be: Khrushchev and his allies Brezhnev, Kuusinen, Mikoyan, Polyanskiy, and Shvernik; the group of Kozlov and Suslov; and the "swamp" of Voronov, Kosygin, and Podgornyy. The Secretariat included only four members of the Presidium: Khrushchev, Kozlov, Suslov, and Kuusinen.[42] Armed with the "conservative" mandate of the 22nd Congress on investment policy, Khrushchev's opponents saw to it that his speech of November 2, 1961, to a conference on questions of agriculture which the party Presidium arranged for Congress delegates was printed in *Pravda* only in summary form and without the original version's espousal of the welfare cause.[43]

THE NEO-STALINIST PHALANX
(NOVEMBER 1961–MARCH 1962)

When Khrushchev left Moscow for the zonal agricultural conferences which followed the 22nd Congress, he knew that immediate relief for the hinterland was not forthcoming. The state's agricultural investment in 1962 was to increase by about 25 per cent over the 1961 level,

[42] The members of the Presidium and Secretariat are listed in *Pravda*, November 1, 1961. The independence of Podgornyy at this stage may be inferred from his remarks about the military importance of heavy industry, in *Pravda Ukrainy*, September 29, 1961.

[43] Cf. *Pravda*, November 3, 1961 (CDSP, XIII, 44, pp. 27-28); and *S.K. v SSSR i R.S.Kh.*, VI, 55-76.

but at the same time its holdings had expanded appreciably through the conversion of many kolkhozes into sovkhozes.[44] Military expenditures now absorbed at least 16.6 per cent of total state investments, or the highest proportion since 1956 (see Chapter V, note 59). Khrushchev's message to farmers gathered in Tashkent was particularly somber: "Indeed, Comrade Guseinov [a district leader] said that capital investments are needed. If we simply followed this path, comrades, why would we hold conferences and discuss urgent measures for increasing production? What are we supposed to do now? Turn out our pockets and count our money? I could turn out my pockets for you and show you that they are empty. All the people's money is in the state bank. I haven't anything, and I have brought you nothing but good wishes. (*Stir in the hall, applause.*)"[45]

Khrushchev now had to reach deeply into his bag of political tricks. One way to get his associates interested in spending large sums of money for farm machinery and chemical fertilizer was to undertake a sweeping restructure of the cropping system. At the Moscow agricultural conference on December 14, 1961, he claimed that 63.7 million hectares, or about 30 per cent of the total arable land, and as much as the area under wheat, was being squandered on grass, oats, and clean fallow. Khrushchev planned to shift 41 million hectares of this area eventually to cultivated crops like corn, sugar beets, fodder beans, and peas. The opposition of Kozlov was known or anticipated, and Khrushchev stigmatized as an advocate of grassland crop rotation one of Kozlov's

[44] *Voprosy Ekonomiki*, No. 1, 1963, p. 71, and No. 5, 1963, p. 21; and *Plenum IV*, p. 388.
[45] *Pravda*, November 19, 1961 (CDSP, XIII, 46, pp. 35-41).

former colleagues in Leningrad, Nikolai Ivanovich Smirnov, who had recently been appointed deputy chairman for agriculture in the State Planning Committee.[46] Kozlov's preserve in Leningrad would soon be exposed as a center of diehard grasslanders (see below).

Kozlov, however, was at no loss to make known and indeed impose his authoritarian will. Some time ago, Khrushchev had proposed a law to punish severely the factory managers who turned out faulty spare parts for agricultural machinery.[47] At a meeting of the party Secretariat held on December 26, 1961, Kozlov as chairman drew attention to an article which appeared in *Komsomol'skaya Pravda* on December 15, 1961, headed "Crime in Balkhash." The article reported the scrapping of new agricultural machinery by peasants, and Kozlov demanded that such actions be investigated and the guilty be harshly punished.[48] This initiative was the basis of an ukase making a criminally negligent attitude toward the handling of farm equipment an offense punishable by from one to three years of imprisonment.[49] Kozlov then stood to gain from *Pravda's* unique manner of reporting the leadership encomiums at the zonal farm conferences. While *Izvestiya* and *Sovetskaya Rossiya* ordinarily told readers that the conferences were electing to their honorary steering committees the party Presidium "with N. S. Khrushchev at the top," *Pravda*

---

[46] *S.K. v SSSR i R.S.Kh.*, VI, 223.

[47] See his speech of January 28, 1954, in *ibid.*, I, 140-141.

[48] P. A. Satyukov, *XXII S"yezd KPSS i Voprosy Ideologicheskoy Raboty. Materialy Vsesoyuznogo Soveshchaniya po Voprosam Ideologicheskoy Raboty, 25-28 dekabrya 1961 goda* (22nd CPSU Congress and Problems of Ideological Work. Materials of the All-Union Conference on Problems of Ideological Work, December 25-28, 1961), Moscow, 1962, p. 331.

[49] *Pravda*, December 30, 1961.

consistently denied preferential treatment to the first secretary.[50]

The ninth anniversary of Stalin's death was chosen as
the proper moment to open a Central Committee session
on agriculture. *Pravda* of January 28, 1962 announced
that the Committee would meet on March 5, 1962, to discuss "The Party's Tasks in Improving the Management of
Agriculture." Khrushchev was confirmed the rapporteur of the session. The next day's lead article in *Pravda*
was devoted to the forthcoming session and listed the
various agropolitical reforms which Khrushchev had
sponsored over the past several years. The list was copied
from one in the Resolution of the 22nd Congress on the
Central Committee Report, but it did not include mention of the decentralization of agricultural management
that Khrushchev had pushed through at the end of 1960.
Izvestiya's analogous leader of January 30, 1962, however, did include the reform in its reproduction of the
standard listing. Thereby the editors of *Pravda* cast
doubt on the wisdom of expanding local autonomy;
Khrushchev's son-in-law at the helm of *Izvestiya* had no
such reservations. Khrushchev himself had stood by the
local party men in his speech of November 2, 1961, declaring: "It is necessary to enhance the role of rural district party committees, which must become real organizers of collective farmers and state farm workers for
the solution of the tasks posed." The same point was
made in the lead article in *Kommunist* for January 10,
1962: "Under present-day conditions the role of rural

[50] Cf. *Pravda* and *Sovetskaya Rossiya*, December 1, 1961; *Pravda*,
Izvestiya, and *Sovetskaya Rossiya*, December 13, 1961; *Pravda* and
Sovetskaya Rossiya, December 21, 1961; *Pravda* and *Sovetskaya
Rossiya*, December 26, 1961; *Pravda*, January 7, 1962; and *Pravda*
and *Sovetskaya Rossiya*, January 12, 1962.

district party committees increases especially."[51] The district partcoms were likewise extolled in an article which S. Puzikov, first secretary of the Lipetsk Regional Party Committee, wrote for the issue of *Party Life* printed about five weeks later.[52] These declarations in behalf of continued reliance on local initiative were augmented by Vinnichenko's headlong attack on Stalin for his authoritarian centralist policies, and commendation of Presidium member Polyanskiy for showing sympathy toward the idea of large-scale kolkhoz unions.[53]

A basic theme of the press agitation for the plenary session was the need to offer adequate payment to farmers. The controlling faction in the editorial board of *Kommunist* polemicized that "Only short-sighted leaders who have become divorced from life can assume that, in connection with the growth of the Soviet people's consciousness, problems of material reward and encouragement for better work supposedly recede in importance. The person who underestimates the role of material interest in the results of labor will surely ruin things."[54] A district party leader in the Ukraine contended in *Izvestiya* on January 30, 1962, that state purchasing prices for kolkhoz output had to be raised in order to stimulate material incentive. The merit of gradually introducing an exclusive system of cash payments to collective farmers was recognized in *Sovetskaya Rossiya*'s editorial article of January 25, 1962, which noted that only one-quarter of RSFSR kolkhozes distributed incomes in cash alone. The system was also urged with-

---

[51] No. 1, 1962, p. 9.

[52] *Partiynaya Zhizn'*, No. 4 (February 16), 1962, pp. 16ff.

[53] "Power of the Desk—On Rural Themes," *Literaturnaya Gazeta*, February 20 and 22, 1962.

[54] No. 1, 1962, p. 6.

out qualification in *Izvestiya* of February 9, 1962, by the Tadzhik Republic's deputy minister of agriculture. He observed that opponents "argue that in the kolkhozes there are too many people who must be provided with work, and that with this excessive labor supply it would be essential to increase the expenditure of labor for a unit of produce." More generally, the prudence of granting concessions to rural workers was an inference to be drawn from Professor D. Kukin's tribute to Lenin's New Economic Policy in a current article on party history which likewise echoed Il'ichëv's reformist message of April 1961 about "the decisive influence of politics on the country's social and economic development."[55] Khrushchev's share in the control of the relatively more cautious party daily also made itself known. The *Pravda* lead article of February 16, 1962, quoted him on the opportunity to increase capital investment in the light and food industries, agriculture, and housing construction. An immediate increase of the production of farm machinery was called for in *Pravda*'s leader of March 4, 1962.

This Khrushchevian agitation must have resulted from several memorandums which the first secretary addressed to the party Presidium before the March 1962 Central Committee session.[56] These documents are not in the eight-volume collection of Khrushchev's agricultural policy papers, which does include his memorandums for the January 1961 and November 1962 Plenums. The omission parallels that of the memorandum which Khrushchev wrote during the discussion of the MTS change, in which he expressed his opinion on

---

[55] *Politicheskoye Samoobrazovaniye*, No. 1, 1962, pp. 63, 66.
[56] The memorandums are referred to in Kunayev's speech at the session, in *Pravda*, March 7, 1962 (CDSP, XIV, 10, pp. 8-9).

the Kolkhoz Center. The information available on the March 1962 Plenum indicates that policy reversals motivated Khrushchev to consign to oblivion his relevant entreaties to the party Presidium.

Khrushchev opened the plenary session with an announcement that its agenda was "*The Present Stage of Communist Construction* and the Party's Tasks in Improving the Management of Agriculture." The underscored topic was not in the public bulletin of January 28, 1962, which carried notification that the Plenum was scheduled. Khrushchev evidently added the new terminology in order to emphasize his conviction that both the old wine and the old bottles had to be discarded. He pugnaciously inquired if any Central Committee members wished to comment on the agenda.[57] The stenographic record does not mention any objection, but the editors of *Pravda* on March 6, 1962, stubbornly maintained that nothing had changed: "On the agenda of the Plenum is the question of the party's tasks in improving the management of agriculture." Khrushchev defended the welfare clauses of the party Program against anonymous critics who saw in material incentive a concession to bourgeois ideology and capitalist pursuit of profit. These critics were far closer to home than the Great Wall of China. Kozlov had remarked on November 6, 1960, that "The Americans are especially worried over the fact that the USSR is rapidly overtaking the United States in steel output." Khrushchev in pseudo-revolutionary language averred that "The imperialists of the USA are especially worried over precisely the fact that the CPSU Program raises the task of creating the abundance of communism."

According to Khrushchev, a serious threat was pre-

[57] *Plenum* IV, p. 3.

sented to fulfillment of the agricultural goals of the Seven-Year Plan and the main purpose of the Central Committee session was "collectively to discuss those urgent measures which must be undertaken in the sphere of agriculture in order to rectify the situation." Stalin had been wrong in trying to economize state funds by not building chemical fertilizer plants and instead relying on the grassland system. Today, 22 million hectares of land had to be removed immediately from grasses and clean fallow and planted to row crops. This required the urgent construction of at least three large industrial plants to serve agriculture. "These enterprises," Khrushchev added, "will probably have to be built by redistributing capital investments and stocks of materials. It would be good to build these plants at forced tempos, enlisting young people in the construction." The ardent tone of Khrushchev's opening-day message is conveyed by these excerpts from his address:

Now we are outlining a large program of development of agricultural production. The growth of material and technical assistance to agriculture must also accord with the new tasks. If we merely call on people to grow more corn and sugar beets and to shift to the milking of cows with "herring-bone" machines but do not provide production with corn-harvesting and beet-harvesting combines, milking apparatus and other machines, we will prove to be merely talkers. You can't call for high labor productivity and chop down corn with axes. (*Applause*). . . .

Serious conclusions must be drawn from this. One must not treat agriculture lightly. It is possible to undermine the entire economy if the lag in agriculture is not noted in good time and overcome. . . .

Increasing material and technical assistance to the collective and state farms is one of the fundamental questions of party policy in the sphere of agriculture. We have adopted a program for creating an abundance of products in the country. This program must be backed up with the entire might of our system. It seems to me advisable to study our potentialities thoroughly and to adopt measures for further increasing material and technical assistance to agriculture.

Questions of farm management were discussed in the party Presidium, and Union-republic leaders consulted before the plenary session. A decision was reached to tighten bureaucratic controls over the farms. State ministries of production and procurement were to be created on the Union-republic level. They would direct a network of kolkhoz-sovkhoz or sovkhoz-kolkhoz production administrations, depending on which kind of farms predominated locally. The majority opinion was that the administrations should function on an interdistrict basis—that is, embrace several territorial-administrative districts. Subsequently, 960 such administrations were created throughout the country and in the RSFSR most were responsible for from 30 to 60 farms.[58]

Khrushchev insisted that inspectors of the administrations confine themselves to supervisory duties and that farm technicians have the final say in agrotechnical matters. But the authority of the party bureaucracy had so risen in the past few years that any directives pertinent to the activities of state administrators would be executed in conformity with its wishes. The general theory of party hegemony was probably supported by

[58] *Ekonomicheskaya Gazeta*, June 9, 1962 (CDSP, xiv, 21, p. 13); and *Pravda*, March 28, 1962 (CDSP, xiv, 14, pp. 8-12).

all top leaders, and the higher-level supervisory bodies established in the new reorganization were to be chaired by representatives of the party bureaucracy.[59] But the party bureaucracy was sharply divided into centralist and decentralizer groupings. Whether farm technicians would actually regulate details of the production process would depend on the settlement of a new controversy over the jurisdiction of regional vis-à-vis district party committees. Khrushchev reported to the plenary session that one of the reasons it had been convened was to act on a proposal that full-time party organizers from Union-republic or regional party headquarters be attached to the production administrations. This proposal was most extraordinary. The posting of commissars in the villages had been an integral part of Stalin's MTS system. After the death of Stalin, Khrushchev had sponsored abolition of the commissar posts and increased the power of district party secretaries. The new party Rules no longer provided for the allotment of party organizers to important sectors of the economy and this change had only recently been hailed in glowing terms.[60] Moreover, the proposal ran counter to Khrushchev's statement of November 2, 1961, and the bulk of propaganda for the March 1962 Plenum.

[59] The first secretaries of Union-republic party organs were to head the Union-republic agricultural committees and Khrushchev's retainer N. G. Ignatov was appointed leader of the USSR Committee for Agricultural Management.

[60] V. Zasorin and N. Vikulin, *O Novom Ustave KPSS* (On the New CPSU Rules), "Znaniye," Moscow, 1961, pp. 35-36 (sent to press on December 3), describes the change as reflective of the "consistent democratization of inner-party life," "application of the elective principle in party agencies," and "enhancement of the role of local party agencies." This booklet ignores the party Presidium in its listing of the top party organs.

In the open discussion, several speakers backed the proposals for a steep increase of farm machinery without delay.[61] The same was true of the material-incentive principle, which connoted a vote for higher state purchasing prices for kolkhoz products.[62] It was felt safer to quarrel in public about party organization in the countryside. The cleavage of opinion over party organizers was essentially between leaders of the RSFSR and the Ukraine. The Great Russian G. I. Voronov was the firebrand of the centralizers. He urged the introduction of party organizers and even the closing-down of district newspapers, with the substitution of interdistrict sheets under regional party committees.[63] Podgornyy of the Ukraine kept silent about party organizers,[64] but his eventual successor as regional party leader, P. Ye. Shelest, challenged Voronov on this matter and local newspapers. Shelest had reason to believe that Khrushchev agreed with him:

If an institution of Party organizers is established, the Party organizers must presumably have the duties of regional Party committee inspectors, similar to the Central Committee inspectors, whose functions apparently will amount to duties of inspection and control rather than those of organization. The main organizational work on the fulfillment of the national

[61] Cf. A. Ya. Pel'she, *Plenum IV*, p. 192; F. D. Kulakov, *ibid.*, pp. 336-337; S. D. Khitrov, *ibid.*, p. 357; V. S. Fedorov, *ibid.*, pp. 359-361; V. G. Komyakhov, *ibid.*, p. 387; P. I. Morozov, *ibid.*, p. 396; M. S. Sinitsa, *ibid.*, p. 409; and G. S. Zolotukhin, *ibid.*, p. 416.
[62] Cf. F. A. Surganov, *ibid.*, p. 148; I. I. Bodyul, *ibid.*, p. 174; Ya. N. Zarobyan, *ibid.*, p. 181; A. Yu. Snechkus, *ibid.*, p. 199; and Z. N. Glukhov, *ibid.*, p. 289.
[63] *Pravda*, March 7, 1962 (CDSP, xiv, 10, pp. 3-5).
[64] *Ibid.* (CDSP, xiv, 10, 5-7).

economic plans by administrations and collective and state farms must be carried out by the primary Party organizations under the leadership of the district Party committees, as is done now, for example, in industry. But by establishing the institution of Party organizers, especially at the expense of the staffs of the district Party committees, we may weaken the activity of the Party apparatus that is closer to production and has the duty of conducting organizational work on the collective and state farms. *Nikita Sergeyevich Khrushchev has spoken more than once about the great role of the district Party committees, and we should not weaken this important link* (Italics added).[65]

The Great Russian Basov, who had profited from the eclipse of Khrushchev's Ukrainian follower Kirichenko, spoke next and seconded the authoritarian centralist proposals of Voronov.[66]

The deliberation on the proposals commenced on the third day of the session, at the fifth of its eight sittings. A 77-man commission was named to draft a decree. Khrushchev chaired the body, which consisted of 14 other members and candidate members of the party Presidium (the candidate Mazurov was absent), 13 Union-republic party first secretaries (three in the Presidium, with Belorussia represented by the republic party's second secretary), and 19 regional party committee first secretaries. The others included ten central government officials, seven functionaries of the central party bureaucracy, the chief editors of *Pravda* and *Izvestiya*, five local practitioners, and at least two district partcom sec-

[65] *Ibid.*, March 9, 1962 (CDSP, xiv, 11, 38-39).
[66] *Ibid.* (CDSP, xiv, 11, p. 39).

retaries.[67] V. I. Polyakov, Central Committee Section Chief for Agriculture in the Union Republics, informed the final meeting of the Plenum that the commission had made certain amendments to a draft decree which it had circulated to members of the Committee and Central Auditing Commission. As usual, the public transcript contains neither the draft nor amendments and merely refers to the final text's unanimous adoption.[68] This censorship was undertaken to obscure the disagreements over investment policy.

Khrushchev disclosed the enormity of his group's reversal in his speech at the close of the plenary session.[69] The party leader denied that he was in any sense retreating from the position which he had taken on the opening day concerning the allocation of additional resources for agriculture. But it was impossible, he said, to supply agriculture with resources earmarked for industrial and defense projects, which was the only source of extra assistance. Khrushchev now echoed the Kozlov-Suslov line that "The strengthening of the might of the Soviet Union, of its defenses, is our most important task, and we will perform it unswervingly. This is the bedrock of the existence of our socialist state, of its development and successes." However, he expressed his own fear that "in a few years we shall perhaps reproach ourselves for not having fully taken into account our possibilities for the development of agriculture." Neo-Stalinism had also been victorious in the struggle over administration. Party organizers would be sent down to

[67] *Plenum IV*, pp. 244-245.
[68] *Ibid.*, p. 457.
[69] "The Soviet People Will Successfully Fulfill the Program for the Further Development of Agriculture," *ibid.*, March 11, 1962 (CDSP, xiv, 12, pp. 5-13).

the production agencies, and district newspapers be subordinated to regional party committees.[70] The decree of the plenary session advertised anew Khrushchev's measures to regularize payment in kolkhozes, but failed to comment on price policy. The sole redeeming feature of the document from the standpoint of Khrushchev was its blanket condemnation of the grassland method. But Khrushchev's suggested target for row crops was overlooked, just as the decree of the June 1954 Central Committee session had neglected to state the estimated quantity of additional range which might be cultivated in the east. As things turned out, the memory of Stalin was in effect honored rather than disparaged on the ninth anniversary of his death.

"Which Way Are We Going?"
(April-December 1962)

The circumspect decision reached on investment policy at the March 1962 Central Committee session proved gratifying to Suslov and Defense Minister R. Ya. Malinovskiy, and still perturbed Khrushchev. Kozlov welcomed the recentralization of farm management as something long overdue, but here too Khrushchev had misgivings. The first secretary's vehement response to the latest obstruction of his program was to seek to dis-

[70] See also the decree of the plenary session, "The Present Stage of Communist Construction and the Party's Tasks in Improving the Management of Agriculture," in *ibid*. (CDSP, xiv, 12, pp. 3-4); "On Reorganization of the Management of Agriculture," Decree of the CPSU Central Committee and USSR Council of Ministers, in *Pravda*, March 24, 1962 (CDSP, xiv, 13, pp. 10-13); and the Central Committee (Presidium or Secretariat) decree on partorgs in *Partiynaya Zhizn'*, No. 8, April 1962, pp. 35-37 (CDSP, xiv, 19, pp. 17-18). The last-mentioned decree is not in the 1963 edition of *Spravochnik Partiynogo Rabotnika*, which covers the period March 1961-January 1963.

credit his enemies by associating them with malpractices of the Stalin era and weaken their organizational strength. Kozlov's friends in Leningrad were exposed for condoning the activities of scientists who clung to the grassland system. The party boss of Leningrad was overthrown and, along with Kozlov, tacitly represented as the protector of medical charlatans. Khrushchev's dependent Kirilenko benefited from the purge in Leningrad, regaining admission to the party Presidium as a full member. Pysin, the line party officer who in 1961 spoke of farming as the economy's "most decisive" branch, replaced the scientist Ol'shanskiy as USSR Minister of Agriculture. A closer watch was set up over Malinovskiy as Yepishev became chief of the politico-military apparatus.

After factional innuendoes were exchanged in public, compromise was reached on the means to ensure the profitability of livestock breeding in kolkhozes. On a broader scale, the party Presidium and Central Committee continued to turn deaf ears to Khrushchev's unremitting pleas in behalf of greater capital improvements in agriculture. Khrushchev sought to keep economic difficulties in the foreground of political attention by dividing the party bureaucracy into industrial and agricultural components, the leaders of which were required to participate in the practical details of day-to-day administration. While the long-range effect of this stratagem was uncertain, its adoption helped to provide Khrushchev with a degree of momentum in the current struggle. The gigantomaniac plan for farm management was slightly modified in the direction of reasonability, and Khrushchev was able to degrade the centralizer Voronov, the technologically "conservative" director of the FMA, Kuchumov, and the Kozlovite Rodionov.

Shortly after the March 1962 plenary session on agriculture, Suslov delivered an address for elections to the USSR Supreme Soviet. He exulted once more that "Heavy industry has developed in an especially tempestuous manner." The Khrushchevite *Izvestiya* would not, however, print his deceptive claim that in the past few years "especially much" had been done to supply farms with machinery.[71] In reality, nothing had changed since Khrushchev's distress call of October 1960.[72] Malinovskiy too concurred with the freeze put on the level of state appropriations to nonmilitary branches of the economy. In *Kommunist* he denied that military spending was excessive and reiterated the traditionalist viewpoint that large conventional forces were needed to wage nuclear war.[73] These tokens of agreement with the do-nothing consensus on investment policy were supplemented by Kozlov's warm approval of tightening the reins of agricultural administration. Kozlov, whom Khrushchev a few years back had represented as someone ignorant of agriculture, vengefully wrote in *Kommunist:* "Until recently there was an insufficiency of strong state agencies of management of this particularly complex and vitally important sphere of production.

[71] Cf. *Pravda* and *Izvestiya*, March 12, 1962.
[72] See M. Terent'yev, *Voprosy Ekonomiki*, No. 9, 1963, p. 12.
[73] No. 7, 1962, pp. 17 and 19. The divergence of opinion on mass armies stands out well in the lead article in *Voyenno-Istoricheskiy Zhurnal* (Military-Historical Journal), Organ of the USSR Ministry of Defense, No. 12 (December 11), 1961, which upholds the belief in the need for multimillion mass armies to fight a possible world war, and Khrushchev's message to President Kennedy in *Pravda*, February 21, 1962, which is very skeptical of such belief.

This hampered the guidance of kolkhozes and sovkhozes and was one of the reasons why the targets of the
first three years of the Seven-Year Plan were not fulfilled."[74] The "conservatives" in the state agricultural
bureaucracy now felt themselves to be on such safe
ground that, despite Khrushchev's tirades against the
grassland method from December 1961 to March 1962,
in 1962 as much as 30 per cent of the plowland at the
experimental farm of the RSFSR Ministry of Agriculture was sown to grasses.[75]

As Stalin in 1947 wished to strike only at the Ukraine,
so Khrushchev in 1962 chose Leningrad as the place to
be singled out for the brazen contempt it had shown for
the ruling against the grassland method. A decree of the
Central Committee (Presidium or Secretariat) adopted
on April 10, 1962, accused the Leningrad City Party
Committee of failure to draw proper conclusions from
the Kremlin's criticism of certain agricultural institutes
in the city and of having abstained from timely and effective measures to overcome the adherence of many
local scientists to the grassland system. The Leningrad
Regional Party Committee was ordered to intensify
control of the municipal committee's guidance of party
organizations in scientific institutes.[76] Khrushchev evidently tabled as well the draft of the April 12, 1962, decree of party and government which asserted the independence of local farm technicians within the limits of
the general plan.[77] But the accretion of power in re-

[74] No. 8, 1962, p. 19.
[75] Khrushchev's speech of March 12, 1963, in *S.K. v SSSR i
R.S.Kh.*, VII, 457. The ministry was abolished later in 1963.
[76] *Partiynaya Zhizn'*, No. 8, 1962, pp. 30-35; and *Spravochnik
Partiynogo Rabotnika*, Moscow, 1963, pp. 489-495.
[77] "On Increasing the Role of Agronomists, Zootechnicians, and

gional party committees had the effect of nullifying this order.[78]

Khrushchev resumed his agitation for more investment in agriculture in an interview of April 20, 1962, with the American publisher Gardner G. Cowles which *Pravda* tardily ran one week later. The outdated livestock structures in many farms had to be rebuilt, he said, electrical and mechanical facilities introduced, and chemical fertilizer plants constructed. All this required capital inputs. Khrushchev assailed Stalin for his "primitive" understanding of agriculture and noted the tyrant's policy of unjustifiably low procurement prices for farm commodities. "Here enthusiasm by itself means little," Khrushchev added. "A man cannot fill his belly with only speeches about communism, a man must eat, he needs clothing, an apartment, other things, without which he cannot live."[79] The recriminations which the Khrushchev and Kozlov-Suslov groups were then hurling at each other behind the scenes found expression in the utterances of party propagandists. Il'ichëv declared that "Only doctrinaires and revisionists can contrast heavy industry and the production of consumer goods or industry and agriculture."[80] The industrial newpaper of the party Secretariat recalled that some members of the "anti-party group" wanted to equalize the growth rates of heavy and light industry.[81]

Other State Agricultural Specialists in Developing Collective and State Farm Production," Decree of the CPSU Central Committee and USSR Council of Ministers, in *Pravda*, April 19, 1962 (CDSP, xiv, 16, pp. 16-17).

[78] See P. Chestnov, *Partiynaya Zhizn'*, No. 1, 1963, pp. 25-29.

[79] *S.K. v SSSR i R.S.Kh.*, vii, 20-27; and *Pravda*, April 27, 1962 (CDSP, xiv, 17, pp. 18-25).

[80] *Pravda*, April 22, 1962.

[81] *Ekonomicheskaya Gazeta*, May 7, 1962.

Organizational thrusts proceeded apace with these verbal maneuvers. Khrushchev upset a few of the bureaucratic arrangements made in the difficult struggles of 1960-1961. Ol'shanskiy of the generally "conservative" body of agricultural scientists was replaced as USSR Minister of Agriculture by a utilitarian party boss, Pysin.[82] Kirilenko, expelled from the ranks of the candidate members of the party Presidium in November 1961, returned as a full member and balanced Voronov as first deputy chairman of the RSFSR Bureau.[83] The first secretary of the Leningrad Regional Party Committee, I. V. Spiridonov, was deprived of the largely honorific title of Central Committee secretary which had been bestowed on him in November 1961, and given the sinecure of chairman of the USSR Supreme Soviet's Council of the Union.[84] Khrushchev soon journeyed to Leningrad to preside over the removal of Spiridonov from the territorial leadership.[85] Both Spiridonov and Kozlov were indirectly criticized in *Pravda* on August 1, 1962, which carried a notice that the Central Committee would not revoke an official ban placed on the use of a drug administered in Leningrad for the treatment of cancer patients. The drug had been erroneously acclaimed in *Leningrad Pravda* on August 4, 1957, and October 27, 1958, or when Kozlov and Spiridonov, respectively, were in charge of the region. Meanwhile, F. I. Golikov, who at the 22nd Congress had paid rare homage to Suslov for his role in the purge of Marshal Zhukov, was replaced by Khrushchev's vassal Yepishev

---

[82] *Pravda*, April 26, 1962.
[83] *Ibid.*, April 26 and 28, 1962.
[84] *Ibid.*, April 26, 1962.
[85] *Ibid.*, May 4, 1962.

as chief of the Main Political Administration of the Soviet Army and Navy.[86]

These personnel shifts of April and May 1962 indicated that Khrushchev was capable of forcing a decision on price policy. But the decision was an act of compromise which vitiated Khrushchev's welfare propaganda of the past 18 months or so. The state purchase prices of kolkhoz beef, pork, mutton, goat's meat, and poultry were to be raised an average of 35 per cent, and the retail prices of meat and meat products were temporarily to be increased by an average of 30 per cent, and of butter by an average of 25 per cent.[87] An explanatory letter of the party and government[88] offers a glimpse into the bickering which went on as this decision was reached. Khrushchev presumably argued in favor of cutting back investments in the metallurgical and machine-building industries or transferring funds earmarked for military projects. Kozlov and Suslov evidently voiced the objection recorded in the letter that this would undermine the economic base of the whole economy and not take into account the "fact" that the Western powers were planning a surprise nuclear-rocket attack on the USSR. These neo-Stalinists assumedly proposed to allocate additional funds to kolkhozes by reducing individual peasant income and restricting housing construction. Khrushchev opposed those alternatives. He also contended on June 27, 1962, that if procurement prices were

[86] The USSR Council of Ministers' decree of May 11, 1962, is in *Pravda*, May 22, 1962. A "chronicle" note in the same day's *Pravda* explained that Golikov was dropped "for reasons of health."

[87] The decree of the USSR Council of Ministers is in *Pravda*, June 1, 1962 (CDSP, xiv, 22, pp. 5-6).

[88] *Pravda*, June 1, 1962 (CDSP, xiv, 20, pp. 3-5).

raised and retail prices kept at the same level, this would provide opportunities for speculation.[89] The disconcerting effect of the price verdict on the liberalizer wing of the party is apparent from Khrushchev's remark in the same speech: "We have heard that there are even certain Communists who are wont to say: 'So we adopted the program for the construction of communism at the 22nd party Congress, and after that we raised meat prices. Which way are we going, then, forward or backward?'" Public disturbances are reliably reported to have followed in the town of Novocherkassk and the Khrushchev group opportunely exploited the incidents. Kirilenko traveled to the provincial capital of Rostov and chaired the meeting of the Regional Party Committee which banished the authoritarian centralist Basov and installed in his place as first secretary V. V. Skryabin of the Ukrainian party apparatus.[90]

The senior bureaucrats who had advanced in the trail of Kozlov during 1960-1961 were indeed special objects of Khrushchev's wrath in the summer of 1962. He used every possible means to undermine confidence in them, including charges of professional ineptitude, Stalinism, and technological conservatism. Newspaper "raiding brigades" were sent into the domain of Kunayev and Rodionov and uncovered gross deficiencies in the train-

[89] *Ibid.*, June 30, 1962 (CDSP, xiv, 26, pp. 6-12, 29). "If purchase prices were raised and retail prices were not, some collective farmers might have to consider whether it would be more profitable for them to produce meat on the collective farm or to go to the state store, buy meat there at the lower price, and sell it back to the state at the higher purchase price, thus making a profit on the deal. Would this approach aid in increasing meat production? No, it would further speculation and lead to reduced production."

[90] *Pravda*, August 16, 1962.

ing of farm machine operators.[91] As early as the 22nd Congress, blame for the lag in supplying farms with electricity from the state power grids had been laid at the doorstep of V. N. Novikov, a former associate of Kozlov, who had been named chairman of the USSR State Planning Committee during the great reorganization of the leadership in May 1960.[92] Novikov was eased out of his post in mid-July 1962 and assigned to integrating the economies of the Communist Bloc states.[93] A few weeks later, Khrushchev opened the Kremenchug hydropower plant and denounced Stalin for ruling that kolkhozes might not use the state power lines even if they ran through their land. Stalin's understanding of agriculture was "somewhat perverted," he said, but "although Stalin has long since passed on, and the party has criticized the negative side of Stalin, little has changed in ensuring kolkhozes and sovkhozes with a supply of electric power. Here there is still rooted the negative heritage of the past, which must be torn out, in order to facilitate a rapid upswing of agriculture."[94]

Khrushchev sent off a memorandum to the party Presidium on August 4, 1962, after he had read the planners' low estimate of farm machinery production in the 1963 economic targets.[95] The estimate was included in a note submitted by the chairman of the USSR Agricultural Committee, N. G. Ignatov, but Khrushchev felt sure that such miserly calculations were the work of N. P.

[91] Cf. *ibid.*, July 4, 6, 7, and 15, 1962.
[92] See the speech of Shkol'nikov in *ibid.*, October 28, 1961.
[93] *Ibid.*, July 18, 1962.
[94] *Ibid.*, July 30, 1962.
[95] "Persistently Introduce the Achievements of Science and Technology into Production," *S.K. v SSSR i R.S.Kh.*, VII, 126-142.

Gusev, chief of the Agricultural Section in the State Planning Committee. The entire bureaucracy concerned with agriculture was advised to check on conditions in their own localities and find what sort of equipment was actually in demand. Kuchumov of the FMA knew that the premier was deeply interested in the construction of a machine to harvest kidney and soy beans, but only after constant nagging did he show Khrushchev the photograph of such a machine in an American magazine. Kuchumov perhaps was unaware of the machine's existence, but if that was so, it was still disturbing. Khrushchev further recommended that metal be economized in the construction of milking machines. A model called "Carousel" was particularly advantageous in this respect and should be manufactured on a planned basis at special factories. Kuchumov's response was evasive and the planners distributed orders for only 1,500 "Carousels."[96]

The capital requirements of specialized sovkhozes around the main cities were brought to the attention of the leadership in Khrushchev's memorandum of September 5, 1962, to the party Presidium.[97] Machinery, swamp drainage, and irrigation were all badly needed to make these farms run profitably. Khrushchev observed that agricultural officials thought that the new system of production management in kolkhozes and sovkhozes was worthwhile, but he was displeased with on-the-spot direction of affairs and believed that "enormous harm" was inflicted by outside interference in the work of farm technicians. The very same complaint was lodged in

---

[96] See Khrushchev's speech of March 12, 1963, in *ibid.*, VII, 461.
[97] "Ripe Questions of the Further Improvement of Agricultural Production," *ibid.*, VII, 143-162.

Khrushchev's memorandum of September 10, 1962, to the party Presidium, which proposed the bifurcation of territorial party committees into industrial and agricultural units.[98] In recommending that party agencies "guide the economy on a daily, genuinely operative basis," Khrushchev apparently intended to induce in the ruling elite an awareness that new solutions were urgently needed if the economy was to achieve its full potential. The reorganization was also designed to advance young, forward-looking cadres into positions of responsibility. Before it was undertaken, only two of the second secretaries of regional party committees in the Russian Federation were under 40 years of age; shortly afterward, 14 second secretaries of industrial regional party committees and 20 of agricultural regional party committees had not reached their fortieth birthday.[99] Understandably, "certain officials" objected to the reorganization.[100]

Khrushchev returned to the theme of agriculture's technical outfitting in his memorandum on grain production, addressed to the party Presidium on November 10, 1962, and carried in *Pravda* three days later.[101] The desperation measure of plowing up millions of acres of grassland without commensurate increases in machinery had to be avoided in 1963 lest farms wind up minus both hay and row crops, which must have often

[98] "On Reorganization of Party Guidance of Industry and Agriculture," *ibid.*, VII, 163-177.

[99] M. Polekhin, *Partiynaya Zhizn'*, No. 1, 1964, p. 26.

[100] F. F. Petrenko, *KPSS v Period Razvërnutogo Stroitel'stva Kommunizma* (CPSU in a Period of Full-Scale Building of Communism), Moscow, 1963, p. 12.

[101] "Summing-up the Results of the Year and Increasing the Production and Purchases of Grain," in *ibid.*, VII, 294-308; and *Pravda*, November 13, 1962 (CDSP, XIV, 46, pp. 9-12).

been the case during the past year. But there was an opportunity to expand the production of chemical fertilizer. The steel addicts still blocked the way to this goal and Khrushchev derided them anew at the Central Committee session on November 19-23, 1962. "Some officials," he said, had "put on steel blinkers. . . . A material appears which is superior to steel and is cheaper and they still cry, 'Steel, steel!' "[102]

The first secretary had achieved a few marginal gains in the most recent discords over agricultural policy. The party Presidium, he related, had adopted a decision to convert one of the biggest machine-building plants, the Kirov plant in Leningrad, to the production of up-to-date tractors. This, of course, was a far cry from the relevant proposals which Khrushchev made at the opening of the March session of the Central Committee. By 1966 the production of chemical fertilizer would amount to 41 million tons, compared with 17 million tons in 1962. The long-range economic targets drawn up in 1961 had foreseen an annual production of 35 million tons of chemical fertilizer by 1965. In practical terms, if the latest mark was reached, farms would be supplied with about one-third of the amount of chemical fertilizer which agronomists deemed essential.[103] Khrushchev disapproved of the unwieldiness of some of the 960 territorial production administrations created in March, and proposed the formation of a total of 1,500 under the

[102] Khrushchev's report on "The Development of the USSR Economy and Party Guidance of the National Economy" is in *Pravda*, November 20, 1962 (CDSP, xiv, 46, pp. 3ff.).

[103] See the figures in N. V. Bautina, *Ekonomicheskiye Zakonomernosti Perekhoda ot Sotsializma k Kommunizmu* (Economic Patterns of Development of the Transition from Socialism to Communism), Moscow, 1962, pp. 124-125.

leadership of internal party committees. This was in line with his theory of the technically functional party and on November 26, 1962, *Pravda* ran on page one a TASS cable from London which noted that in Soviet Russia, "a special party apparatus will manage agriculture." One of the devotees of state authoritarian centralism had to pay for this reversal of viewpoint, and Voronov was chosen for the sacrifice. He was overrun by L. N. Yefremov, first secretary of the Gorky Regional Party Committee and the graduate of an agricultural institute, who was appointed to candidate membership in the party Presidium and named first deputy chairman of the RSFSR Bureau.[104] Voronov, still a member of the Presidium, sank to the inferior executive post of RSFSR premier.[105]

Kozlov and Suslov held their ground on investment policy. State outlays for agriculture were to rise by 17.8 per cent in 1963 and the delivery of machines and chemical fertilizer by only 10.5 per cent.[106] The economist Buzdalov commented in the vein of Khrushchev's latest messages to the oligarchy: "In the future these appropriations must be increased." For the moment, Khrushchev had to rest content with the degrading of Kuchumov and the Kunayev-Rodionov team in Kazakhstan.[107] Meanwhile, there were conflicting opin-

[104] *Pravda*, November 24, 1962.
[105] *Ibid.*
[106] V. F. Garbuzov, *Pravda*, December 11, 1962 (CDSP, xiv, 52, p. 11); and I. Buzdalov, *Voprosy Ekonomiki*, No. 1, 1963, p. 71.
[107] Kuchumov's replacement as FMA chief by the Ukrainian-schooled official of the Machine-Building Section in the USSR State Planning Committee, A. A. Yezhevskiy, was reported in *Pravda*, December 22 and 27, 1962. Five days later, the same daily announced that Rodionov was discharged from the party second

ions about the proper appraisal of Stalin's historical role and the effect of his policies.[108] The declining indices of agricultural production[109] and Khrushchev's personal aspirations at the age of 68 ensured the resumption of intergroup hostilities in the near future.

One of the main points which stands out upon inquiry into the events of 1961-1962 is the predominant importance of internal over foreign political considerations in the budgeting of state resources. There was no such thing as an "objective" estimate of the world situation in order to determine the appropriate levels of government spending for producer and consumer goods. Instead, policy-makers were sharply divided over the implications of recurrent tension in East-West relations. As during the Korean War, Khrushchev was absorbed

---

secretaryship of Kazakhstan and Kunayev was shifted to the republican premiership.

[108] In 1959-1962, an explanatory note on the newspaper *Pravda* was reprinted in successive editions of the republished transcripts of party congresses and conferences. One sentence in this note listed famous editors of *Pravda*, including Stalin and Molotov. This sentence appeared in the note in the volumes signed for printing on November 18, 1959, January 5, 1960, and March 17, 1961. The sentence was expunged from the note in the volume signed on February 10, 1962, or shortly after Khrushchev's denigration of Stalin at the 22nd party Congress. However, the sentence reappeared in the note as carried in the volume signed for printing on December 6, 1962. Khrushchev's propagandist Bugayev wrote in *Pravda* of December 26, 1962: "Sometimes the question is asked: Have we not put enough blame on the consequences of the cult of the individual? No, not enough! It will not be enough until they are completely overcome not only on the ideological and theoretical plane, which has already been done with revolutionary decisiveness and courage, but also in all spheres of practical activity" (CDSP, XIV, 52, p. 39).

[109] In the period 1953-1958, farm output rose an average of 8.5 per cent annually, but the same increment for 1954-1962 was 5.5 per cent (V. Khlebnikov, *Voprosy Ekonomiki*, No. 7, 1962, p. 49; and *Kommunist*, No. 8, 1963, p. 20).

in matters of domestic reconstruction and his group stubbornly fought for the adoption of its reformist platform, unrestrained by thoughts of the regime's external difficulties. In the summer of 1961, the Soviet government formally expressed grave concern about the Berlin question in an *aide-mémoire* to the American President, increased its defense expenditures by one-third, erected the Berlin Wall as its local armored forces confronted their opposite numbers, and resumed nuclear testing in the atmosphere. However, simultaneously with these forboding occurrences, the draft party Program brightly heralded a "new period" of industrialization to benefit the consumer, most members of the editorial board of *Pravda* anticipated that the Soviet Union would overtake the United States in per capita output of consumer durables by 1971, and various propagandists continued to laud Khrushchev's doctrinal innovation which stressed the value of consumption over production. A corollary of this reformist agitation was moderate definition of the main goal of Kremlin foreign policy: "to provide peaceful conditions for the building of a communist society in the USSR," etc.

The opposition no less doggedly championed its productionist outlook and emphasized the national security aspect of the foreign policy complex, believing that its main tendency should be "to foil the sanguinary designs of the imperialists." Concurrent divergencies over the reputation of Stalin excluded the possibility of an inadvertent crossing of wires in the propaganda machinery. The sources urging a higher standard of living for the masses integrally upheld flexibility in the conduct of external affairs and trod down on Stalin, while the reverse was true of the partisans of austerity. The ultimate decision reached at the 22nd party Congress to observe a relatively cautious line in foreign policy but avoid serious modification of the production-weighted scale of national priorities demonstrated again the primary significance of factional compromise in governmental budgeting.

In 1962, as well, Khrushchev ignored the strident professions of the danger of war, which were rife in Soviet home propaganda, and called for the redistribution of capital funds to build agricultural machinery plants. Defense requirements, as these were perceived in a section of the dictatorship, turned out to be overriding. It is tempting to speculate that the premier hoped to end the running controversy over military preparedness by initiating the risky decision to establish intermediate-range ballistic missile sites in Cuba. But shortly after the Kremlin's ignominious retreat in the face of American pressure, the military's share of state investments was officially reported to have decreased slightly, and Khrushchev was strong enough to demote several inconvenient bureaucrats and, in due course, replace the Chief of the General Staff.[110] Moreover, a decree secretly

[110] On defense spending, see Chapter V, note 59. Marshal M. V. Zakharov commanded the Leningrad Military District from 1955 to 1957, or when Kozlov was first secretary of the Leningrad Regional Party Committee. He was named first deputy USSR Minister of Defense and Chief of Staff of the Soviet Army and Navy shortly prior to Kozlov's entry into the Central Committee Secretariat. The press organ of the Defense Ministry, *Krasnaya Zvezda*, reported on March 28, 1963, that Zakharov had been replaced as chief of staff by Marshal S. S. Biryuzov. In January-February 1963, on the occasion of the 20th anniversary of the Battle of Stalingrad, one group of marshals, including Biryuzov, ascribed authorship of the victory plan to the local military figures and political overlord, Khrushchev. Another group, headed by Malinovskiy, alleged that Stalin's war chiefs at the center had both drafted the plan and said the last word on it. (Cf. the

adopted on January 8, 1963, obviously upon the insistence of Khrushchev, authorized the building of 150 new poultry factories for the production of eggs and 70 for the production of broilers. An official estimate put at 5,000,000 rubles the building of a poultry factory for 250,000 hens.[111] Thus, there can be no certainty about which side in the argument over investment and defense policies was responsible for the Cuban missile venture. In any event, the standoff on resource allocation persisted until one of the major contestants in that argument was physically immobilized.

---

articles of Marshals A. I. Yerëmenko, *Pravda*, January 27, 1963; V. I. Chuykov, *ibid.*, January 30, 1963; Biryuzov, *Politicheskoye Samoobrazovaniye*, No. 2, 1963, p. 37; N. N. Voronov, *Pravda*, January 31, 1963; and Malinovskiy, *ibid.*, February 2, 1963). Zakharov's September 1962 review of the latest volume of a multivolume history of the Soviet-German war indicated that he belonged to one of the anti-Khrushchev officer cliques (Cf. Zakharov, *Kommunist*, No. 14, 1962, pp. 42-43; and Lt. Gen. N. Radetskiy, *Pravda*, October 5, 1962).

[111] See Khrushchev's memorandum "To the Presidium of the CPSU Central Committee: On Certain Questions Linked with the Implementation of the Party's Course Toward the Intensification of Agriculture," *Pravda* and *Izvestiya*, April 24, 1964 (CDSP, xvi, 17, pp. 3ff.).

ADDENDUM

On May 4, 1963, three years to the day after F. R. Kozlov was formally promoted to membership in the CPSU Central Committee Secretariat, *Pravda* ran on page two a brief notice by the Committee that he had been unable to participate in the May Day festivities because of illness. The validity of the reason given for the absence of Kozlov cannot be determined. But in view of Kozlov's embroilment in recent political disputes, the timing of this notice seemed ironic and created an impression that his enemies—above all, Khrushchev—had at last managed to square a long-standing account. This impression was reinforced by subsequent shifts on the levels of policy and personnel appointment. The policy of an all-out drive in metallurgical production, which Kozlov had verbally championed with remarkable consistency, was modified in line with Khrushchev's urging for economy in the use of costly metal and greater attention to chemistry. Personalities whose intimacy with Khrushchev stretched back to his career in the Ukraine now amassed more executive power and the influence of those who had emerged from the apparatus in Leningrad receded.

After Khrushchev had tongue-lashed the steel enthusiasts at the November 1962 Central Committee session, Kozlov evidently felt that he had to tread more cautiously. He told a public meeting in Leningrad on February 26, 1963, that "needed" tempos of metallurgical development had to be preserved and "significantly more attention" paid to the chemical industry. He was much less equivocal about the construction of new industrial giants: "In many branches of our industry there is not sufficient capacity or supply of machines and equipment to assure the uninterrupted planned growth of a particular product. In order to liquidate this 'shortage,' we must construct a larger number of new machine-building or other enterprises and invest huge funds in this."[1] The inveterate Stalinist Chesnokov had since made sure that a "philosophical" anthology which he edited linked the causes of metallurgy and machine-building.[2]

On June 4, 1963, *Pravda* announced that the USSR Council of Ministers had met recently to examine Khrushchev's proposals to change the practice of allocating funds and manpower to various industrial branches on the basis of previously established ratios. The change was intended to facilitate priority development of the chemical industry in order to pull up light industry and agriculture. The planners were also ordered to avoid diffusing capital investment over numerous projects and instead to concentrate efforts on important ones so that these might be put into operation in the shortest time. (Since 1959, 24 billion rubles' worth of central capital investment funds had been tied up in unfinished construction work.[3]) Kozlov's viewpoint was

[1] *Leningradskaya Pravda*, February 27, 1963.
[2] "The production of metal and fuel is the foundation of modern industry. Without a powerful metallurgical base the development of the basic branches of the national economy is entirely impossible. At present, although our country has achieved enormous successes in the development of the metallurgical industry, a shortage of metal is asserting itself, and this is limiting the development of a number of branches of the national economy—such, for example, as machine-building and the manufacture of oil and gas pipe." (*Nekotorye Aktual'nye Voprosy Marksistsko-Leninskoy Teorii. Sbornik Statey pod Redaktsiey prof. D. I. Chesnokova* [Some Current Problems of Marxist-Leninist Theory. Collection of Articles Under the Editorship of Professor D. I. Chesnokov], "Vysshaya Shkola" Publishing House, Moscow, (February 20) 1963, p. 91).
[3] *Kommunist*, No. 10, 1963, p. 77.

discredited when the planners were asked to "foresee on a large scale the direction of capital investment to increase productive capacity at the expense of restoring and technically reoutfitting the existing enterprises, which will enable an increment of ouptut in shorter times and with less expenditure." In a few weeks' time, the steel production goal of 95-97 million tons annually by 1965, which was set in 1961, was lowered to 86-91 million tons, or the figure of the Seven-Year Plan ratified in 1959.[4]

The breaking of Kozlov's power eventuated in a flow of statements in behalf of the "collective leadership" principle.[5] The responsibilities of the fallen leader for senior personnel appointments and general supervision of affairs at party headquarters were parceled out to Brezhnev and Podgornyy, who were formally recruited into the party Secretariat at the Central Committee session of June 18-21, 1963.[6] Khrushchev's greater trust in Brezhnev may be inferred from the protocol evidence which was immediately available.[7] One of the first acts of the new, "Ukrainian" directorate at the center was to cut short the career of a "Leningrader" and rehabilitate

[4] See P. Ye Sledzyuk, deputy chairman of the State Committee for Ferrous and Nonferrous Metallurgy in the USSR State Planning Committee, in *Krasnaya Zvezda*, July 21, 1963. Sledzyuk declared that "Metallurgy is the basis of strength of the military power of the Soviet Union. It is tanks, planes, rockets, and submarines."

[5] Cf. *Partiynaya Zhizn'*, No. 9, (April 29) 1963, p. 22; *Kommunist*, No. 7, (May 4) 1963, p. 25; *Voprosy Istorii KPSS*, No. 7, (June 28) 1963, pp. 42-43; *Kommunist*, No. 10, (July 12) 1963, pp. 44-45; and *Partiynaya Zhizn'*, No. 14, (July 17) 1963, p. 25.

[6] *Pravda*, June 22, 1963.

[7] In contrast to *Pravda*, Adzhubey's *Izvestiya* on August 6, 1963, named only Khrushchev and Brezhnev (without Podgornyy and Kirilenko) among Soviet leaders present at an evening reception in the Kremlin held in connection with the signing of the limited nuclear test-ban treaty.

one of their own. *Pravda* on August 16, 1963, announced that A. K. Korovushkin, who like Kozlov worked in Leningrad in the late 1930's, was released as chairman of the USSR State Bank. Simultaneously, *Pravda* reported the bureaucratic comeback of V. A. Kucherenko. An associate of Khrushchev in the Ukraine during the period 1939-1950, Kucherenko served as chairman of the USSR State Committee for Construction Affairs from 1955 to January 1961. He was then displaced by I. A. Grishmanov, an ex-associate of Kozlov in Leningrad, who held that post until November 1962. Kucherenko was made president of the USSR Academy of Construction and Architecture and in 1962 revived in *Kommunist* the controversial agro-city scheme of Khrushchev.[8] Now Kucherenko returned to government service as a USSR minister of undisclosed portfolio.

One outstanding personnel change of the day served as a reminder that no bureaucracy, territorial or professional, is solidly unified. Shortly after the Central Committee met in June, V. V. Shcherbitskiy, premier of the Ukraine and candidate member of the party Presidium since November 1961, tumbled to the lower station of regional party secretary.[9] The devious behavior of the "Ukrainian" Podgornyy helps to explain Khrushchev's imminent ordeal in the matter of allocations to the chemical fertilizer industry.

Underscoring the close interdependence of problems of domestic and foreign policy, a new stage in the struggle for funds began during the diplomatic talks which resulted in the signing of an agreement with the

[8] No. 7, 1962, p. 25.
[9] *Pravda*, June 30 and July 8, 1963.

United States for a limited ban on nuclear testing. On July 12, 1963, Khrushchev sent to the party Presidium a memorandum calling for an expansion of the output of chemical fertilizer from the 1963 planned level of 15.8 million tons to 100 million tons in 1970. The cost of this project was estimated at 5.8 million rubles.[10] The premier restated a goal of 80-100 million tons of chemical fertilizer by 1970 when he met with American farm experts on July 30, 1963. The estimated cost had since risen to 10 billion rubles and was to be defrayed partly by a cutback of military spending. "Now we shall reduce expenditures on defense," Khrushchev pointed out, "and this money as well we shall direct to the production of chemical fertilizers."[11] Shortly thereafter, Khrushchev outlined to the Presidium a multibillion-ruble scheme for irrigating arid farm regions.[12]

Bad weather conditions and the depressed state of farm inventories and treasuries led to serious crop failures throughout the country in 1963. Khrushchev mustered enough votes in the leadership to undertake extremely costly purchases of wheat and flour in overseas markets. He convincingly absolved himself of blame for the crisis by waving his October 1960 memorandum to the party Presidium.[13] The supporters of Khrushchev rightfully could point to the guilt of "some leaders" who had turned their backs on the technological needs of agricul-

[10] "On Developing the Production of Chemical Fertilizers for Complete Satisfaction of the Requirements of Agriculture," *S.K. v SSSR i R.S.Kh.*, VIII, 23-43.

[11] "Talk with Delegation of Agricultural Specialists of USA," *ibid.*, VIII, 44-61.

[12] "On Developing Irrigated Agriculture in Order to Receive a Guaranteed Harvest of Grain Crops," memorandum of August 14, 1963, in *ibid.*, VIII, 91-102.

[13] See *Kommunist*, No. 13, 1963, pp. 8-10.

ture.[14] But Khrushchev inexplicably backtracked from his stand on irrigation at a meeting with Ukrainian farm workers held on September 27, 1963. Notwithstanding his memorandum of the previous month, the premier stated that efforts to speed up the production of chemical fertilizer took precedence over irrigation work "because a solution of both tasks simultaneously is, evidently, beyond our capabilities."[15] It may be hazarded that the dimensions of the reduction of defense spending which the premier had contemplated had since come under acrimonious review.

Foreign Minister A. A. Gromyko enumerated in *Izvestiya* of October 26, 1963, the following diplomatic priorities and made it clear that Khrushchev had authorized the listing: (1) disarmament; (2) German peace treaties; (3) non-aggression treaty between NATO and Warsaw Pact members; (4) *reduction of military budgets;* (5) efforts to inhibit the spread of nuclear arms; (6) measures to ensure against surprise attack; and (7) diminishing the number of foreign troops in Europe. But on November 6, Podgornyy emerged as the spokesman of military interests. He aired a new, less practicable order of diplomatic priorities in a speech made on the occasion of the anniversary of the Revolution: (1) European security and "eliminating the vestiges of World War II" (i.e., the German question); (2) nonaggression pact; (3) nuclear-free zones in all parts of the world; (4) preventing spread of nuclear weapons; and (5) ensuring against surprise attack, including the thinning-out of foreign troop strength in West and East Germany. Only if settlements were reached on

[14] See L. Korbut, *Voprosy Ekonomiki*, No. 8, 1963, p. 89.
[15] *Pravda*, October 1, 1963.

these matters would a serious improvement of international relations have occurred and the proper conditions be created for general and complete disarmament.[16] The epauletted section of the Central Committee was so appreciative of Podgornyy's intractable outlook on arms control and disarmament that he was granted prominence in the daily of the Defense Ministry when the Khrushchevite *Izvestiya* saw fit to slight him.[17]

In spite of Podgornyy's remarks of November 6, Khrushchev was determined to impose his will in the matter of chemical fertilizer production. *Izvestiya* on November 13, 1963, cited an annual target of 100 million tons to be attained by 1970, and *Pravda's* leader of November 14 stressed that Comrade N. S. Khrushchev had said: *"Our goal is to reach in 1970 the productive level of 100 million tons of chemical fertilizer. Why must we pose and solve such a task? If we are to speak of the real possibility of increasing grain production, it is necessary to see it foremost in wide use of fertilizer."* But complications shortly arose. *Pravda* on November 16 raised doubt about Khrushchev's preeminence when it violated established protocol and reported that a public meeting in the capital had elected to its honorary steering committee the Central Committee Presidium, without "Comrade N. S. Khrushchev at the top," which is the usual formula. A day later, *Pravda* and *Izvestiya* carried a letter to the Central Committee which was signed by a number of agricultural scientists.

[16] *Ibid.*, November 7, 1963.
[17] On January 14, 1964, *Pravda* on page one featured a photograph of Premier Castro's arrival in Moscow. It included Podgornyy, as did the photo in *Krasnaya Zvezda* of the Defense Ministry. But Podgornyy was cut off in the analogous photos in *Izvestiya* and *Sovetskaya Rossiya*.

The letter knowledgeably disputed a claim of the USSR Ministry of Agriculture that 86.4 million tons of chemical fertilizer were required and insisted that a lesser amount would suffice if the commodity was properly utilized. State planners were requested to "formulate more precisely" the essential quantity of chemical fertilizer. This proposal drew conflicting reactions in the editorial offices of *Pravda* and *Izvestiya*. In keeping with the essentially "conservative" tone of the party organ, the editors of *Pravda* tacitly endorsed the contents of the letter by remarking in an appended note inviting comment that it offered "important proposals of great importance for the national economy." On the other hand, the reformists in charge of the government newspaper merely welcomed comment on the letter and thus observed the ritualistic silence of dissent insofar as its substance was concerned. The past activities of Lysenko and Laptev gave indication that the latest political bombshell had hardly been prepared in the laboratories of agricultural science, but instead within the circle of Khrushchev's adversaries in the leadership.

When calm finally prevailed, Khrushchev had obtained much, but had to settle for less than he wanted. One-quarter of the 42 billion rubles earmarked for chemistry over the next seven years would directly benefit agriculture.[18] The state outlays for standard agricultural needs were considerably increased (from a total of 10 billion rubles during the past four years to 11.5 billion rubles in 1964-1965). Moreover, kolkhozes were to receive

[18] The economic plans for 1964-1965 and their implications are outlined in the speeches of P. F. Lomako and V. F. Garbuzov to the USSR Supreme Soviet session in *Pravda*, December 17, 1963. Like the new steel goal, the allocations to chemistry were those originally established in the Seven-Year Plan.

long-term credits of 2.8 billion rubles in the next two years. On the other hand, the volume of chemical fertilizer planned for 1970 was fixed at 70-80 million tons rather than the 100 million which Khrushchev demanded. The premier's irrigation scheme was held in abeyance, albeit he had advised combining it with the fertilizer program. The old guard element in the defense and industrial bureaucracies lost some ground, as the overt military budget was reduced by 600 million rubles and cutbacks were ordered for metallurgy, conventional machine building, and electric power projects. But the recosting operation also entailed less expenditure for housing and footwear. In all, the "hidebound dogmatists" whom Khrushchev later criticized for opposition to his chemical venture[19] and who were probably equally obdurate about the irrigation plan, had not done too badly. The opposition, furthermore, was able to postpone the replacement of the debilitated Kozlov. Ukrainian party leader Shelest, who was awarded Shcherbitskiy's seat as a candidate member of the party Presidium, turned out to be a vocal advocate of the orthodox policy of preferential growth of heavy industry.[20] Thus, despite the absence of Kozlov and the temporary disappearance of Suslov,[21] effective challenges to Khrushchev persistently arose.

[19] *Pravda*, February 15, 1964.

[20] The changes in Presidium membership were announced after the December 1963 Central Committee session in *ibid.*, December 14, 1963. On heavy industry, see the polemical article of V. Mazur in *Pravda Ukrainy*, January 17, 1964.

[21] The whereabouts of Suslov were unreported in the press from September 17, 1963, to January 2, 1964.

CONCLUSIONS

STRUGGLE FOR power has never been merely a raucous pastime in the Kremlin. It has always been a fundamental factor motivating the behavior of Soviet leaders in dealings with outsiders and one another. This has been no less true of the formation of policy in the post-Stalin period. The heads of succeeding regimes could not master anything like the plenitude of power which Stalin accumulated during the timespan of fifteen years and under hypertense conditions, internally and abroad. Malenkov, and Khrushchev after him, had to seek to achieve their major goals through resort to persuasion and intrigue within a structure of diffused power. At the same time, other leaders had both the right to express personal dissent and, most important, the capability to marshal support for opposing viewpoints. The general effect of this systematized competition for personal prestige and sovereignty of ideas was the creation willy-nilly of "checks and balances" in the mechanics of government. This in turn led to dilatory and half-hearted solution of pressing national problems that required the kind of prompt and bold action urged by more forward-looking elements in the leadership, chiefly Khrushchev.

ISSUES AND ATTITUDES

The internal political disputes of the last decade originated in whirlpools of vendetta, patronage, opportunism, and rival convictions. The personal antagonisms of Khrushchev and Beriya dated back to the war years, those between Khrushchev and Malenkov were recurrent in the postwar period, and Kozlov and Suslov in all probability deeply resented Khrushchev's organizational insult to them in 1957-1960. The ties of some leaders with the directors of certain bureaucratic departments evidently were too close for them to resist distress calls to block unsettling changes in departmental routine. (The relationships of Malenkov—agricultural planning —Benediktov's ministry, and of Kozlov—investment planning procedures—V. N. Novikov's state committee, are suggestive here.) The lure of temporary advantage may be inferred to have figured in the insurrections of Malenkov's economic deputies in 1954-1955, Matskevich in 1959-1960, and Podgornyy in 1963.

The typical leader of stature, however, did not appear to be a mere "careerist" or political weathercock, but someone of definite attitude who strove for the adoption of mutually reinforcing decisions. The patterns of oratory and career movement in the upper stratum tended to confirm Mikoyan's characterization of the 1956-1957 struggle in the party Presidium: "These differences with the conservative-dogmatic group were not over particular organizational or isolated political questions. No. They concerned the determination of the entire policy of the party in the new stage of historical development, its general line."[1] The same might be said of the arguments between the Khrushchev and Kozlov-Suslov groups in 1958-1963.

Hardly by chance did the competing groups devote so much attention to manipulation of the Stalin symbol. There basic divergencies of outlook concerned Stalin's method of government. In economics, the neo-Stalinists were uninterested in short-term improvement of the welfare of the broadest circles of the population. In

[1] *Pravda*, October 22, 1961.

administration, they favored curtailment of local autonomy and reliance on authoritarian centralism. The neo-Stalinists' low estimate of the moral cohesiveness of the nation, masked by their stress on inner unity in regard to "contradictions," made them wary of badly needed measures to decentralize the topheavy bureaucracy and provide broad scope for a display of initiative on the periphery. Austerity and regimentation for the multitude; material and order-giving privileges for the metropolitan elite—such were the nostalgic values of conservative politicians from Malenkov and Molotov in the 1950's to Kozlov and Suslov in the 1960's. Small wonder that Mao Tse-tung as well as Stalin cropped up as a hero of the conservatives in the 1961 struggle over the draft party Program.

The alternative course of conciliation found its partisans in older leaders like Khrushchev and Mikoyan and younger ones like Polyanskiy. They persistently championed the underdog causes of higher priority for agriculture, meaningful labor rewards for the largest number of citizens, and the shifting of administrative gravity to local levels. This reform party emphasized the cohesion of the regime, but argumentatively and with simultaneous focus on inner "contradictions" like the production-consumption dilemma. It also made strenuous efforts to debunk the Stalin myth. The distinguishing features of the reformists' propaganda and the nature of their proposals betrayed an awareness of serious flaws in the basic arrangements of national life. The reformists' definition of underlying problems may in time overshadow the magnitude of their setbacks in party forums.

Some of the main determinants of attitude among those who exercised influence in the system of closed politics were professional interes, age, and regional affiliation. Besides priding himself on being a *narodnik*, or peasant socialist, Khrushchev asserted his "weakness for agriculture" and happily recalled his contacts with farmers on his days off.[2] These statements cannot be dismissed as sheer demagoguery. A self-made agronomist who retained a farm technician as a personal secretary, Khrushchev consistently utilized institutional prerogatives to advance agricultural questions to a high position on the political agenda. Moreover, his frank diagnoses of conditions on the land were accompanied by specific recommendations heedful of the state's commitments and potential. Again, it was scarcely a coincidence that the rivals of Khrushchev were trained in fields not merely remote from the interests of agriculture, but antithetic to them. Malenkov and Kozlov were educated as industrial engineers and henceforth were intimate with business executives whose sprawling empires were founded on the expropriation of rural wealth. Like other industrial trainees of the Stalin era, Malenkov and Kozlov assumedly were prone to regimentation and might be expected on that basis alone to have favored tighter control of farming—as indeed the case appears to have been. The "generalist" type of leader like Molotov and Suslov, whether out of conviction or to justify his position of authority, acted as the guardian of a corpus of doctrine which ruthlessly legitimated the total supremacy of cities over villages. The reorganization of the party along production rather than territorial lines, which Khrushchev sponsored in 1962, was fashioned to undercut the authority of these technically inexperienced bosses.

Khrushchev's spokesmen maintained that a rejuve-

[2] *S.K. v SSSR i R.S.Kh.*, II, 280.

nating current amongst office-holders of the party bureaucracy was one of the most salutary effects of the 1962 reorganization. Of course, no absolute statements regarding the age factor can be made in searching for the roots of conflicting orientations in the elite. Reformers and conservatives existed at all points on the age scale. But, generally speaking, the men who embarked on apparatus careers in the late 1920's and early 1930's leaned toward bland acceptance of the established order. They in particular were tagged for replacement in the periodic "efficiency" and "integrity" campaigns which Khrushchev's innovator group launched for ulterior, political reasons. In short, the alleged power of Communist doctrine to unify the generations proved more illusory than real. This may have especially important consequences for the Soviet future.

Regional diversity also had its impact on behavior in the hierarchy. The Great Russian-Ukrainian dichotomy made itself felt in the conflicts over the kolkhoz federation in 1959 and the role of district party committees in 1962. Northerners by and large abided by their heritage of centralized administration, while southerners individualistically favored the dispersal of authority in their own bailiwicks. The sectional jealousies help to explain the otherwise scholastic arguments over Ukrainian party history which raged in 1960-1962, paralleling the shifting fortunes of Khrushchev's "Ukrainian" protégés Brezhnev, Kirichenko, and Kirilenko.[3] Indeed, Khrushchev appears to have made references at that time

[3] The conflicting interpretations of Ukrainian party history are to be found in *Kommunist*, No. 16, 1960, pp. 18ff.; *XXII S"yezd KPSS i Zadachi Kafedr Obshchestvennykh Nauk*, pp. 228, 251, and 260ff.; and I. Mints, *Pravda*, July 25, 1962.

to Stalin's hostility toward the Ukrainian bureaucracy with a view to denigrating the anti-Ukrainian cabals of the Great Russian traditionalists Kozlov and Suslov.

LEGISLATIVE PROCEDURE

The sham parliament which the Soviet leaders maintain in the form of the USSR Supreme Soviet has deservedly received little attention from Western students of Soviet affairs. But without carefully reading the Soviet press and under the enthrallment of deterministic theories about "totalitarianism," some of these students have constructed a no less ingenuous model of legislative procedure in Soviet Russia. It is an essentially apolitical model of dispassionate staff studies, cool discussion in the top leadership, and finally of autocratic whim. As indicated, however, by the 1947 incident over the projected waterworks at Kakhovka, factionalism basically influenced the course of decision-making even in the Stalin period. Once intuition is discarded and hard research undertaken, a notable regularity is observable in the sequence of major events attending changes of policy in Soviet economy and administration. This regularity in the post-Stalin period enables one to detect a genuinely oligarchic procedure for policy-making, and its most outstanding feature is conflict.

While the proposal for change was still in embryonic form, organizational maneuver commenced. A bureaucratic department might have to be overhauled for the purpose of instilling the proper bias in its staff work. The allegiance of a local party caucus might have to be secured. Always, opinion leaders of the bureaucratic elite had to be told to utilize the press and conference hall to shape the appropriate consensus. These opinion leaders included party and government operatives, economic experts, the editors of newspapers and magazines, "theorists" in party and academic work, and literati. A substantial body of empiricist, doctrinaire, and opportunist talent resided in opinion-shaping circles and was at the disposal of feuding groups at the highest level. Next, the proposal, and perhaps a counterproposal, were submitted to the party Presidium or Central Committee. Deliberation occurred at expanded meetings of the Presidium, with as many as 90 persons involved. The proposal might be adopted by a majority vote of Presidium members or be tabled for additional study. The cycle was usually terminated with the rise and fall of underlings of patronage chiefs in the top leadership (see Appendix: The History of Some Decisions of the Post-Stalin Period).

The Chief Executive

The record indicates that in 1959-1963 Khrushchev aspired to major reform of domestic policy and was effectively opposed. How then could he stay on as party first secretary and premier? This question must arise in view of the death-struggle image of Soviet politics which was created by the collapse of the Malenkov regime in just less than two years and the showdown in the party Presidium which occurred about two years after that. It brings to mind the wise teaching of Boris Nicolaevsky about the Fabian quality of post-Stalin strife in the Kremlin: "This struggle for power need by no means at each moment be a struggle for the overthrow of the government or removal of the Central Committee first secretary. Such 'maximalist' goals always are fixed at the end of a long road of development which is marked by heightening animosities. On this road there are always many intermediary phases, when the contending groups set 'limited objectives. . . .' "[4] Nonetheless, since the crisis of 1957 there appear to have been times when Khrushchev was in danger of enforced retirement. He seems to have responded by turning into controversies the ultimate issues of "collective leadership" and "peaceful coexistence." Khrushchev strongly hinted to the few thousand constituents of the top leadership that his rivals were disposed toward courses of action which would jeopardize the principle of group rule and world tranquillity. The elite's paramount desire for normality and the inquisitorial backgrounds of Khrushchev's main adversaries, Kozlov and Suslov, would have sufficed to dampen any ardor for impeachment proceedings similar to those of 1957. If all this seems reminiscent of Stalin's tactic of playing on bureaucratic fears of Trotsky's militaristic reputation in the power struggles of the 1920's, it can only be said that the issues, attitudes, and gambits in Soviet politics are notably predictable. It is only the capricious resolution of individual conflicts which eludes accurate prophecy, but usefully reminds us that we are dealing here with the classic instance of a government of men.

The ability to make controversies of issues is in itself an instrument of power and Khrushchev on occasion has skillfully wielded it. He repeatedly attempted to transfer discussion from the smaller to the larger party organ, where the influence of rivals might not count for as much. However, the independent behavior of Central Committee members was so flagrant that

[4] *Sotsialisticheskiy Vestnik* (Socialist Courier), New York, No. 3/4 (763-764), March-April 1962, p. 46.

Khrushchev's play often miscarried. There is reason to believe the claim that Malenkov was boastful of his successes over Khrushchev in the closed meetings held at Central Committee plenums after the death of Stalin.[5] The latter-day standard-bearers of conservatism, Kozlov and Suslov, presumably formed majorities of their own in the debates on administrative and investment policy at the December 1959 and March 1962 Central Committee sessions, respectively. The evidence of such free-wheeling conduct of Committee members tends to refute the notion that the party first secretary controls the appointment of key personnel. Along with the fact that the Malenkovite Ponomarenko was intrusted with implementing Khrushchev's policy of land expansion in Kazakhstan, it indicates that such appointments are negotiated among equals in the party Presidium. Viewed in perspective, the foremost consequence of Khrushchev's frequent resort to the Central Committee as a political tool was that it enabled him to stabilize his interim regime. It was at once the source of his executive longevity and of the muddled nature of internal policies which, however unfairly, will often be associated with his name.

Over the long run, expanding the arena of conflict by familiarizing the public with the nature of some policy differences may have been Khrushchev's most im-

---

[5] The following passage in the speech of Furtseva to the 22nd party Congress relates to a meeting of the party Presidium held shortly before the crisis of June 1957. Khrushchev asked for the rehabilitation of generals shot in 1937 and accused Malenkov and Molotov of implication in the crimes: "Malenkov even said to Nikita Sergeyevich: Are you frightening us with a plenum? The plenum is like our own home; we shall go and tell all to the plenum." (*XXII S"yezd KPSS*, i, 396. This is not in the original version of Furtseva's speech, in *Pravda*, October 22, 1961.)

portant contribution to the betterment of his country-men. It was a step toward developing a kind of public opinion which in time may alter the thinking of the ruling class at large. (Encouraging public opinion polls and fostering in the party Program of the idea of pop-ular referendums on internal and foreign policy ques-tions were rudimentary moves in the same direction.) It was one of the more hopeful signs that eventually the Soviet regime may forsake its conspiratorial demeanor and act in a fully responsible manner toward its own people and those in the rest of the world.

APPENDIX

THE HISTORY OF SOME DECISIONS OF THE POST-STALIN PERIOD

Issue	Organization	Propaganda	Proposal	Action
1. Land expansion in semi-arid regions (1953-1954) (raised by Khrushchev after secret meetings during the September 1953 Central Committee session).	(a) Pro *Khrushchev's protégé L. R. Korniyets appointed USSR Minister of Agricultural Procurement (November 25, 1953). *Malenkov's protégé V. M. Andrianov released as first secretary, Leningrad Regional Party Committee, and Khrushchev's ally F. R. Kozlov appointed (November 29, 1953).	(a) Pro *Ts. Stepanyan on "contradictions," in *Pravda*, December 7, 1953. *N. I. Belyayev on need to plow up Siberian ranges, in *Pravda*, December 11, 1953. **Pravda* leader of January 7, 1954, for cultivating virgin soil massifs in east.	Memorandum of Khrushchev to party Presidium, January 22, 1954, for expansion of grain plantings in east by 13 million hectares in next two years with promise to recoup investment in one year's time.	*Policy:* March 28, 1954, decree of government and party based on Khrushchev's memorandum.
	(b) Con	(b) Con *V. S. Dmitriyev's lecture at December 23-28, 1953, conference of USSR Academy of Sciences and USSR Ministry of Agriculture. *Suppliers in USSR State Planning Committee.	COUNTERPROPOSAL Plow and harrow virgin soil, but leave uncropped for one or more years and then sow to perennial grasses as well as grain, in Malenkov-controlled *Izvestiya*, February 7, 1954.	*Organization:* Purge of leadership in Kazakhstan with charge of equivocal attitude toward land expansion, February 1954.

ISSUE	ORGANIZATION	PROPAGANDA	PROPOSAL	ACTION
2. Sale of heavy machinery to kolkhozes (1958) (raised by Khrushchev).	(a) Pro *Central Committee Secretariat expanded by adding Khrushchev's protégés N. G. Ignatov, A. I. Kirichenko, and N. A. Mukhitdinov (December 17, 1957). The "conservative" Secretary Suslov is now isolated. *The "conservative" F. R. Kozlov transferred from Leningrad to inferior post of RSFSR premier (December 19, 1957). *The "conservative" I. Benediktov released as RSFSR Minister of Agriculture (January 18, 1958, identified in other post).	(a) Pro *I. Vinnichenko in *October*, November 1957. *Khrushchev's Kiev speech of December 26, 1957 (unpublished). *Fedoseyev on "contradictions" and "dogmatists" in *Pravda*, January 17, 1958. *Khrushchev's Minsk speech of January 22, 1958. (b) Con *Osad'ko in *Herald of Moscow University*, January 11, 1958. *Academic Council of All-Union Scientific Research Institute for Agricultural Economics ("on eve of the MTS reorganization"). *Suslov refuses to admit doctrinal legitimacy of sales in speeches of March 11 and April 29, 1958.	Report of Khrushchev to Central Committee session, February 25, 1958.	Law of March 31, approving sales.

Issue	Organization	Propaganda	Proposal	Action
3. Kolkhoz unions beyond the district level (1958-1959) (raised by protégés of Khrushchev).	(a) Pro * G. I. Vorobyëv replaces V. P. Mylarshchikov as chief of Central Committee Section for Agriculture in RSFSR (April 1959). * G. A. Denisov replaces P. Ye. Doroshenko as chief of Central Committee Section for Agriculture in Union Republics (October 1959). (Khrushchev in 1960 notes that both sections worked out broad, but unacceptable, proposals for December 1959 Central Committee session). (b) Con * Kapitonov, purged in March on grounds of moral turpitude, appointed first secretary,	(a) Pro * M e m o r a n d u m of Khrushchev to Central Committee (or Presidium) with remarks on USSR Kolkhoz Center, February-March 1958. * Various participants in public discussion of MTS reform, March 1958. * Academician Strumilin in *Voprosy Ekonomiki*, May 1958. * Vinnichenko in *Oktyabr'*, June 1958. * P. Rukavets in *Oktyabr'*, October 1958. * M. Kovalenko in *Pravda Ukrainy*, November 13, 1959. * Staff correspondent of *Pravda Ukrainy*, December 15, 1959. * Kolkhoz chairman in *Sovetskaya Kirgiziya*, November 28, 1959.	Speeches of Polyanskiy, Podgornyy, Kirilenko, and Belyayev at December 1959 Central Committee session. (b) COUNTERPROPOSAL Conversion of economically weak kolkhozes into sovkhozes, speech of Matskevich at December 1959 Central Committee session.	*Policy:* December 1959 Central Committee session resolves that question of unions be studied in party Presidium. No comment on the counterproposal for transforming weak kolkhozes into sovkhozes. *Organization:* Degrading of Kazakhstan party leader Belyayev and "manager" of December 1959 Central Committee session, Kirichenko, January 1960.

(b) Con	(a) Pro
Ivanovo Regional Party Committee, September 22, 1959. *Kalnberzins, critic of opponents of MTS reform, dismissed as first secretary, C.P. Latvia, after local scandal over "Right opportunism" in industrial policy, November 25, 1959.	*Memorandum of Podgornyy, December 1959. (b) Con *Various participants in public discussion of MTS reform, March 1958. *Kovalevskiy at June 1958 conference of USSR Academy of Sciences. *Baranov in *Oktyabr'*, October 1958. *District party secretary in *Pravda Ukrainy*, December 19, 1959. *Matskevich's note to the Central Committee.

BIBLIOGRAPHY

1. PRIMARY SOURCES

PROCEEDINGS OF CPSU CENTRAL COMMITTEE MEETINGS

Plenum Tsentral'nogo Komiteta Kommunisticheskoy Partii Sovetskogo Soyuza, 15-19 dekabrya 1958 goda, stenograficheskiy otchët (Plenum of the Central Committee of the Communist Party of the Soviet Union, December 15-19, 1958, Minutes), Moscow 1958.

Plenum Tsentral'nogo Komiteta Kommunisticheskoy Partii Sovetskogo Soyuza, 22-25 dekabrya 1959 goda, stenograficheskiy otchët (Plenum of the Central Committee of the Communist Party of the Soviet Union, December 22-25, 1959, Minutes), Moscow, 1960.

Plenum Tsentral'nogo Komiteta Kommunisticheskoy Partii Sovetskogo Soyuza, 10-18 yanvarya 1961 goda, stenograficheskiy otchët (Plenum of the Central Committee of the Communist Party of the Soviet Union, January 10-18, 1961, Minutes), Moscow, 1961.

Plenum Tsentral'nogo Komiteta Kommunisticheskoy Partii Sovetskogo Soyuza, 5-9 marta 1962 goda, stenograficheskiy otchët (Plenum of the Central Committee of the Communist Party of the Soviet Union, March 5-9, 1962 Minutes), Moscow, 1962.

PARTY CONGRESSES

XXII S"yezd Kommunisticheskoy Partii Sovetskogo Soyuza, 17-31 oktyabrya 1961 goda, stenograficheskiy otchët (22nd Congress of the Communist Party of the Soviet Union, October 17-31, 1961, Minutes), 3 vols., Moscow, 1961-1962.

DOCUMENTS

Direktivy KPSS i Sovetskogo Pravitel'stva po Khozyaystvennym Voprosam (Directives of the CPSU and Soviet Government on Economic Problems), Moscow, 1958.

Istoriya Kolkhoznogo Prava (History of Kolkhoz Law), 2 vols., Moscow, 1958.

Meisel, James H., and Kozera, Edward S., eds., *Materials for the Study of the Soviet System*, 2nd revised and enlarged edition, Ann Arbor, Mich., 1953.

295

BIBLIOGRAPHY

2. Books and Pamphlets

Arutyunyan, Yu. V., *V Soyuze Edinom—Molot i Serp* (Hammer and Sickle in a Unified Alliance), Moscow, 1963.

Bautina, N. V., ed., *Ekonomicheskiye Zakonomernosti Perekhoda ot Sotsializma k Kommunizmu* (Economic Patterns of Development of the Transition from Socialism to Communism), Moscow, 1962.

Boffa, Giuseppe, *Inside the Khrushchev Era*, New York, 1959.

Bol'shaya Sovetskaya Entsiklopediya (Large Soviet Encyclopedia), Vol. 33, Moscow, 1955.

Bugayev, Ye. I., *O Nekotorykh Zakonomernostyakh Razvitiya Marksistko-Leninskoy Partii* (On Some Developmental Patterns of a Marxist-Leninist Party), Moscow, 1961.

Buyanov, P. S., Karavayev, A. A., and Kulagin, N. A., eds., *Novyy Etap v Razvitii Kolkhoznogo Stroya* (A New Stage in the Development of the Kolkhoz System), Moscow, 1959.

Carr, E. H., *A History of Soviet Russia: Socialism in One Country, 1924-1926*, New York, 1960.

Churayev, V. M., *O Edinstve Partii* (On Party Unity), Moscow, 1958.

Conquest, R., *Power and Policy in the USSR: The Study of Soviet Dynastics*, New York, 1961.

Embree, George D., *The Soviet Union Between the 19th and 20th Party Congresses, 1952-1956*, The Hague, 1959.

Gorbunov, Ye. P., *Sovetskiye Tempy i ikh Burzhuaznye Kritiki* (Soviet Rates and Their Bourgeois Critics), Moscow, 1961.

Jasny, Naum, *The Socialized Agriculture of the USSR: Plans and Performance*, Stanford, 1949.

Karelina, M. L., Nadtocheyev, D. I., Ryabtsev, I. G., eds., *Lektsii po Istorii KPSS (prochitany aspirantam Akademii Obshchestvennykh Nauk pri TsK KPSS v 1961/62 g.)*, *vypusk pervyy* (Lectures on CPSU History [read to candidates of the Academy of Social Sciences attached to the CPSU Central Committee in 1961-1962], part one), Moscow, 1963.

Khrushchev, N. S., *Stroitel'stvo Kommunizma v SSSR i Razvitiye Sel'skogo Khozyaystva* (Building of Communism

296

in the USSR and Development of Agriculture), 8 vols., Moscow, 1962-1964.

Kopteva, A. M., *Iz Istorii Bor'by V. I. Lenina za Edinstvo Partii* (From the History of V. I. Lenin's Struggle for Party Unity), Moscow, 1961.

Meissner, Boris, *Sowjetrussland Zwischen Revolution und Restauration* (Soviet Russia Between Revolution and Restoration), Cologne, 1956.

Narodnoye Khozyaystvo SSSR v 1958 Godu (USSR National Economy in 1958), Moscow, 1959.

Narodnoye Khozyaystvo SSSR v 1959 Godu (USSR National Economy in 1959), Moscow, 1960.

Narodnoye Khozyaystvo SSSR v 1961 Godu (USSR National Economy in 1961), Moscow, 1962.

Nekotorye Aktual'nye Voprosy Marksistsko-Leninskoy Teorii. Sbornik Statey pod Redaktsiey prof. D. I. Chesnokova (Some Current Problems of Marxist-Leninist Theory. Collection of Articles under the Editorship of Professor D. I. Chesnokov), Moscow, 1963.

O Nekotorykh Problemakh Stroitel'stva Kommunizma v Svete Resheniy XXI-ogo S"yezda KPSS (On Some Problems of Building Communism in Light of the Decisions of the 21st CPSU Congress), Moscow, 1960.

Petrenko, F. F., *KPSS v Period Razvërnutogo Stroitel'stva Kommunizma* (The CPSU in the Period of Full-Scale Building of Communism), Moscow, 1963.

Ponomarëv, B. N., *et al.*, *Istoriya Kommunisticheskoy Partii Sovetskogo Soyuza (Izdaniye vtoroye, dopolnenoye)* (History of the Communist Party of the Soviet Union [2nd, supplemented edition]), Moscow, 1962.

Rozental', M. M., ed., *Dialektika Razvitiya Sotsialisticheskogo Obshchestva* (Dialectic of Development of Socialist Society), Academy of Social Sciences attached to the CPSU Central Committee, Department of Philosophy, Moscow, 1961.

Schapiro, Leonard, *The Communist Party of the Soviet Union*, New York, 1960.

Shatagin, N. I., *Edinstvo Partynykh Ryadov—Glavnoye Usloviye Sily i Mogushchestva KPSS* (Unity of the Party Ranks Is the Main Condition of the Power and Might of the CPSU), Moscow, 1954.

Spravochnik Partiynogo Rabotnika (Handbook of the Party Official), Moscow, 1959 and 1963.

Stalin, J., *Problems of Leninism*, Moscow, 1953.

Tikhonov, G. P., ed., *Voprosy Kolkhoznogo Prava* (Problems of Kolkhoz Law), Leningrad, 1961.

Ukraintsev, B. S., Koval'chuk, A. S., Chertkov, V. P., *Dialektika Pererastaniya Sotsializma v Kommunizm. Osobennosti Deystviya Osnovnykh Zakonov Dialektiki v Razvitii Sotsializma* (Dialectic of the Growing of Socialism into Communism. Peculiarities of the Action of the Basic Laws of the Dialectic in the Development of Socialism), Moscow, 1963.

Velikoye Torzhestvo Idey Leninizma (Great Triumph of the Ideas of Leninism), Moscow, 1960.

Voprosy Istorii KPSS. Sbornik Statey (Problems of CPSU History. Anthology), Moscow, 1959.

Voprosy Istorii KPSS Perioda Velikoy Otechestvennoy Voyny (Problems of CPSU History of the Period of the Great Patriotic War), Kiev, 1961.

Voprosy Stroitel'stva Kommunizma v SSSR. Materialy Nauchnoy Sessii Otdelenii Obshchestvennykh Nauk Akademii Nauk SSSR (Problems of Building Communism in the USSR. Materials of a Scholars' Meeting of the Department of Social Sciences of the USSR Academy of Sciences), Moscow, 1959.

XXII S"yezd KPSS i Voprosy Ideologicheskoy Raboty. Materialy Vsesoyuznogo Soveshchaniya po Voprosam Ideologicheskoy Raboty. 25-28 dekabrya 1961 goda (22nd CPSU Congress and Problems of Ideological Work. Materials of the All-Union Conference on Problems of Ideological Work. December 25-28, 1961), Moscow, 1962.

XXII S"yezd KPSS i Zadachi Kafedr Obshchestvennykh Nauk. Materialy Vsesoyuznogo Soveshchaniya Zaveduyushchikh Kafedrami Obshchestvennykh Nauk Vysshikh Uchebnykh Zavedeniy. 30 yanvarya-2 fevralya 1962 goda (22nd CPSU Congress and Tasks of Social Science Departments. Materials of the All-Union Conference of Heads of Social Science Departments of Higher Educational Institutions. January 30-February 2, 1962), Moscow, 1962.

Zasorin, V. and Vikulin, N., *O Novom Ustave KPSS* (On the New CPSU Rules), Moscow, 1961.

Zorin, Valentin S., *Monopolii i Politika SShA: Monopolii i Vnutrennyaya Politika Respublikanskoy Partii SShA v 1953-1960 gg.* (Monopolies and US Policy: Monopolies and the

Internal Politics of the US Republican Party, 1953-1960),
Moscow, 1960.

3. JOURNALS AND NEWSPAPERS

Bakinskiy Rabochiy (Baku Worker), organ of the Central
Committee and Baku City Committee of the Communist
Party of Azerbaidzhan.

Bol'shevik, theoretical and political journal of the Central
Committee of the All-Union Communist Party (B).

Current Digest of the Soviet Press, New York, N.Y.

Daily Report, USSR and East Europe, Foreign Broadcast Information Service.

Ekonomicheskaya Gazeta (Economics Newspaper), organ
of the CPSU Central Committee.

Istoricheskiy Arkhiv (Historical Archive), journal of the
Institute of History of the USSR Academy of Sciences.

Izvestiya (News), organ of the USSR Supreme Soviet
Presidium.

Kazakhstanskaya Pravda (Kazakhstan Truth), organ of the
Central Committee of the Communist Party of Kazakhstan and Kazakhstan Supreme Soviet and Council of Ministers.

Kommunist, organ of the Central Committee of the Communist Party of Armenia.

Kommunist, theoretical and political journal of the CPSU
Central Committee; successor to *Bol'shevik*.

Kommunist Tadzhikistana (Communist of Tadzhikistan),
organ of the Central Committee of the Communist Party
of Tadzhikistan and Tadzhikistan SSR Supreme Soviet.

Kommunist Ukrainy (Communist of the Ukraine), theoretical and political journal of the Central Committee of the
Communist Party of the Ukraine.

Komsomol'skaya Pravda (*Komsomol* Truth), organ of the
Central Committee of the All-Union Leninist Communist
League of Youth.

Leninskoye Znamya (Lenin's Banner), organ of the Moscow
Province Party Committee and Moscow Province Soviet
of Worker Deputies.

Literaturnaya Gazeta (Literary Newspaper), organ of the
USSR Union of Writers' Board.

Molodoy Kommunist (Young Communist), journal of the
Central Committee of the All-Union Leninist Communist
League of Youth.

Moskovskaya Pravda (Moscow Truth), organ of the Moscow City Party Committee and Moscow City Soviet of Worker Deputies.

Nash Sovremmenik (Our Contemporary), literary and current affairs journal of the USSR Union of Writers.

Oktyabr' (October), literary and current affairs journal of the RSFSR Union of Writers.

Partiynaya Zhizn' (Party Life), organizational journal of the CPSU Central Committee.

Partiynoye Stroitel'stvo (Party Organization), journal of the CPSU(B) Central Committee.

Politicheskoye Samoobrazovaniye (Political Self-Education), study journal of the CPSU Central Committee.

Pravda (Truth), organ of the CPSU Central Committee.

Pravda Ukrainy (Truth of the Ukraine), organ of the Central Committee of the Communist Party of the Ukraine and Ukrainian SSR Supreme Soviet and Council of Ministers.

Pravda Vostoka (Truth of the East), organ of the Central Committee of the Communist Party of Uzbekistan and Uzbek SSR Supreme Soviet and Council of Ministers.

Problems of Communism, bimonthly magazine of the United States Information Agency, Washington, D.C.

Sel'skaya Zhizn' (Rural Life), organ of the CPSU Central Committee.

Sotsialisticheskiy Vestnik (Socialist Courier), central organ of the Russian Social-Democratic Labor Party, New York.

Sovetskaya Belorussiya (Soviet Belorussia), organ of the Central Committee of the Communist Party of Belorussia and Belorussian SSR Supreme Soviet and Council of Ministers.

Sovetskaya Estoniya (Soviet Estonia), organ of the Central Committee of the Communist Party of Estonia and Estonian SSR Supreme Soviet and Council of Ministers.

Sovetskaya Kirgiziya (Soviet Kirghizia), organ of the Central Committee of the Communist Party of Kirghizia and Kirghiz SSR Supreme Soviet and Council of Minsters.

Sovetskaya Latviya (Soviet Latvia), organ of the Central Committee of the Communist Party of Latvia and Latvian SSR Supreme Soviet.

Sovetskaya Litva (Soviet Lithuania), organ of the Central Committee of the Communist Party of Lithuania and Lithuanian SSR Supreme Soviet Presidium and Council of Ministers.

Sovetskaya Rossiya (Soviet Russia), organ of the CPSU Central Committee Bureau of RSFSR Affairs and RSFSR Council of Ministers.

Sovetskoye Gosudarstvo i Pravo (Soviet State and Law), journal of the Institute of Law of the USSR Academy of Sciences.

Soviet Studies, A Quarterly Review of the Social and Economic Institutions of the USSR. Edited on behalf of the Department for the Study of the Social and Economic Institutions of the USSR, University of Glasgow, by J. Miller and R. A. J. Schlesinger.

Turkmenskaya Iskra (Turkmen Spark), organ of the Central Committee of the Communist Party of Turkmenistan and Turkmen SSR Supreme Soviet and Council of Ministers.

Vestnik Leningradskogo Universiteta: Seriya Ekonomiki, Filosofii i Prava (Herald of Leningrad University: Series on Economics, Philosophy, and Law), Leningrad.

Vestnik Moskovskogo Universiteta: Seriya Ekonomiki, Filosofii i Prava (Herald of Moscow University: Series on Economics, Philosophy, and Law), Moscow.

Voprosy Ekonomiki (Problems of Economics), journal of the Economics Institute of the USSR Academy of Sciences.

Voprosy Filosofii (Problems of Philosophy), journal of the Philosophy Institute of the USSR Academy of Sciences.

Voprosy Istorii KPSS (Problems of CPSU History), journal of the Institute of Marxism-Leninism attached to the CPSU Central Committee.

Yezhednevnyi Informatsionnyi Byulleten' (Daily Information Bulletin), Radio Liberty, Munich.

Zarya Vostoka (Dawn of the East), organ of the Central Committee and Tbilisi City Committee of the Communist Party of Georgia.

INDEX

Abalin, S. M., 43, 43n, 53, 53n, 57, 62
Academy of Sciences, 78f
Afonov, 86
age, of cadres, 262
Agitprop, 50n
agricultural decollectivization, 104f
agricultural equipment, 25-27, 77f, 81, 90-91, 97-99, 113-53 *passim*, 185-87, 206-10, 216-20 *passim*, 229, 240-41, 246-47, 249, 254, 256, 260-64, 267
agricultural investment, 25ff, 68, 200, 205, 208-09, 211-14, 216-17, 219, 223-24, 239-40, 244, 246-47, 251-54, 256, 264, 267-68, 270-77 *passim. See also* resource allocation.
agricultural management, 51f, 101-07, 131-35, 194, 202-08, 216-17, 221, 230, 242-43, 245, 247-49, 251-55, 261-64
agricultural procurement prices, 67, 67n, 124, 216-17, 231, 243, 249, 256, 258-59
agricultural production 27, 41-42, 68, 265, 265n, 273
agricultural taxes, 57, 67, 185f, 191, 206
"agro-cities", 46-50, 66, 99, 144-45n, 149, 152, 272
agro-technical policy, 34-39 *passim*, 41, 41n, 48, 48n, 63, 67, 74, 240f, 246, 252-53, 255, 262f
Alekseyev, L., 193n
Alekseyevskiy, Ye., 37n
All-Union Scientific Research Institute for Agricultural Economics, and MTS, 120; App. p. 2
Andreyev, A. A., 10, 22n, 30, 32-33, 45-46
Andrianov, V. M., 75-76; App. p. 1

Anisimov, N., 168
anti-peasant policies, 216-17, 226f, 229-30n, 241, 258f, 260; and prejudice, 22, 22n
Aristov, A. B., 137, 170, 177n, 180n, 191, 215
arts, and politics, 137-38
Arutyunyan, Yu. U., 108n
Audonin, N., 64n
austerity, bureaucratic pressure for, 208, 212, 214

Baranov, App. p. 3
Barayev, A. I., 194f, 202
Basou, A. B., 192, 250
Baulin, A., 128n
Bechin, A., 91
Belyayev, N. I. 78-79, 114, 149, 155, 163, 173, 175, 178-81, 192; App. pp. 1, 3
Benediktov, I. A., 74, 87, 92, 101, 101n, 119, 123, 123n, 187, 279; App. p. 2
Beriya, L. P., 5, 9-10, 28, 37, 37n, 40, 42-44, 49-59 *passim*, 62-66, 138, 278
Berklau, Ye. K., 172, 172n
Bernal, John, 69, 95n
Bialer, S., 51n
Biryuzov, S. S., 267
Bodyul, I. I., 249n
Boffa, Giuseppe, 62n
Bogdanov, 55
Bolgov, A. V., 128n
Bol'shevik, 42f, 44
Borkenau, Franz, 6n, 19n
Bovin, A., 197n
Braginskiy, L., 165
Brezhnev, L. I., 86f, 137, 137n, 177n, 180n, 191, 239, 271, 271n, 282
Bronshteyn, M., 158f
Bugayev, Ye., 198-99, 221, 221n, 265n
Bukharin, 9, 55

303

INDEX

Literaturnaya Gazeta, 51, 226
livestock, 27, 30, 41, 57, 97, 109-
12, 185, 196, 199-200, 253, 256
Lobanov, P. P., 100n
Logacheva, P., 63n
Lomakin, N. L., 19n, 189n
Lomako, P. F., 276n
Lysenko, T. D., 31n, 36, 48, 74,
82, 88-89, 100n, 151n, 194-95,
202-03, 276; and virgin lands
program, 79-82

Machine and Tractor Stations
(MTS), 27, 33, 55-56, 69, 72-
74, 101-07, 225, 244f, 248; and
kolkhoz payments, 81; reorganization of, 113-53 *passim*,
App. pp. 2, 3
Malenkov, G. M., 8-10, 12, 12n,
14, 18, 20, 22n, 28, 30, 36-37,
39-40, 42-44, 49-58 *passim*, 114,
127, 137-38, 152f, 168f, 181-82,
189-90, 194, 221-23, 225f, 236-
37, 278-81, 284, 286, 286n,
App. p. 1; and the grain
crisis, 59-101 *passim*
Malinovsky, R. Ya., 252-54,
267n
Mal'tsev, T. S., 35, 151n, 195,
195n, 203
Malyshev, I., 128n, 226
Mao Tse-tung, 197, 199, 233,
280
Marx, 233-34
Matskevich, S. P., 69, 99n, 101,
106f, 134n, 152, 177, 179, 186-
87, 193-94, 200, 203-05, 279,
App. p. 3
Maynard, John, 31n
Mazur, V., 277n
Mazurov, K. T., 104, 131, 152,
203-05, 250
Meisel, James H., 41n, 48-49n,
53
Meissner, Boris, 94n-95n
Mel'nikov, L. G., 48, 66
Mikhaylov, V., 187n

Mikoyan, A. I., 31n, 57, 57n,
67, 96, 100, 236, 236n, 239,
279-80; and virgin lands program, 83
military expenditures, 41-42,
42n, 44-45, 52-54, 95, 95n, 98,
208, 211, 219, 231, 240, 254,
254n, 266-67, 273-74, 277. *See
also* resource allocation
military provisioning, 96
Miller, J., 92n, 93n, 145n
Miller, J. D. B., 3
Ministries of Agriculture (Union-republic level), 114, 159-
60, 179, 185, 213n
Ministry of Agricultural Procurement, 75, 81f
Ministry of Agriculture, 34,
71-72, 79, 81f, 92-93, 101, 103,
107, 154f, 159-61, 174, 179-80,
185-88
Ministry of Procurements, 102-
03
Ministry of State Farms, 78,
81f, 93, 103
Ministry of Trade, 42
Mitin, M., 128n
Mnatsakanyan, M. O., 22n
Molotov, V. M., 9, 12-13, 15,
18, 20, 22n, 100, 107, 107n,
109-10, 127, 137-38, 152f, 168f,
189-90, 221-22n, 225f, 236-37,
265n, 281, 286n; and virgin
lands program, 82-84ff
"monolithism", 4-5
moral turpitude, charges of,
161f
Moscow Conferences of Communist Bloc powers, 1957,
115f; 1960, 205
Mukhitdinov, N. A., 116, 129,
177n, 191, 213, 239, App. p. 2
Mylarshehikov, V. P., App. p. 3
Mzhavanadze, V. P., 175, 205n

Nadtocheyev, D. I., 84n, 108n
Nagy, Imry, 137
Nicolaevsky, Boris, on post-

Gabriel A. Almond, *The Appeals of Communism*

Gabriel A. Almond and James S. Coleman, editors, *The Politics of the Developing Areas*

Cyril E. Black and Thomas P. Thornton, editors, *The Strategic Uses of Political Violence*

Robert J. C. Butow, *Tojo and the Coming of the War*

Bernard C. Cohen, *The Political Process and Foreign Policy: The Making of the Japanese Peace Settlement*

Bernard C. Cohen, *The Press and Foreign Policy*

Percy E. Corbett, *Law in Diplomacy*

Charles De Visscher, *Theory and Reality in Public International Law*, translated by P. E. Corbett

Frederick S. Dunn, *Peace-making and the Settlement with Japan*

Herman Kahn, *On Thermonuclear War*

W. W. Kaufmann, editor, *Military Policy and National Security*

Klaus Knorr, *The War Potential of Nations*

Klaus Knorr, editor, *NATO and American Security*

Klaus Knorr and Sidney Verba, editors, *The International System: Theoretical Essays*

Lucian W. Pye, *Guerrilla Communism in Malaya*

James N. Rosenau, *National Leadership and Foreign Policy: A Case Study in the Mobilization of Public Support*

Rolf Sannwald and Jacques Stohler, *Economic Integration: Theoretical Assumptions and Consequences of European Unification*, translated by Herman F. Karreman

Richard L. Sklar, *Nigerian Political Parties: Power in an Emergent African Nation*

Glenn H. Snyder, *Deterrence and Defense*

Thomas P. Thorton, editor, *The Third World in Soviet Perspective: Studies by Soviet Writers on the Developing Areas*

Sidney Verba, *Small Groups and Political Behavior: A Study of Leadership*

Myron Weiner, *Party Politics in India*